# Tales of the
# Grove Park Inn

Take from this hearth its warmth,
From this room its charm,
From this inn its amity,
Return them not -- but return.

~ The Great Hall Fireplace ~

# Tales of the Grove Park Inn

## Bruce E. Johnson

author of

~ *Built For the Ages:*
*A History of the Grove Park Inn* ~
~ *An Unexpected Guest* ~
~ *Grove Park Inn Arts & Crafts Furniture* ~
~ *The Dark Side of Paradise:*
*A Novel About F. Scott Fitzgerald* ~

No portion of this book may be used or reproduced in any fashion,
either by print, photocopier, recording, scanning, electronic device,
internet or by any method yet to be developed
without the prior written permission of the copyright holder.

Knock On Wood Publications
Wood-Care, Incorporated
25 Upper Brush Creek Road, Fletcher, N.C. 28732

Printed in the United States of America.

ISBN 978-1-4675-5960-7

Designer: Alexandra Fisher.
Editor: Melissa Jadron Luxmore.
Photographs courtesy of the Grove Park Inn.
Cover photograph by John G. Robinson (1880-1921).

# Tales of the Grove Park Inn

# Other Books by Bruce E. Johnson

*The Dark Side of Paradise: A Novel About F. Scott Fitzgerald (2014)*
*Arts and Crafts Shopmarks (2012)*
*An Unexpected Guest* (2011)
*Grove Park Inn Arts & Crafts Furniture* (2009)
*Hand Wrought: The Artistry of William Waldo Dodge* (2005)
*The Official Price Guide to American Arts & Crafts* (1988, 2003)
*Built for the Ages: A History of the Grove Park Inn* (1991, 2013)
*The Pegged Joint* (1995)
*Fifty Simple Ways To Save Your House* (1995)
*The Wood Finisher* (1993)
*The Weekend Refinisher* (1989)
*Gustav Stickley's 1912 Craftsman Furniture Catalog* (1989)
*Dedham Pottery Catalog* (1987)
*The Collector's Guide to Arts & Craft Shopmarks* (1987)
*How To Make $20,000 a Year in Antiques* (1986)
*Knock On Wood: Antique Repair and Restoration* (1984)

# Websites

www.ArtsAndCraftsCollector.com
www.Arts-CraftsConference.com
www.AnUnexpectedGuest.com
www.AskBruceJohnson.com

Dedicated To

# Frederick Loring Seely
## (1871 - 1942)

The man who designed and defined
the character of this historic hotel.

*If I should leave Asheville, it would be with no little regret.*
*It is the most wonderful place to live, and I am sure I*
*would find my way back here in my old age, if I am blessed*
*with one. The landscaping is now finished, and the place*
*is more beautiful than any I have ever seen. Of course,*
*you must grant me the privilege of feeling this way,*
*for it seems like a child to me.*

Frederick L. Seely to E. W. Grove
November 1, 1914

**She lay on her back,** her long blond hair silhouetted by a small pool of blood slowly creeping out from beneath her head. He avoided looking at her eyes, bright blue eyes staring blankly at the skylight 60 feet above the Palm Court. Her long, delicate fingers quivered once, then slowly relaxed. "Black boys don't touch no white girls," he could hear his mama say. "Don't you touch 'em, Robert. Never!"

And so begins the most talked about murder-mystery written about the Grove Park Inn and her famous ghostly guest -- the Pink Lady. Set on the night of August 27, 1918, this novel will transport you back to an era of grand hotels, famous guests, and a family feud spinning out of control amid a maze of hidden doors and secret tunnels beneath this famous hotel.

An Unexpected Guest

A Novel
by Bruce E. Johnson

Grove Park Inn
Asheville NC.
Robinson

"... an unexpected marvel."
- *Asheville Citizen-Times*          Mature readers only.

# Forward

It has been more than 26 years since the first article I ever wrote about the Grove Park Inn appeared in print. A short while later I followed it with a story for the 1988 *Arts & Crafts Conference Catalog* about F. Scott Fitzgerald's disastrous summer in room 441. In the nearly three decades since then, I have lost count of how many magazine articles, newspaper stories, columns and books I have written about some aspect of this famous hotel. Yet, here I am, more than a quarter of a century later, still discovering and documenting more stories about the Grove Park Inn and its guests.

This paperback is intended as a companion to another book I have written. *Built For The Ages: A History of the Grove Park Inn* is a more formal hardback book, complete with color photographs. *Tales of the Grove Park Inn* is a collection of related stories, all true and each based on historical research. Each chapter was written to stand alone, so they do not have to be read in chronological order. As a result, some important historical information will appear more than once in the book.

Millions of people, from the original workmen and ordinary guests to the hotel employees and staff who guide this mountaintop cruise ship toward its daily destination, have each had their own Grove Park Inn experience. Many of them have left behind stories we should never forget, which is precisely why I have written this book.

I would hardly know how to begin listing all of the people who have shared with me their stories about the Grove Park Inn. Rather than risk leaving anyone out, let me say "thank you" to everyone who has helped me gather information for this modest contribution to the heritage of the famous Grove Park Inn.

Without you, neither its history nor this book would be what it is today.

Bruce E. Johnson
January 1, 2013

*Original circa 1900 advertising poster.*

# Chapter 1

# "As Fat As Pigs"

*Adults: Take two tablespoons, three times a day.*
*In all cases to be taken for a period of eight weeks*
*or during the entire malarial season.*

Grove's Tasteless Chill Tonic

In 1874, a young man by the name of Edwin Wiley Grove stepped off the Memphis & Ohio Railroad in a small town with the unlikely name of Paris, Tennessee. In his pocket he carried a letter he had read a hundred times, a letter from Dr. Samuel Caldwell, offering him a position as pharmacist in the doctor's small drug store on the east side of the town square.

Grove had been just twelve years old when his father, James Grove, left him in charge of their small farm outside Bolivar, southeast of Memphis, while he fought alongside the men of the 3rd Tennessee Confederate Calvary. Edwin and his mother waited three years for his return, while James Grove served under General Nathan Bedford Forrest, the controversial slave trader, plantation owner, riverboat gambler and military commander who reportedly killed more than thirty Union soldiers in hand-to-hand combat.

It was during the Civil War that James Grove met Dr. Samuel Caldwell, a prominent citizen of Paris. Pressed into service as a Confederate battlefield surgeon, Dr. Caldwell was later captured by Union raiders and sent to Camp Douglas, Illinois, one of the largest prisoner of war camps with more than 12,000 Southern soldiers. Dr. Caldwell tended to the wounded and dying Confederate men until nearly the end of the war, when he was released in a prisoner exchange between the two sides.

After the war, Dr. Caldwell returned to his medical practice in Paris, where he and banker A. B. Mitchum established a small pharmacy on the east side of the square. James Grove had by then returned to his farm, but when his only son expressed an interest in pharmacy, he wrote to Dr. Caldwell. By 1874, when 24-year-old Edwin Grove had finished his classes in Memphis, Dr. Caldwell was ready to retire to his farm, where he loved raising horses and experimenting with new strains of tobacco. Dr. Caldwell met Edwin Grove at the railway station that day, gave the young man a quick tour of the town and brought him to the pharmacy to meet Mr. Mitchum.

With a room waiting for him in a local boarding house, Grove quickly settled into his new position and the daily routine at the small town pharmacy. Word of the young, single pharmacist undoubtedly spread quickly through Paris, prompting the curious to drop in for a refill of their peppermint oil, mercurial pills or camphorated oil.

Among those who met the new pharmacist in those first few months was Mary Louisa Moore, an attractive young woman from nearby Milan. Friendship soon turned to courtship, and the young couple was married in the Paris Presbyterian Church in September of 1875. He was 25 and she was 20, and they soon moved into a one-story brick home at 607 North Poplar Street, an easy ten-minute walk to the pharmacy. Two years later, in 1877, their daughter Evelyn was born in their home.

Ambition was never lacking in Edwin Grove's character, and by 1880 he had purchased the pharmacy from Dr. Caldwell and Mr. Mitchum, renaming it Grove's Pharmacy. In addition, whenever he had the chance, he began experimenting with a number of different medical remedies, most notably those attempting to ward off the deadly malaria.

Malaria had ravaged the world for centuries before being carried to America by European settlers and African slaves. Missionaries were among the first to note that Indian tribes in Central and South America avoided the deadly disease by chewing the inner bark of the "fever tree" -- their name for the cinchona tree. When stripped, dried and processed, the bark of the cinchona tree yielded a powder called quinine, a bitter yet effective preventive for malaria.

For those living in the South during the nineteenth century, malaria had become one of the leading causes of death, especially among infants and the elderly. One of its victims was Irma Grove, the second daughter of Edwin and Mary Louisa Grove. Then, in 1884, just a year before their tenth wedding anniversary, the 34-year-old Mary Louisa Grove died in their home, presumably during an outbreak of either yellow fever or malaria.

Their seven-year-old daughter Evelyn survived.

As he grieved over the deaths of both his second daughter and his wife, Edwin Grove redoubled his efforts to find a remedy that would protect people from the deadly grip of malaria. His first product, called Feberlin, was a liquid form of quinine sold by prescription only through other pharmacies. Encouraged by its initial success, Grove set about to perfect a quinine formula that would be mild enough to be sold without a doctor's prescription, yet strong enough to be effective. In 1886, after countless experiments with various formulas mixed in a large drum equipped with wooden paddles spun by high school boys, Grove began marketing his first six-ounce bottles labeled as Grove's Tasteless Chill Tonic.

By disguising the bitter taste of quinine with sugar and lemon-flavored syrup, Grove created a tonic that, as he claimed, "makes it especially fine for children, who do not have to be coaxed to take this fine preparation regularly." In addition to "medically-proven anti-malaria ingredients that fight malaria infection right in the bloodstream," Edwin Grove also added iron particles as "a valuable help in overcoming and offsetting the ravages of this disease."

One other ingredient which undoubtedly spurred sales, yet was never mentioned on the label, was revealed in a letter which E. W. Grove had written to one of his employees in 1900: "I would advise that you reduce the alcohol to 15 percent, but don't reduce the [cinchona tree] bark, letting the quality remain as you had it in the formula sent me. We want to make it as strong as we can afford...."

A typewritten copy of the formula, which for decades remained a closely guarded secret, reveals the original ingredients in Grove's Tasteless Chill Tonic:

| | | |
|---|---|---|
| Cinchona Bark | 2 ounces | Quinine to ward off malaria. |
| Black Root | .1 ounce | Tonic for upset stomach. |
| Dogwood Bark | .1 ounce | A malaria preventative. |
| Poplar Bark | .1 ounce | A sedative. |
| Prickly Ash Bark | .1 ounce | For chronic pain relief. |
| Sarsaparilla | .1 ounce | Sugared flavoring (root beer). |
| Alkaloid | 20 grams | A stimulant. |
| Lemon Syrup | 30 percent by volume | |
| Alcohol | 20 percent by volume | |

As his personal guarantee and to guard against confusion with other products of similar names and claims, Grove printed his signature on each box and bottle of Tasteless Chill Tonic and later his Bromo-Quinine cold tablets.

Even so, for Grove to market his Tasteless Chill Tonic beyond the boundaries of Henry County he had to tap a financial source deeper than the till of his pharmacy's cash register. He turned to his friends and associates in Paris, offering them the opportunity to buy shares issued by the Paris Medicine Company at an initial offering of $100 each. Men of vision, such as O. C. Barton, A. H. Duncan and George Musselman, saw their $100 shares increase in value to as much as $3,500 each. In addition, the corporation proved so successful that each year Grove paid stock dividends ranging from 50 percent to 100 percent of their value to those first and only investors, making them, as one Paris farmer observed, "rich enough to burn a wet mule."

With enough cash to finance the necessary equipment, a proven product ready to manufacture, and a growing demand for it, Edwin Grove lacked only one thing: a marketing plan. Anyone who had watched a family member or close friend die a slow death from either yellow fever or malaria recognized the debilitating chills and rapid weight loss signaling those final days. Grove, too, knew from first-hand experience, and so he hit upon an advertising slogan designed to assure people of the healing qualities of Grove's Tasteless Chill Tonic: "Makes Children and Adults As Fat As Pigs." To drive his point home, each piece of Grove's sales literature featured the smiling face of a happy baby superimposed on the body of a plump, healthy pig.

And if that were not enough, he included a guarantee at the bottom: "No Cure, No Pay."

Even so, in 1889, fifteen years after he had arrived in Paris, Tennessee, nine years after he had opened Grove's Pharmacy on the town square, and just three years after he had incorporated the Paris Medicine Company to produce, market and distribute Grove's Tasteless Chill Tonic, 39-year-old Edwin Wiley Grove realized he had a problem.

While he had been warmly embraced and encouraged by the townspeople of Paris, the fact remained that the town of less than 2,000 people was located nearly 100 miles from Nashville and nearly 150 miles from Memphis. Grove needed an available, convenient and reliable means of shipping thousands of cases of Grove's Tasteless Chill Tonic across the country -- and around the world.

Promising never to forget those close friends who had enabled him to pursue his dream, Grove announced that he was moving the Paris Medicine Company to St. Louis, where he planned to construct offices and a factory for producing Grove's Tasteless Chill Tonic not far from the bustling Union Station. Destined to become the largest train station in the country, Union Station served 22 different railroads and more than 100,000 people a year, far more than any other train station in the United States.

Grove remained true to his word, maintaining close ties with his friends back in Paris. In 1905, he provided $50,000 to endow the town's first free public high school, along with $4,000 per year to help offset operating expenses. To show their appreciation, the school board named its football team the "Chill Tonics." Grove remained a lifelong member of the Paris Presbyterian Church, contributing funds for new stained glass windows and for the maintenance of the cemetery where he eventually was buried.

The move to St. Louis took more than two years to complete, but the results were soon evident as Grove sold more bottles of his

Tasteless Chill Tonic in 1890 than Asa Candler did of another Southern favorite: Coca-Cola.

But the low-lying warehouse district of West St. Louis was plagued with smoke and smog produced by hundreds of inefficient coal-fired furnaces and sluggish steam locomotives. At times the air would become so dense and foul that the streetlights would burn throughout the day. To escape the pestilent air, Grove purchased a stately three-story Victorian house in the prestigious Westminster Avenue neighborhood, near the site of the planned 1904 World's Fair in the lush and sprawling Forest Park. Nevertheless, the combination of long hours in the factory, late nights in the office, constant worry about production, sales and advertising, and the effect of the smoke and smog on his lungs soon began to take its toll on Edwin Grove.

Even though he was not yet 45 years old and enjoyed walking whenever possible, Grove's health began to decline. He developed insomnia, began to lose his hearing and suffered from extended periods of hiccups, quite possibly as a result of internal irritation caused by the smoke and smog in the factory district where he continued to work long hours.

Neither home remedies nor medical treatment seemed to lessen the effect of the constant hiccups, which further weakened his physical state. As a last resort, one physician suggested that he travel to Asheville, nestled in the foothills of the Blue Ridge Mountains and rapidly gaining a reputation for its clean air, outdoor activities and curative qualities for people suffering from respiratory ailments, including asthma, emphysema, chronic bronchitis and tuberculosis. With a growing number of sanitariums, boarding houses and pulmonary physicians in Asheville, his family hoped that Edwin Wiley Grove might find a cure or, at the least, some relief for his constant hiccups.

In 1897, the Grove family, consisting of Edwin, second wife Gertrude, 20-year-old Evelyn and seven-year-old Edwin Wiley Grove Jr. began spending extended summer vacations in Asheville. The pharmaceutical manufacturer eventually built a spacious home for his family on a grassy knoll in North Asheville. The early springs, mild summers, colorful falls and brief winters appealed to Grove, who took great delight in walking the tree-lined streets around his neighborhood. As one of the youngest millionaires in Asheville, Grove certainly could have afforded one of the early, experimental automobiles, but refused his entire life to ever learn to drive. Although he purchased a car for his son in 1905, when young Edwin was but fifteen years old, the senior Grove preferred to have his chauffeur drive him around town in his gleaming Pearce-Arrow.

Ever mindful of the opportunities around him, Grove soon began investing in land around his North Asheville home. In little more than ten years after his 1897 arrival in Asheville, Edwin Wiley Grove had accumulated nearly 1,000 acres of prime real estate directly in the path of what he accurately predicted would be Asheville's route of residential expansion.

Now he just had to decide what to do with it.

*Edwin Wiley Grove*
*1850 - 1927*

*Fred L. Seely seen here in a c. 1898 photograph taken shortly before his marriage to Evelyn Grove, which took place in St. Louis.*

# Chapter 2

# "The Dandy from Detroit"

*From what I know of you, I see no reason why I should
not grant Evelyn's request to correspond with you, and if
there are any defects in Evelyn's character and disposition,
or in yours, I trust they will be brought out and known
to both of you before it is too late.*

Edwin Wiley Grove to
Fred L. Seely, 1898

While many men might have been content by age 48 to have
invented a popular and effective preventative against the spread of
malaria, to have formed a successful business for its manufacture,
and to have become a millionaire several times over -- with luxurious homes in St. Louis, St. Petersburg and Asheville -- that was not
the case with Edwin Wiley Grove.

The president of the Paris Medicine Company never tired of
searching for the next product that might equal or surpass the success of Grove's Tasteless Chill Tonic, those six-ounce bottles of quinine, sugar, lemon syrup, iron particles and alcohol found in nearly

every medicine cabinet across the South. In the years after 1890, when he moved his offices, factory and family from Paris, Tennessee, to St. Louis, Missouri, the men and women who worked for E. W. Grove were producing Febriline, Dr. Porter's Antiseptic Healing Oil, Pazo Anointment, Laxative Bromo-Quinine and, of course, Grove's Tasteless Chill Tonic.

But Dr. Grove -- the title was self-assumed, as he had no training or advanced degrees beyond a Memphis pharmacy school certificate -- continued to search for the next patent medicine he could produce. And when a product was in the developmental stage, he never hesitated to experiment with it by either taking it himself or urging his family and employees to try it as well.

Recognizing the struggle parents had to endure when coaxing their children to swallow even just a tablespoon of quinine, whose bitter taste could never be completely disguised by sugar or lemon syrup, Grove was determined to invent the first malaria tablet. Finding the perfect combination of ingredients that would not crumble in the box, while at the same time would quickly dissolve when swallowed -- and still containing the necessary amount of quinine to be effective -- proved to be more of a challenge than Grove alone could conquer. In 1897, after hearing of the strides being made in the Parke, Davis & Company's tablet department in Detroit, he wrote to them asking for assistance

Anxious to secure a lucrative contract with the renowned inventor of Grove's Tasteless Chill Tonic, the general manager at Parke, Davis & Company, William Warren, invited Grove to inspect their facilities and to meet with his small staff of chemists. As was the practice when a potential client arrived at Parke, Davis & Company, Warren always assigned one of his department heads to escort each visitor through the plant and to entertain him during his stay.

Once an appointment with E. W. Grove had been set, William Warren asked 26-year-old Frederick Loring Seely from his Experimental Department to greet the president of the Paris Medicine Company at the Michigan Central railway depot.

Since Seely's arrival in Detroit three years earlier, the young man from New Jersey had risen rapidly through the ranks at Parke, Davis & Company. In 1885, at the age of fourteen, he had begun working after school at Seabury & Johnson in New York City. He stayed on after graduation and remained there until he was 23, when he accepted a position in 1894 in the Experimental Department at Parke, Davis & Company. Demonstrating an aptitude for mechanical engineering, along with a quick grasp of chemical components, Seely soon rose to become head of their fledgling tablet department. It seemed only logical to William Warren that the serious young man from New Jersey -- who never went to the saloons with his fellow workers, who attended church every Sunday morning and who apparently had no life other than his work -- would be the ideal guide for the staunch Edwin Wiley Grove.

As their initial meeting progressed, Grove and Seely began sizing each other up -- and liked what they saw. The 48-year-old Grove recognized in Fred Seely, who was young enough to have been his son, many of the same traits that had carried him to the pinnacle of his success: determined, inventive, frugal, religious and impatient for success. As they talked on their way to the Cadillac Hotel, where the two men dined that evening, Seely sensed Grove's longing to step back from his responsibilities as founder, president, chairman and majority stockholder of the Paris Medicine Company. Grove talked of his new home in Asheville and his desire to spend more time there, where he had established an experimental laboratory under the name of the Tasteless Quinine Company, organized as a subsidiary of the Paris Medicine Company. Grove's health had suffered under the strain of his business, and his business had suffered under the strain of his health, but Grove felt there was no one he could yet trust to manage his multi-million dollar company. His only son Edwin was not yet even eight years old, and his daughter Evelyn, who had just turned twenty, had shown no interest in the family business.

Evelyn Grove.

Young, single, attractive -- and heir to a business and real estate portfolio worth millions of dollars.

And, as any potential suitor could not help but note, with a chronically ill stepmother and an exhausted, overweight and over-burdened father seemingly on track to an early heart attack.

The following morning William Warren greeted Fred Seely and Edwin Grove, then sent them on their tour of the Parke, Davis & Company's tablet department. Seely and Grove spent the day together discussing chemical formulas, sales promotions and plans for the future. Grove listened intently as Fred Seely hinted at ideas he had for being able to increase the capacity of the Excelsior tablet-making machines Parke, Davis & Company had been purchasing from the J. H. Day Company in Cincinnati. Realizing for the first time, perhaps, that Parke, Davis & Company did not hold a patent on their tablet machines, Grove began to rethink his initial idea of paying the Detroit firm to stamp out his tablets. Pressed by William Warren later that day to sign a contract, Grove deferred, claiming the need to return to St. Louis to discuss the proposition with his associates.

A few days later, Fred Seely wrote Edwin Grove, thanking him for making the trip to Detroit to discuss the problems Grove had been experiencing with his formula, and offering to travel, at his own expense, to Asheville to inspect the laboratory where Grove had been experimenting with his tablets. He followed this correspondence with another letter on February 5, 1898, asking if he could visit Grove in Asheville the following week.

On Monday, February 14, which happened to be Valentine's Day, Edwin Grove and his liveryman picked up Fred Seely in front of the Swannanoa Hotel on Biltmore Avenue, just down the hill from Pack Square, and brought him back to Grove's residence at the corner of Liberty and Broad Streets. There, before they sat down to dinner together, he introduced Fred to his wife Gertrude, his son Edwin and his daughter Evelyn.

A few days later, Fred Seely returned to his office, reporting to William Warren on the progress he had made improving Grove's formula. Seely's suggestions had eliminated the unpleasant greenish appearance, as well as the unfortunate side effects of occasional vomiting and diarrhea some people had experienced. Back at his desk, Seely also took time to write a personal letter to Edwin Grove. While his letter has not surfaced, the handwritten reply Edwin Grove mailed on February 25 contained the following response to what must have been a rather bold request by the young man:

*Evelyn's mother died when she was only about five years old and for a long time I had to act as both mother and father to her, and no one knows but myself how dear she is to me and the interest I feel in any change affecting her future. Evelyn has become a devoted Christian from her infancy and I know she could not be happy with any man who was not a Christian, and it was what I saw of your Christian character that influenced her to honor, trust and respect you.*

*Evelyn has had many admirers, but she only seemed to look upon them as friends, as their Christian character was not up to the standards which she had enacted for her ideal man.*

*I am frank to say to you, Mr. Seely, that your Christian character and your high ideal of what it takes to constitute a perfect man before God has made a favorable impression upon me, and I have said as much to Evelyn, but at the same time I advised her that I did not think you had seen enough of her and that she had not seen enough of you to come to a definite conclusion on so important a matter on such short acquaintance.*

*Evelyn is just out of school and I feel that she is too young for me to think about her assuming the responsibilities of matrimony and womanhood for some time yet. From what I know of you, I see no reason why I should not grant Evelyn's request to correspond with you, and if there are any defects in Evelyn's character and disposition, or in yours, I trust they will be brought out and known to both of you before it is too late.*

While the prospect of a matrimonial union between Fred Seely and Evelyn Grove already seemed to have been on their minds, Edwin Grove and Fred Seely proceeded at an even faster pace in regards to their business relationship. A short time later Grove boarded a train for Cincinnati, where he introduced himself to John Day, owner of J. H. Day & Company, which designed machinery for "Bakers, Millers, Druggists, Perfumers, Spice Mills, Manufacturers, Baking Powders, Self-Rising Flour, Putty, Paints, Soaps, Etc." Among their clients was the firm of Parke, Davis & Company, for whom they manufactured machines for stamping out tablets. After their meeting, John Day wrote to his friend Fred Seely about Grove's visit:

*He stated that he was going on to see you and wanted to know what I thought or knew about you. I, of course, could not say anything about you but what was good and I have given that to him in a very forcible manner; however, I do not think I overstated facts. From what he intimated to me, I believe that before this time he will have made arrangements with you and that in course of time will want several of our Excelsior Tablet machines. We certainly trust that you have closed a deal with him and that it will not be long before you will be running a place of your own and getting a more just recompense for your services than you are now getting. I honestly believe that Mr. Grove should also be congratulated if he is able to secure as a son-in-law a young man of your ability and integrity.*

As he had indicated to John Day, Edwin Grove returned to Detroit on Friday, May 13, but, rather than proceeding to Parke, Davis & Company, he took a room at the Russell Hotel, where he and Seely had dinner that evening. Their weekend discussions culminated on Monday evening, when they reached an agreement whereby Fred Seely would become manager of the Tasteless Quinine Company in Asheville. His primary responsibilities would be to secure tablet-making machines for Edwin Grove from J. H. Day and to oversee production of Grove's Laxative Bromo-Quinine tablets for its parent company, the Paris Medicine Company.

Grove left the following day for Washington, D.C., to attend a meeting of pharmaceutical manufacturers concerned over proposed legislation that would eventually become the Pure Food and Drug Act of 1906. As it was finally written, the law mandated federal inspection of meat production facilities, prohibited the inclusion of poisonous chemicals in patent medicines, and forced manufacturers such as E. W. Grove to list on their labels specific drugs, including alcohol, cocaine, morphine and heroin, included in their formulas. Neither Grove nor the Paris Medicine Company were targeted as specifically as was the Coca-Cola Company, which until 1903 had secretly included small amounts of cocaine in its formula, later replaced with large doses of caffeine. Grove, however, worried that the required disclosures would diminish sales of his best-selling Grove's Tasteless Chill Tonic.

While Grove was en route to Washington, Fred Seely boarded a train to Asheville, arriving on May 21 for what would have been just his second meeting with Evelyn Grove. He remained in Asheville for four days, returning to Park, Davis & Company on May 27, at which time he submitted his resignation to William Warren.

Incensed at the prospect of losing the head of his tablet department as well as what could have been a major account with the world-renown Paris Medicine Company, William Warren took out a warrant for Fred Seely's arrest, insisting that Seely had stolen Park, Davis & Company formulas, drawings and measurements of their tablet machines. When Grove learned of Warren's actions, he advised Fred Seely to immediately return to Asheville to make a sworn statement under oath in front of the county clerk contesting William Warren's accusations. Meanwhile, Grove took an overnight train to Detroit, where he confronted William Warren and, in the presence of two stenographers, grilled the supervisor until Warren admitted that his accusations had been based solely on reports from other employees.

After a third meeting with Evelyn, Fred Seely then left Asheville for Cincinnati, where he spent most of June, July and August working on behalf of Edwin Grove and the Tasteless Quinine Company in the machine shop of John H. Day. There he worked with Day's machinists, increasing the production capability of the Excelsior tablet machines as well as developing an invention of his own -- an attachment to the Excelsior that would automatically count tablets and insert a specified number into Grove's small cardboard boxes. Prior to this time, John Day's machines would simply stamp out the tablets and drop them into a large wooden barrel. Later, employees would scoop out the tablets, count and hand-fill the boxes with the required number of tablets.

By the end of August, Grove's tablet machines had arrived in Asheville, where Fred Seely and his foreman, A. G. Lang, soon had them stamping out and boxing thousands of Grove's improved Bromo-Quinine tablets. Despite their rapid advancements, Seely and Grove continued to experiment with the various components in the anti-malaria tablets, trying various combinations of chemicals, including a small dose of morphine. Along the way, what had originally been intended to be a tablet that would ward off malaria was found to have an unexpected side effect. During his experiments, which included testing each new combination of ingredients on himself, his family and his employees, Grove discovered that his tablets also eliminated headaches and many of the symptoms associated with the common cold.

This discovery of an effective cold tablet could not have come at a better time for the Paris Medicine Company. As medical researchers began to trace a connection between mosquitoes and the transmission of malaria, they recommended filling in low, wet areas where mosquitoes thrived. As the number of mosquitoes declined, so did the number of malaria victims -- along with the demand for Grove's malaria-prevention products. Recognizing this trend, Grove soon switched the focus of his marketing from "Makes Children and Adults As Fat As Pigs" to "Cures A Cold In One Day."

Thus, with the assistance of Fred Seely, Edwin Wiley Grove now had another new invention to his credit: the first cold tablet.

And in the process he also gained a new son-in-law, as on October 24, 1898, Frederick Loring Seely and Evelyn Grove were married in the chapel of the Second Presbyterian Church of St. Louis, just a short walk from the Grove's home on Westminster Place.

The newlyweds, however, had to postpone any plans for a honeymoon, as Gertrude Grove, Evelyn's stepmother, had scheduled surgery to correct a partial bowel obstruction the week following their wedding. As a result, after their wedding Fred and Evelyn boarded the Southern Railway train bound for Asheville, accompanied by eight-year-old Edwin Grove Junior and Gertrude Grove.

E. W. Grove saw the group to Union Station, where he also boarded a train, but Grove's was headed to Texas, where he claimed he needed to meet with his salesmen. Writing from Texas the following week, Grove reminded his new son-in-law, "As soon as you try the experimental Tasteless Tablets which I gave you before you left, let me know the result."

And this was just a taste of what lay ahead for Fred Seely and his life with Edwin Wiley Grove.

Fred and Evelyn spent their first two years of marriage living in her father's home in Asheville. Grove remained in St. Louis much of this time, struggling to deal with internal management problems developing among his minority stockholders from Paris. Fred Seely soon perfected both the formula for Grove's Bromo-Quinine cold tablets, as well as the machinery for stamping, counting and boxing them, for which he received a United States patent and a sizable monthly royalty from the Paris Medicine Company for exclusive rights to it.

By 1900, however, Grove and Seely had decided to close the Asheville branch and move the tablet machines to St. Louis. Fred and Evelyn made the move as well, effectively trading houses with her father and stepmother. While Fred stepped into the role as operations manager at the Paris Medicine Company with his customary energy and efficiency, the Grove family returned to Asheville, where Grove spent the next year recovering from a bout of near-exhaustion. In a matter of months, Fred Seely had reorganized every department, from factory production and traveling salesmen down to the advertising and accounting departments. Along the way he more than ruffled a few feathers, firing salesmen who were not meeting his quotas and releasing slackers on the factory floor, many of whom had been hired by Grove simply on the basis that they were related to Grove's longtime friends and early supporters back in Tennessee.

In the fall of 1901, however, E. W. Grove was ready to return to the helm of his smoothly running operation in St. Louis. Fred Seely also seemed ready for a change, as the two men soon decided that Fred and Evelyn would finally take their long-overdue honeymoon, embarking in October on a round-the-world cruise paid for by the Paris Medicine Company. Their trip was also business-related, as the couple spent nearly a month on the remote island of Java, where Evelyn was the only English-speaking woman, while Fred negotiated a long-term contract for Grove with a major producer of quinine, a vital staple for the Paris Medicine Company.

Company employees predicted that the couple's return to St. Louis in 1902 would signal a new era at the Paris Medicine Company. Fred Seely appeared ready to assume control of the daily operation, while E. W. Grove, at age 52, would begin to enjoy his well-deserved retirement. Grove had even developed interests outside St. Louis and the Paris Medicine Company, investing in a cattle operation in Texas, timber fields in Arkansas, coal mines in West Virginia, residential real estate in Atlanta and new homes in both St. Petersburg and Asheville, where he had also begun buying real estate for future development.

But E. W. Grove had other ideas about his future.

Unable or unwilling to share the management of the Paris Medicine Company with his son-in-law, who might have been as equally unable or unwilling to share management with his father-in-law, Grove and Seely soon reached an impasse. Their two totally different styles of organization and management left their employees confused as to whose orders they were to follow. While their conversations that long, hot summer in St. Louis can only be imagined, the result was painfully obvious: in 1902, at the age of 31, Fred Seely tendered his resignation from the Paris Medicine Company.

The reasons for his abrupt departure varied according to whom was asked. As Grove later recounted, Fred Seely had caused confusion among the employees, prompting several to leave the Paris Medicine Company. According to his version, Grove had offered Seely the opportunity to move to Atlanta where, in exchange for overseeing the development of Grove's two new residential neighborhoods, Grove would pay him a salary, provide him and Evelyn with a home, and would assist him in setting up a business of his choosing, all the while permitting Seely to remain as a stockholder and secretary to the board of the Paris Medicine Company.

Publicly, Fred Seely, now also a father, told friends and a St. Louis newspaper reporter that he was considering enrolling in either Yale or Princeton, possibly to study law.

Years later, when Grove and Seely were pitted against each other in a bitter family feud over the Grove Park Inn, Fred Seely testified in court that, in fact, he had been forced to resign by Grove, who cited "his wife's jealousy of her step-daughter Evelyn."

In truth, all three reports bear some claim of validity. Just as Grove and Seely each proved too headstrong, too stubborn and too egotistical to make any partnership work, Grove's constant and at times inappropriate expressions of his affection for his only daughter sparked both jealousy in his own wife and resentment on the part of his son-in-law. Four volatile ingredients -- Gertrude's jealousy, Grove's pride, Evelyn's meekness and Fred's ambition -- combined to sabotage any possibility of a pharmaceutical empire with profitable subsidiaries in real estate developments, ranching, mining, timber and, of course, the hotel business.

In 1906, after failed attempts to patent a bottling machine, to further his education at Princeton or to become a real estate developer in Atlanta, Fred Seely convinced E. W. Grove that they should start a new daily newspaper called the *Atlanta Georgian*. Despite his misgivings, Grove, who had hoped his son-in-law would find a career in banking or real estate, reluctantly agreed to provide the financial backing to lease the buildings, buy the presses and hire the employees required to do battle with such established papers as the *Atlanta Constitution*, the *Atlanta News* and the *Atlanta Journal*.

Despite having absolutely no experience in the newspaper business and being considered, rightly so, as an outsider by Atlanta businessmen, Fred Seely carved out a distinguished reputation as a newspaper publisher and editor. During his tenure at the *Georgian* from 1906 until 1912, Seely supported the candidacy of Woodrow Wilson and led the call for a repeal of Georgia's corrupt practice of leasing out convicts to favored land and railroad developers.

Unfortunately, his personal zeal and untiring work ethic could not lure enough advertisers away from Atlanta's established newspapers to make the *Georgian* profitable. Frustrated and exhausted, by 1912 Fred Seely was looking for a respectable exit, one that would preserve his personal reputation while also repaying his father-in-law the nearly $200,000 Grove had already invested in the enterprise.

That same year Fred Seely began to take more seriously his father-in-law's idea for building a hotel in Asheville. Grove had accumulated enough land for such an undertaking and, as Seely knew from his regular visits back to Asheville, the aging Battery Park Hotel no longer dominated the hotel scene in the rapidly growing city.

Perhaps, he soon imagined, if he could find a buyer for the *Atlanta Georgian*, he could escape the daily grind of running a newspaper, while also providing his father-in-law with the one missing ingredient in his plan for a hotel -- the financing.

And, perhaps, a new career for himself as well.

*Since 1886, the original Battery Park Hotel had served both residents of Asheville and the growing number of tourists, including George Vanderbilt, Fred L. Seely and E. W. Grove on their initial visits to the region.*

*People from smog-besieged cities, such as St. Louis, Pittsburg and Chicago, soon began hearing about the natural features and healing qualities of the Asheville region, prompting them to begin vacationing there.*

# Chapter 3

# "Tobacco, Tuberculosis or Tourists?"

*Gradually Asheville became a city of palaces and shacks;*
*of hotels and tenants; of the rich and the poor. If there*
*was an Asheville of magnificent hotels, ramshackle*
*boarding houses, and health resorts, there was also a town*
*of immigrants living above stores around Pack Square,*
*of blacks squeezed into shacks, and of mountaineers*
*pressed together in mobile home parks on the city's outskirts.*

Milton Ready, Historian

When Edwin Wiley Grove first arrived in Asheville in 1897, the future of the city stood at a crossroads. Sitting on a mountain plateau high above the French Broad River in a fertile valley that for decades had supplied Indians and early settlers with an abundant source of fish and game, the city seemed much younger than its sister cities to the east -- Durham, Winston-Salem and Raleigh.

Its growth had long been stymied by the very feature that was soon to attract people from across the country: the Blue Ridge Mountains.

Though worn and much older than the craggy peaks of the Rocky Mountains and nowhere near as daunting to those first settlers, the Blue Ridge Mountains encircling Asheville served as an effective barrier to the expansion of the railroad. Poor management, bitter politics and blatant corruption had derailed every attempt made after the Civil War to wind a set of tracks through narrow passes and up the steep slopes surrounding the city. Fueled with luck, determination and convict labor -- coupled with new machinery capable of drilling tunnels through hundreds of feet of solid granite -- the Western North Carolina Railroad burst through the final mountainside into the French Broad River Valley on October 2, 1880. The new rail line provided a direct route from the East through the mountains and into Asheville, whose population doubled in the next three years.

Contact with the central and eastern portions of the state brought more reports of the economic boom taking place in Durham, where the thin, sandy soil was found to be ideal for the growing of what was to become North Carolina's premier cash crop: tobacco.

Despite stories to the contrary, the English could not lay claim to having introduced tobacco to the American colonies. Long before the first explorers set foot on their beaches, Native American Indians had been growing tobacco for use in their religious ceremonies. The Jamestown colonists soon discovered, in fact, that their new American-grown tobacco was far superior to that being sold to the English by Spain, and eventually began exporting tobacco to London. By 1700, their treasured tobacco seeds were traveling south into the Carolinas with new bands of settlers. Demand for quality tobacco in England, where it was considered a luxury, provided plenty of financial incentive for the first farmers in what was to become the state of North Carolina.

As the domestic population of the state increased, so did the demand among its settlers for tobacco. Prior to the Civil War, most tobacco leaves were chewed, smoked in a pipe or rolled into cigars. Less frequently, the dried leaves were ground and hand-rolled into cigarettes. The first tobacco grown in North Carolina, however, was considered inferior to that being harvested in neighboring Virginia, prompting tobacco growers to find new ways to utilize their product. At the close of the Civil War, a young man by the name of Washington Duke returned to his decimated family home outside Durham, where he resurrected their small tobacco farm. Rather than competing with the Virginia growers and their higher grade of tobacco, Duke began grinding his dried leaves to be hand-rolled by former slaves into cigarettes.

His son, James "Buck" Duke, also believed that the future of tobacco lay in cigarettes rather than cigars, pipes and snuff. In 1885, he signed an agreement with James Bonsack of Virginia, who four years earlier had invented the first automated cigarette-rolling machine. Believing the American public would reject the notion of a machine-rolled cigarette, other tobacco manufacturers had earlier snubbed Bonsack. Together Duke and Bonsack improved the efficiency of his first machines and soon began installing them in Duke's factory in Durham. Bonsack's first model could roll 120,000 cigarettes a day and, within a few years, their factory in Durham was producing nearly one billion cigarettes a year, aptly named the Duke of Durham.

Aggressive and innovative marketing -- including the lure of the first baseball trading cards in each pack -- along with a restrictive contract that prevented Bonsack from leasing his machines to other firms, soon made Washington Duke, Sons & Company one of the largest tobacco companies in the United States. In 1890, in a move that ultimately attracted the unwanted intrusion of federal regulators, James Duke negotiated the merger of his firm with four other leading manufacturers into the giant American Tobacco Company. For nearly two decades this monopoly dictated everything from the price of raw tobacco to the cost of cigarettes around the world, effectively stimulating the demand for tobacco while at the same time controlling both the price and the supply of cigarettes.

In turn-of-the-century Asheville, many civic leaders pointed to how the growing and processing of tobacco had catapulted Durham from a sleepy farm town to a major center of commerce. Area farmers had already grown enough burley tobacco, the variety used for pipes and cigarettes, to see the first market and warehouse built in Asheville in 1870. Before long they were raising more than seven million pounds of tobacco a year. By the turn of the century, a total of twenty tobacco dealers and six warehouses prompted one civic leader to predict that Asheville "would become the tobacco center of North Carolina."

But the proponents of tobacco soon found themselves fighting a losing battle.

First came the discovery that while tobacco could be grown on a number of different types of soil, the largest yields came from fields of sandy, well-drained loam, typical of what was found in the central part of the state. Farmers around mountainous Asheville were forced to utilize the river bottoms, small valleys and 'hollows,' where the soil had a high organic content and too much nitrogen for tobacco to flourish.

In addition, the burley tobacco typically grown in western North Carolina proved less suited to cigarette production than the flue-cured or 'bright' tobacco grown in the flat, hot Piedmont portion of the state. The harvesting of burley tobacco left farmers at the mercy of the elements, as the stalks were typically cut and stacked "teepee-style" in the fields. They remained in the open for three or four days, during which time the farmers prayed for dry weather to prompt the initial curing. The families would then gather the wilted stalks and carry them to their tobacco barn, where the stalks were hung upside down on hooks and allowed to air-dry for six to eight weeks. Once cured, the stalks were removed, the leaves stripped and sorted by size and quality, then bundled and hauled to the nearest market to be auctioned to one of the tobacco buyers.

As an additional hindrance, most tobacco farmers in western North Carolina grew tobacco as a supplement to their regular incomes, whether that be raising other crops or working in town. Stubbornly independent, many of the mountain farmers resisted the advice offered by agriculture specialists who had studied crop rotation, new insecticides and means of preventing such diseases as 'black shank' and 'blue mold.' Their family fields were small and scattered amid the steep hillsides, forcing farmers to rely heavily on hand labor, generally from their own children. But when those children grew up and found there was not enough income from the farm to support them, they left, and many tobacco plots grew up in weeds.

Finally, the concentration of both tobacco fields and factories in the Durham and Winston-Salem area, where corporations had already invested the money required for faster, more efficient machinery to process tobacco into packaged cigarettes, hindered any real growth of the industry in Asheville.

So while tobacco remained a family tradition on many farms around Asheville, the tobacco industry never gained a foothold.

Yet while tobacco was failing to gain support, an even more vocal group of citizens believed they had found the key to Asheville's economic future -- tuberculosis.

Asheville's existence had once depended on the influx of cattle drovers and fur traders into its mountain plateau, but word soon spread of its mild climate and natural healing qualities: clean air, unpolluted rivers, hot springs, mountain trails and lush landscapes. One doctor who had studied the entire United States in search of the perfect location for a healing center, "selected Asheville as having the optimum combination of barometric pressure, temperature, humidity and sunlight."

As drovers and traders were slowly replaced by frail invalids and tired businessmen, taverns evolved into inns, then inns became hotels. The hotels spawned boarding houses, and many boarding houses soon were called sanitariums.

Among those outsiders whose doctors had prescribed a train ticket to Asheville and who had arrived with a nagging cough, asthma, bronchitis, rheumatism or emphysema -- or who simply suffered from exhaustion or seemed on the verge of a nervous breakdown -- were men who would rise to shape the city's future.

Men such as George Vanderbilt and Edwin Wiley Grove.

Over the years, the stories of how each of these two men came to western North Carolina have become a part of Asheville folklore.

In 1887, the 25-year-old George Vanderbilt, the ninth and youngest child of industrialist William Henry Vanderbilt, decided on a lark to accompany his mother from their Fifth Avenue Manhattan mansion to rustic Asheville. Her family physician had recommend that she seek treatment from Dr. Samuel Westray Battle, a former New York and United States Navy surgeon who had established a medical practice in Asheville. Mrs. Vanderbilt and her son booked rooms in the city's newest and finest hostelry -- the Battery Park Hotel -- and, while his mother recuperated from a severe case of social exhaustion, George became enamored with the panoramic views of the Blue Ridge Mountains from his balcony. He leased a horse and, accompanied by a local guide and real estate attorney, began riding through the farms and forests south of the city, emerging on a wide bluff with a commanding view of the French Broad River and Mt. Pisgah in the distance.

It was then and there that the young bachelor decided to build his home, a 250-room palatial mansion modeled after the Chateau de Blois in France. Money was not a problem, at least not then, as he stood to inherit six million dollars (a small fraction of what his older brothers received), the family farm, their Fifth Avenue mansion and his father's extensive art collection. By the time his acquisitions were complete, George Vanderbilt had accumulated nearly 125,000 acres of farmland and forest, including the 80,000-acre Pisgah Forest.

In 1898, at the age of 36 and three years after the completion of the Biltmore House, George Vanderbilt quietly married Edith Stuyvesant Dresser while in France. Two years later, she bore their only child, Cornelia, who later embarked on a scandalous married life, most of it spent touring France with her artist lover. But in 1914 George Vanderbilt suddenly died, most likely of a blood clot formed as he recuperated in their Washington, D.C., home after an appendectomy.

Ironically, it was Edith Vanderbilt, not George, who ultimately had the greatest impact on Asheville.

Strapped for cash after George's death and in charge of raising their 14-year-old daughter, Edith began divesting herself of tangent responsibilities. She sold Biltmore Estate Industries, the hamlet of Biltmore Village and the land for what later became an upscale residential development called Biltmore Forest. Later, she sold nearly 100,000 acres to the United States government for what became the Pisgah National Forest, and in 1930 threw open the doors to the famed Biltmore House, collecting an admission fee from those who wished to see how the infamous Vanderbilts had lived.

Dr. Westray Battle, who arrived in Asheville in 1885, had not been the only physician to tout the healing powers of the mountain environment and Asheville as the region's health center. Some had come to restore their own health, then stayed to establish a medical practice. As Asheville's reputation grew, so did the number of boarding houses -- and the number of physicians specializing in pulmonary health care. One of the most well known was the Brexton Boarding House in the Montford neighborhood. Initially run by a series of women, in 1906 it was leased by St. Joseph's Hospital for treating their tuberculosis patients. The hospital soon enlarged the building, adding several sleeping porches to provide easy access to sunlight and the mountain air deemed critical to their patients' care and recuperation.

Along with Dr. Battle, Dr. Karl Von Ruck was influential in positioning Asheville as a center for tuberculosis care. Von Ruck arrived in Asheville in 1886 and opened the Winyah Sanitarium two years later. Many of the physicians who came to work for him later opened their own practices, further expanding Asheville's reputation for medical care, especially in the treatment of tuberculosis.

While this influx of physicians and the infirm swelled Asheville's population at the turn of the century, residents gradually learned more about the disease and how it might affect them and their children. Tuberculosis, they learned, was spread from person to person through tiny droplets of infected saliva propelled through the air by coughing or sneezing. Once in the lungs, the tuberculosis bacteria entered the victim's bloodstream and spread throughout the body. Over time, infected persons would gradually waste away, their strength and immune system so drained that death often seemed inevitable.

With no known cure for tuberculosis, the logical approach seemed to be isolation, preferably in a setting that provided clean, fresh air and proper nutrition. As one historian noted, the sanatoriums located in areas such as Asheville "provided a dual function: they isolated the sick [and] the source of infection from the general population, while the enforced rest, together with a proper diet and the well-regulated hospital life, assisted the healing process."

"The idea of caring for patients in a setting removed from the general populace was considered wise and necessary for preventing the spread of the disease," one writer explained. "At the time, cities were considered by many to be pestilential and insalubrious places, so the notion of patients taking in the fresh air and sunshine of healthful and mountainous, rural settings was persuasive. It is not surprising, then, that pastoral settings, often former farms, were viewed as the ideal locations for sanatoria and that many maintained their own agricultural operations, particularly dairies, in order to supply the patients with fresh and healthful food."

While Edwin Wiley Grove did not suffer from either tuberculosis or emphysema, by 1897 his physician had recommended that he spend several weeks each year in Asheville. Working long hours in the sweltering heat and polluted air of the manufacturing district of St. Louis, Grove suffered from near-exhaustion. In addition, the pharmaceutical manufacturer also endured prolonged bouts of hiccups his entire life. They, too, contributed to his declining health and prompted him to spend more and more time each year in Asheville recuperating.

With the addition in 1898 of Fred L. Seely to both his family and the management of the Paris Medicine Company, E. W. Grove was able to spend even more time in Asheville with his wife, young son and daughter Evelyn.

His move there coincided with the increase in the number of sanitariums and boarding houses catering to tuberculosis patients. While Grove was not alone in warning of the repercussions to Asheville's economy an association with tuberculosis could have, he was among the most vocal. Fearing Asheville could become a leper colony for the highly contagious tuberculosis, he urged the city's leaders to regulate the size and location of sanitariums. He also advocated closing down shanty boarding houses which accepted infected patients who could not afford to stay at reputable sanitariums run by trained medical personnel.

E. W. Grove's first purchase was the large lot at 43 Liberty Street, where James Tennent designed and constructed a sprawling three-story home for him. As he spent more time there, Grove recognized the opportunities in residential real estate that Asheville offered. The majority of new homes were clustered in the Montford neighborhood northwest of downtown and Kenilworth to the south. With Beaucatcher Mountain blocking expansion to the east and the French Broad River to the west, Grove calculated that the demand for housing would soon drive up the value of land further north of downtown. One of the first major purchases he made was of the Kimberly Farm, largely rolling pasture land at the foot of Sunset Mountain and adjacent to the Swannanoa Hunt Club's nine-hole golf course.

Ever impatient, Grove soon hired a crew of surveyors and graders who began laying out neighborhoods, plotting building lots, installing curbstones and paving streets, many which he named after members of his family: Gertrude Avenue, Edwin Place and Evelyn Place. Grove had learned a great deal about real estate development in both St. Louis and Atlanta, and applied those lessons to his developments in Asheville. At the north end of Charlotte Street, at the point where Macon Avenue winds up Sunset Mountain toward the present day site of the Grove Park Inn, Grove first donated land to the citizens of Asheville for a public park. Aptly named Grove Park, it included a fountain, a low rock wall separating it from Charlotte Street and two roofed streetcar stations for people awaiting the arrival of the streetcar. His gift to the city of Asheville, however, contained one provision: that Grove would be able to erect a stone cottage in the corner of Grove Park to serve as the office of the E. W. Grove Real Estate Company. Today both the park and the fieldstone cottage remain intact, appearing much as they did more than 100 years ago.

As his land holdings in Asheville grew, so did Grove's concern over the future of Asheville and the direction civic leaders might choose to follow. In a letter dated November 24, 1909, to his son-in-law Fred Seely about a recent purchase, "I was almost forced to buy this property to protect my holdings there. If consumptive sanitariums had gone up on [Sunset] mountain, it would have injured my property very much. Now I am fully protected on all sides, and I regard it as a very profitable investment because Asheville cannot grow any other way."

Grove, however, knew that it could all come to a halt unless he took special precautions with each sale. After conferring with his attorney, each of the deeds for any residential property he sold included a ban on "any commercial or manufacturing establishment or factory or tenement or apartment house of any kind, at any time; or use any buildings erected thereon for such purpose." In addition, whenever possible Grove purchased boarding houses catering to tubercular patients and had them torn down.

The Recession of 1908, however, sharply curtailed sales of residential building lots, prompting E. W. Grove and his real estate manager William Randolph to begin considering fresh marketing plans. It was about this same time that civic leaders in Asheville began approaching E. W. Grove about the possibility of building a tourist hotel on his property. The once stately Battery Park Hotel, built in 1886 in downtown Asheville, was beginning to show its age, and residents and business owners were concerned about losing the tourist trade. Recalling, no doubt, the problems he had encountered with his early stockholders in the Paris Medicine Company, Grove declined any partnership offers to either buy or build on his land.

But the idea of building and owning a major tourist hotel, located in the midst of the residential building lots he had for sale, had certainly captured his attention.

Never one to make a hasty decision, Grove discreetly discussed the idea at great length with both Randolph in Asheville and Fred Seely in Atlanta. Late in 1910, Fred Seely wrote back to Grove, "when it is known that there is a first-class hotel such as we propose for Sunset [Mountain] in Asheville, and that no sick people are taken, there will be no trouble in filling the house."

Grove, Randolph and Seely spent most of 1911 and the first part of 1912 discussing various plans both for the design and financing of a luxury resort hotel. While Randolph quietly began contacting architects, Fred Seely began negotiations for the sale of the *Atlanta Georgian*, the newspaper he and Grove had founded in 1906, to William Randolph Hearst. Once completed, Grove and Seely agreed to use that money to build the Grove Park Inn, under the supervision of Fred Seely.

To their great consternation, however, at the same time a group of Asheville citizens and business owners, concerned over the recent drop in tourism, announced plans to construct "a national sanitarium, national in the sense that it will be large enough to accommodate all comers, and will be so conducted that persons of almost every class can be admitted…. a great building erected on some peak near in, and conducted by skilled directors, [where] the sick of the world could come, and it would be but a short time until this city would be famous the world over as a resort indisputably beneficial to those afflicted with tuberculosis. Instead of speaking in hushed tones about tuberculosis, we are shouting abroad the fact that this section has properties for the cure of lung troubles far superior to those of Denver, and all are invited to come."

The proposal set off a firestorm.

Almost immediately, the recently-formed Asheville Hotel Men's Association vehemently opposed the plan, demanding that the Board of Trade, which endorsed the plan, forego any plans to advertise and promote Asheville as a destination of people suffering from the highly contagious tuberculosis, stating that, "the advertising of Asheville as a tubercular health resort would make it impossible to secure Asheville the usual summer and winter tourists." Furthermore, they declared that they would no longer provide any financial support for the Board of Trade.

A representative from the Southern Railway Company wrote that he had "received hundreds of letters in the course of the year from all parts of the country, stating that they were anxious either to come or to send members of their family to Asheville, but that they would not come until assured by me that they could find quarters where the patients would not be thrown in contact with sufferers from tubercular troubles."

The chairman of the Sanitary Committee of the City of Asheville seemed to have struck the chord marking the middle ground in the battle: "I am heartily in sympathy with their efforts to throw certain restrictions and safeguards around places which keep tubercular people.... such as segregation [of patients], reporting cases to the Health Department, and enforcement of the law [in regards to] hotels and boarding houses [that are falsely] advertising that they keep no tubercular patients. I do think when we do that we, as officials, have done our duty, and feel that it is going beyond our duty to advertise Asheville as specially fitted for that class of people."

During the height of the controversy, E. W. Grove, while not an official member of the Hotel Men's Association, made it clear that if the City of Asheville were going to publicly encourage people with tuberculosis to come to Asheville for treatment, then he would drop his plans to build the Grove Park Inn. To emphasize his point, he instructed William Randolph to send this telegram to all of the architects who had previously submitted sketches: "The various hotel plans submitted do not meet with Mr. Grove's approval; he is not desirous of continuing the competition. I am sending your plans to you per express with much appreciation for the interest you have shown in the matter."

To understand how important the proposed Grove Park Inn was to the people of Asheville, on October 28, 1909, when Grove's name was first linked to the hotel project, the *Asheville Gazette-News* stated: "The completion of the plans will mean an advertisement for Asheville second only to that afforded by Biltmore Estate and will bring here many people of wealth, and its building will give employment to hundreds of workmen for a long term of years. Dr. Grove is a far-sighted man and eventually, of course, will be the gainer by his enterprise, but it is Asheville which will immediately profit and that in no measurable degree. Dr. Grove is so well-known for his unfailing success in all that he has undertaken means that even more will be done than he has promised."

Faced with the likely prospect that E. W. Grove was about to cancel his plans, the city leaders and businessmen huddled together, attempting to mend the damage done by their proposal for a national sanitarium in Asheville. On March 7, 1912, Fred Seely wrote to Grove from Asheville, where he had been following the hearings:

*In reply thereto I beg to say that the 'agitation' has about died out; the Aldermen will not consent to have the health conditions exploited; they will not appropriate any money for that purpose. The report of the committee that started all the trouble has been knocked out, and the members of said committee agree that the matter was ill-advised, and they are more than willing that no more be said about it.*

*We can now safely go ahead.*

*Fred Seely's original 1912 sketch that Edwin Wiley Grove approved.*

# Chapter 4

# "A Groundbreaking Surprise"

*The sketch proved, strangely, to be entirely satisfactory*
*to Mr. Grove and he approved it, and requested that*
*I go to Asheville with him to locate the building and*
*start the work.*

Fred L. Seely

May 1912

When, in the spring of 1912, Fred Seely reluctantly boarded the Asheville train bound for Atlanta, he had to have been thinking about his future. To those who knew him, Fred Seely seemed on the road to success. At age 41, he was the founder, co-owner, publisher and editor of a respected Atlanta newspaper, was married to the only daughter of one of the wealthiest men in St. Louis, had four lovely children and a modern home, and found his name being mentioned by the leaders of the Georgia Democratic party as a possible candidate for public office.

But Fred Seely was unhappy.

Behind the façade he saw a man who was tired of fighting the daily battle of trying to lure major advertisers away from the established Atlanta newspapers, of explaining to his father-in-law and business partner why, after five years, the paper had yet to show a profit, of urging his wife to take a more active role in the prestigious Atlanta Woman's Club, and of hiding from himself the knowledge that his decision to move his family to Atlanta had been a mistake.

He also knew, however, that he could not go crawling back to his father-in-law, asking to return to work as vice-president of the Paris Medicine Company. Grove's only son, Edwin, had now turned 22 and, after dropping out of school, had come to realize just how wealthy his father really was. Edwin had moved into Fred Seely's former office and was going through the motions of learning the various departments at the Paris Medicine Company under the watchful eye of his vigilant father. The elder Grove no longer needed Fred Seely to reorganize and run his business, as he had fourteen years earlier. At age 62, he had his son primed to assume control of his company and his fortune.

For a while it had seemed as if Fred Seely's role as a vocal supporter of Woodrow Wilson's candidacy for president in the summer of 1911 might land Fred an appointment in Washington. He had carefully nurtured his friendship with Secretary of State William Jennings Bryan, whom he had met while Bryan was campaigning in Atlanta in 1906. But the call to serve his country, the call that could have permitted him to escape Atlanta with his dignity intact, never came. Any thoughts of returning to St. Louis, Detroit or Princeton, cities that had once held great hope and promise for him, were all tainted with disappointment. There was but one place where he and Evelyn had both been happy.

Asheville.

Evelyn and their children always looked forward to their trips aboard the Southern Railway to her father's sprawling home on the grassy knoll at the corner of Liberty and Broad Streets. Fred and his father-in-law seemed to get along better walking along the freshly paved streets near his new sub-divisions, Norwood Park, Grove Park and Kimberly Avenue, than they ever had in St. Louis or Atlanta. But Grove did not need his son-in-law to manage his real estate investments in Asheville, especially since sales of his residential building lots had stalled during the recent recession. More recently, however, their talks had turned to another building project, one in which Grove lacked any real experience: a resort hotel.

At first Fred Seely had paid little mind to Grove's idea of building a resort hotel on the western slope of Sunset Mountain, judging it to be yet another of his father-in-law's fleeting ideas of increasing property sales on his adjoining land. But as he read the newspaper reports and editorials in the Asheville papers urging E. W. Grove to provide the city with a modern facility to replace the aging Battery Park Hotel, he began to take the idea more seriously. Like Grove, Fred Seely had no experience in hotel construction or management, but he had learned in his five years at the helm of the *Atlanta Georgian* that his ability to plan, to organize and to direct people could enable him to undertake any new project.

As he listened to his father-in-law talk about the possibility of building a resort hotel on Sunset Mountain, he realized that Grove was more concerned with the benefit of having a completed hotel in the midst of his developments than he was with the actual design, construction and management of it. He advised Grove to proceed cautiously, inviting architects from across the region to submit preliminary sketches for a proposed hotel. In 1910, William Randolph, Grove's property manager, began sending out the following notices:

*Relative to the hotel proposed in E. W. Grove Park, we beg to state that we will be glad to consider any sketches or plans that you wish to submit, provided such sketches or plans are to be without any expense to Mr. E. W. Grove.*

The site which Grove had selected lay on the western slope of Sunset Mountain, nearly halfway to the summit and overlooking the Asheville Country Club golf course, downtown Asheville and the lush French Broad River valley. It was high enough to offer guests a panoramic view of the Great Smoky Mountains to the west, yet not so high on the mountain that it could prove inaccessible during Asheville's occasional winter storms.

As Grove later explained, "After a long mountain walk one evening, at the sunset hour, I sat down here to rest, and while almost entranced by the panoramic view of these encircling mountains and a restful outlook upon green fields, the dream of an old-time inn came to me -- an inn whose exterior, and interior as well, should present a home-like and wholesome simplicity, whose hospitable doors should ever be open wide, inviting the traveler to rest awhile, shut in from the busy world outside."

While Grove studied the numerous sketches arriving from architects across the country anxious to secure the lucrative commission, Fred Seely returned to Atlanta, where he began negotiations to sell the struggling *Atlanta Georgian* to newspaper magnate William Randolph Hearst. He completed the sale in the spring of 1912, just as Grove, frustrated with the sketches he had received, was about to drop the idea of building a hotel on Sunset Mountain. Seely gently intervened, offering to review the sketches for Grove back in his Atlanta office.

## "A Groundbreaking Surprise"

Upon his return to Asheville a short while later, Fred Seely presented Grove with a drawing of his own. Borrowing elements from several different proposals, Seely conceived of a six-story, 150-room hotel constructed not of wood, but of granite boulders collected from Grove's mountainside holdings. Two wings would branch from the towering central section, built around a mammoth lobby flanked at either end by twin fieldstone fireplaces. They had been inspired by none other than the fireplace in the Old Faithful Inn at Yellowstone National Park, which Grove's assistant had earlier visited, bringing back a brochure with photographs of the inn's spacious lobby.

Reinvigorated both by the sale of the *Atlanta Georgian* and by his son-in-law's plan for a six-story hotel, Grove made the decision to push forward with the hotel project, but with a change in leadership. Rather than hiring the services of one of the architects who had submitted plans for the hotel, Grove offered Fred Seely the opportunity to move his family to Asheville, where Seely would oversee construction of the hotel. In exchange for his services, Grove offered his son-in-law $7,500 a year, plus thirteen acres of land at the top of Sunset Mountain where Fred and Evelyn could build a home.

Seely quickly accepted his father-in-law's offer, then in May of 1912 began sending out notices to the architects. "We did not succeed in getting a satisfactory plan from any of the architects," he explained in one letter, "and for that reason I undertook it myself. The sketch proved, strangely, to be entirely satisfactory to Mr. Grove, and he approved it and requested that I go to Asheville with him to locate the building and start the work."

Up until this point in time, the proposed hotel did not yet have a name. It fell to Grove's daughter Evelyn to suggest that it be called the Grove Park Inn.

After making additional sketches and notes reflecting some of Grove's ideas, Seely contacted William G. McKibbin, an Atlanta architect he had met earlier. McKibbin had a reputation as a competent architect, structural engineer and draughtsman, but reportedly had struggled with alcohol problems. In all likelihood, McKibbin was both willing to work for the frugal Seely for less money than other architects would charge, and would be content to provide the detailed blueprints and engineering calculations required without interfering with Seely's design or the construction process.

While McKibbin was busy transforming Seely's sketches and notes into detailed blueprints (now in the collection of Asheville's Pack Memorial Library), Seely paid a visit to Oscar Mills, an Atlanta contractor. Mills had earlier been hired by E. W. Grove to grade and pave the streets in his two sub-divisions, Atkins Park and Fortified Hills, which Seely had supervised after his arrival in Atlanta in 1904. Seely convinced Mills to come with him to Asheville to serve as his general contractor on the hotel project, scheduled to begin just two months later in July of 1912.

Oscar Mills arrived in Asheville in June to familiarize himself with the site and to oversee unloading of the wagonloads of rocks and boulders already being hauled to the site by area farmers. After conferring with McKibbin and Mills on the plans for the digging of the foundation trenches, Fred Seely wired Grove at the Paris Medicine Company offices, letting him know that they would be ready for the official groundbreaking to take place on Tuesday, July 9. Knowing Grove's aversion to any unnecessary public attention, Seely suggested that Gertrude Grove turn over the ceremonial first shovelful of dirt.

On July 1, 1912, Seely again sent a telegram to Grove in St. Louis:

"A Groundbreaking Surprise"

*Work begins on Hotel foundation tomorrow Tuesday. Will be ready to open July first, 1913. Everything working out satisfactory. When are you coming? All well. - Fred*

As an article in the newspaper the following day explained:

# CONSTRUCTION OF GROVE HOTEL STARTED

## Work Will Be Pushed and New Hotel Will Probably be Ready in Another Year

The actual construction of the Grove hotel on the slope of Sunset Mountain has begun and the building will be pushed to completion as rapidly as is consistent with good workmanship. It is expected that it will be ready for occupancy by the first of July of next year and for the next twelve months the ideal site, just at the summit of Sunset Mountain, will present a busy scene.

The plans for the hotel were worked out by F. L. Seely, who has recently removed here for permanent residence. Mr. Seely's plans follow the simple, but strong lines of a period in English architecture that built for homely comforts, and this feature is carried out in the plans for the local hotel.

J. Oscar Mills, of Atlanta, who has developed the property of E. W. Grove in that city, is here, and will be the foreman of construction of the new hotel. His family will join him here within the next few weeks.

J. W. McKibbin, of Atlanta, is the architectural engineer on the extensive work and the establishment of his foundation lines has been completed.

The first shovel of dirt in the excavation work was turned yesterday morning by Mrs. E. W. Grove, in the presence of a few friends, and the work was begun immediately afterward in earnest.

An article appearing in the competing Asheville newspaper provided some additional information, but it still left with one key question unanswered.

*At ten o'clock this morning, Mrs. E. W. Grove turned the first shovelful of dirt in the excavations to be made for the Grove hotel on Sunset Mountain, and at 12:30 about fifty workmen began in earnest the excavation for the foundations for the structures.*

*At the formal beginning of the work there were only a few people present besides Mr. and Mrs. Grove and W. F. Randolph, but the occasion marked the beginning of the erection for Asheville of one of the finest hotels that the country will possess.*

*The statement was made by Mr. Randolph this morning that they hoped to have the structure complete within fifteen months. This is a very conservative estimate, as it is felt that there should be no unnecessary push of time at the expense of something else, but Mr. Randolph said also that, if it should be possible, an attempt would be made to have the opening of the hotel on July 1, 1913.*

The question left unanswered was simple:
Where was Fred Seely?

Where, indeed, was the man who had sketched, designed and agreed to oversee construction of this 150-room hotel?

The man who had sold his daily newspaper of six years to start this project?

The man who little more than a week earlier had wired E. W. Grove from Asheville imploring, "When are you coming?"

The man who knew full well the power of the press in generating interest?

Where, indeed, was Fred Seely?

Seely had sent a telegram to Grove from Asheville on July 1, but Grove's reply was addressed to Fred Seely care of the Ritz Carlton Hotel in Manhattan. It is believed Seely was meeting William Randolph Hearst, possibly to discuss the payment plan for the *Atlanta Georgian*. By July 9, the day of the groundbreaking, Fred Seely appears to have returned to Asheville, as he wrote a letter that day stating that "Oscar [Mills] arrived this morning...."

Strangely, Seely made no mention in his letter of the groundbreaking ceremony taking place that day.

Assuming, then, that Fred Seely was in Asheville on the day of the groundbreaking, along with his foreman Oscar Mills, there could only have been one place where Seely could have been at 10:30 that morning that he would have considered more important than the groundbreaking ceremony -- at the far end of the building site, supervising the marking of the foundation, and getting Oscar and his fifty men started correctly.

For in Fred Seely's mind, he only had 356 days to build a six-story, 150-room hotel -- and the clock had just started ticking.

# "A Groundbreaking Surprise"

*Construction of the Grove Park Inn provided employment for hundreds of men and boys, some of whom are seen here cutting the road leading into the hotel grounds.*

*Crates of clay roof tiles stand ready, as workmen lace 90,000 pounds of reinforcing bar in preparation for the pouring of the concrete roof.*

# Chapter 5

# "A Marvel of the Builder's Art"

*Ground hogs and snakes couldn't get a toehold in the*
*upper portion of this section. I feel very certain of our*
*position as to stone, plenty of it, and that we can land*
*it on the hotel site quickly and cheaply.*

Fred L. Seely

While it may not bear comparison to the building of the Great Pyramid of Giza, the completion of the Grove Park Inn in little more than one year was nothing short of amazing.

Work began in earnest after the official groundbreaking on Tuesday, July 9, 1912, when Gertrude Grove turned over the first ceremonial shovelful of dirt on the site. Exactly one year and three days later, the opening night banquet took place on Saturday, July 12, 1913, when master of ceremonies Fred L. Seely and owner Edwin Wiley Grove greeted their invited guests.

Although he missed his personal deadline of July 1 by a few days, what Fred Seely accomplished in 368 days was a true testament to his organizational skills.

In comparison, construction on the Biltmore House, another Asheville landmark, began in earnest in 1889. Six years later, in the summer of 1895, it was still not finished. Frustrated, George Vanderbilt had announced to his architect and contractor that he would be hosting a lavish party for his friends and family from New York that Christmas. Work that fall on the Biltmore House assumed a feverish pace, but by December the house remained unfinished. Vanderbilt instructed his workmen to seal up any rooms that remained unfinished, and the Christmas party took place as planned. As soon as the last guest departed, the workmen returned and work on the house continued for several more years.

As the date of the official opening for the Grove Park Inn drew closer, Fred Seely faced a similar situation. Late in June, he made the decision to pull his workmen off the sixth floor, leaving those sixteen guest rooms temporarily unfinished in order to be sure that the dining room, the Great Hall, the Palm Court and essential sleeping rooms would be ready.

So, despite falling short by a few days and a few rooms, how did Fred Seely pull off this amazing feat?

Freed from the restraints of his responsibilities as both publisher and editor of the *Atlanta Georgian,* Fred Seely threw himself into the hotel project with unbridled enthusiasm and tremendous energy. His initial move had been to hire two men he had already met in Atlanta. The first was architect and structural engineer William G. McKibbin. Seely sat down with McKibbin in his office at the *Atlanta Georgian* and showed him the sketch that E. W. Grove had approved, along with the list of features the hotel would require: 150 guest rooms, a dining room to accommodate 400 people, a spacious lobby measuring 80 feet by 120 feet and flanked by two towering fireplaces, a lower level recreation room with a three-lane bowling alley and swimming pool, and a number of ground floor offices, a ladies lounge and a writing room.

While McKibbin went to work on the blueprints, nineteen pages of which are preserved in Asheville's Pack Memorial Library, Fred Seely had a similar meeting with Oscar Mills, a general contractor who had worked with Seely on Grove's two residential developments in Atlanta. Seely convinced Mills to come to Asheville to serve as the foreman in charge of the 400 stonemasons, carpenters, plumbers, electricians, tile setters and roofers who would be building the hotel.

Even before Gertrude Grove posed beside her shovel on July 9, 1912, local farmers had already begun bringing wagonloads of rocks and stacking them in piles in anticipation for the laying of the foundation. In 1911, when Grove had first acknowledged the rumors that he was about to begin construction on a hotel in Asheville, his preliminary plan had been to build it of "logs, stone, and hewn and rough sawn lumber, using mill stuff only where the details of construction demand it. The stone and timber needed for the various buildings are on the property and accessible." Later he added, "The nature of the surrounding scenery suggests a picturesque construction that will appear to be a part of the forest -- built of logs and stone, of which we have an abundance."

Grove's vision for his hotel had largely been shaped by photographs his secretary had given him of two recent hotels, both erected within the boundaries of Yellowstone National Park: the Grand Canyon Hotel and the Old Faithful Inn. Grove marked a passage in one of the park's early brochures that read, "The distinctive feature of the new Canyon Hotel will be the 'lounge.' This part of the structure will be 175 feet long and 84 feet in width, and will project out from the lobby of the main building toward the Grand Canyon."

Beside it Grove had written in pencil, "Our lounge room should be as long as this."

It remained for Chicago architect Henry Ives Cobb, who until the arrival of Fred Seely had been Grove's architect of choice, to convince Grove to forego his idea of using logs. Instead, Cobb suggested utilizing granite boulders. As Grove relayed in a letter of March 26, 1912, to his real estate manager in Asheville, "Mr. Cobb also states that when you have concluded you have enough stone to complete this building, to go ahead and haul twice as much more. [He] also suggested very attractive columns could be made in the big lobby room out of boulders." Later he added, "All of us at home have been admiring the plans of the stone hotel sent in by Mr. Cobb, and the more we study it, the more beautiful and original it appears."

Two months later Fred Seely informed Henry Cobb that his services as architect would not be required, explaining, "I was at the time working on a sketch of my own. The sketch proved, strangely, to be entirely satisfactory to Mr. Grove."

Strangely, Henry Cobb's original plans have not been seen.

Regardless of the source of inspiration for his own sketch, Fred Seely latched onto the idea of building the hotel from stone. "There is a veritable mountain of stone in the cove," he reported to his father-in-law, "running up the mountain from the switchback all the way to the top of the mountain. Ground hogs and snakes couldn't get a toehold in the upper portion of this section. I feel very certain of our position as to stone, plenty of it, and that we can land it on the hotel site quickly and cheaply."

When he arrived in Asheville in June of 1912, Fred Seely ordered a large canvas tent to be placed at the edge of the site to serve as an office for him and Oscar Mills until the carpenters could erect a temporary wood shanty next to the road. Mr. and Mrs. Grove, who a few days earlier had been ill and confined to bed, took the train from St. Louis to preside over the groundbreaking. As soon as Fred Seely and Oscar Mills were hunched over their plans in the canvas tent, E. W. Grove, knowing the project was in safe hands, returned to the offices of the Paris Medicine Company in St. Louis.

The hotel project attracted the attention of a number of Asheville photographers, both professional and amateur, whose work created a historical record of the year. What becomes startlingly clear is the fact that the Grove Park Inn was constructed with but one major piece of construction equipment: a solitary steam shovel.

The operator of the steam shovel began by cutting a road to the site from what today is known as Macon Avenue. He then proceeded to carve out a level ledge on the western slope of Sunset Mountain where the hotel would soon rise, looking, as one observer noted, "more like it grew out of the mountain." After staking out the footprint for the lower level, which would house a swimming pool, a three-lane bowling alley, a recreation room, dining rooms for children and the hotel staff, plus a barber shop, Oscar Mills assigned his first group of men the task of digging the trenches for the concrete foundation on which the walls would rest.

As a reporter later noted: "The building rests upon a strong foundation of concrete, rocks and steel. Twelve concrete columns five feet square extend to the top of the building, the concrete bases on which they rest being eleven feet square. All walls are seven feet thick at the base and are three and one-half feet wide at the places at which they furnish support for the flooring. At the top they are eighteen inches across. All of the concrete foundation work and the columns of concrete are reinforced with steel rods, 100 tons of steel being used in the reinforcement of the building."

While to the untrained eye the walls of the Grove Park Inn

appear to have been constructed solely of boulders laced with mortar set deeply in their crevices, both Fred Seely and Oscar Mills knew from experience that rocks alone would not suffice. Supporting columns and walls were first laid of hollow concrete blocks or poured concrete to provide straight lines and sufficient support for the weight of the upper floors and roof. That summer they hired 36 stonemasons, along with 28 carpenters and 300 laborers, to lay up the block, cover it with boulders and rocks, and, as the walls rose in the sky, to build scaffolding and inclined ramps for the men hauling wheelbarrow after wheelbarrow of concrete blocks, mortar and rocks to the masons.

Unfortunately, all but a few of their names have been forgotten, lost along with early payroll records. Among those men who worked on the Grove Park Inn was a stonemason and tile setter by the name of John T. Corbin (1871-1955), who, while in his early twenties, learned his trade working on the Biltmore House. Later, he worked for an Asheville contractor by the name of Samuel Bean and, as noted in his obituary, laid stone, rocks and tile for several major projects in Asheville, including the Grove Park Inn.

As an article in the *Asheville Citizen* explained, "The walls are being constructed of stones as they appear on the mountainside. They are being placed without being finished or surfaced and on many of them the moss is still growing. It is the desire of the owner of the hotel to make it as rustic as possible, and the huge rocks that form the walls are rugged and rough. They are being placed in cement mortar, although the appearance of the hotel will not indicate this, as the mortar is being used in such a manner that it will not be visible."

The same reporter who visited the site that fall also wrote, "The rocks are large and heavy and the manner in which they are raised to their positions of various heights is interesting. An inclined roadbed has been built to the top of the structure and the stones are carried over it by pulleys. All of the windows are capped with one large stone, some of which will weigh over three tons. They are being hauled about five miles from Schartle's cove, where a large force of hands is being kept at work loading the wagons with the boulders. They are being transported to Sunset Mountain by teams [of mules] and at the beginning of the automobile highway several wagons are trailed behind a large motor truck to the hotel site."

In 1984, just before his death, Noah Stewart, one of the original workmen, recalled, "My mother died when I was nine years old, and when I was about fourteen years old I went to where they were building the Grove Park Inn. I got a job there. I was what people called a 'water jack.' I carried water to the men when they were digging ditches for the foundation for the Grove Park Inn hotel. When I first started to work there as a water jack, I got big pay: $1.25 a week!

"When I was a water jack, I had to go way round a hollow to get water from a cold spring. Well, as you know, Mr. E. W. Grove was the owner of the Grove Park Inn hotel. Well, one morning when I was coming from the spring, I met Mr. Grove. I did not know him well. It was a hot morning. And he had a large fancy walking cane. So, he asks me if he could have a drink of water, and I said, 'Sure, sir.' He drank a large dipper full and he thanked me. And you know he gave me a one-dollar bill. Boy, I thought I was rich!"

Noah Stewart's daughter, Gertrude Stewart, added, "When [my father] carried water from a spring to the work crews, he said he carried two buckets at a time. They had a dipper for the white men to drink from and another dipper for the Negro workers. One dipper hung on one side of the bucket and one dipper hung on the other side -- to keep them separated!"

"He said he worked up to ten hours a day on this job and did it for about three months. He said they walked 'rain or shine' to the inn, and used the road called the Automobile Road -- a dirt road. In the winter time they walked in snow a foot deep to get to work at the hotel during its construction -- and if the snow got too bad, they would stop under a tree for shelter."

As Noah Stewart explained, "Then I got larger and older, and I got bigger pay. My brother Harry and me hauled rock from all over that Sunset Mountain, back as far as Mount Meadows Inn. We had a five-ton Packard truck, and I think we had eight wagons. We would take the wagons up on the mountainside and men would load up the rocks. I think they had these wagons made special for the job. They were very large wagons!"

Noah Stewart's daughter recounted another story her father had also told her:

*There was a crew of men who were doing rockwork, and one of them who was on a scaffold fell off. My father said he was a Negro man. He said when he fell, he hit his head on a rock, and cracked his skull, dying from the injury.*

*As you know, mountain people are very superstitious, and after his death, the workers were unnerved. That included my father. When they would go to work and the sun not up yet, still just "dusky dark," they were afraid they would see the ghost of the dead man. With every little unexplained noise, they knew it was "HIM" who had returned from the grave!*

During the first four months of construction, the people of Asheville could see little of the fabled stone walls rising from the foundation of the Grove Park Inn, as their view was blocked by the jungle of wooden scaffolding the carpenters continued to build alongside the stonemasons. When they awoke on Saturday morning, October 26, however, they found a front-page story announcing the removal of the scaffolding in front of the hotel. In a letter written the next day to E. W. Grove in St. Louis, Fred Seely exclaimed:

*You should have been here yesterday to look over the crowd viewing the hotel. The scaffolding in front of the north section was removed Saturday and a fine opportunity to see the real stonework was had. Everybody was enthusiastic about everything connected with the construction, outlook, etc. The streetcar company doubled their cars out our way all afternoon. The delightful weather we are having induces many people to walk in the mountains now and a large majority of them use the trails. The Wander Trail is so attractive to them that I believe that we shall have to tie it down to keep them from carrying it away.*

Seely's enthusiasm for the hotel project had from the beginning prompted some concern on his father-in-law's part, for Grove could still recall a time ten years earlier when Fred Seely had worked himself to a state of near-exhaustion at the Paris Medicine Company. As Grove warned just before the groundbreaking, "I fear you want to hurry too much in getting the hotel built. There is no reason for any special hurry and I do not want you to go into this and overtax yourself in trying to do too much in this short time. You know from past experience this is something you must learn to control. Again, to exercise any undue haste in building the hotel, it might not be what we started out to build. I only mention this so that you can take time and not go ahead unless you know you are right."

Fred Seely, however, remained undeterred, believing that if he did not have the hotel ready to be open for business no later than July 1, 1913, they would miss the lucrative summer season of business. As he explained, apparently not for the first time, in a letter written a few months after the groundbreaking:

*I know you fully realize what a tremendous undertaking it is for us to finish this work in eleven months from the time we started, as we are compelled to do unless we let it run over another year, and I have explained to you so many times why this would not be wise, that I won't mention it again. We are working under the highest pressure we can put on, and I am spending every night here until midnight, and sometimes later. But since I am well, and it is not affecting me in any way, I do not object to it in the least. And while I am trying to get every bit of quality into the building that I can, yet I am fighting to keep the cost down.*

Fred Seely appears not to have been exaggerating the number of hours he and the others had been putting in at the hotel, for a reporter noted that "night work is being carried on regularly by the carpenters in erecting and removing scaffolds, and the material is being hauled at night. The grounds have been equipped with electric lights and various portions of the building are well lighted for the convenience of the night laborers."

In that same letter to E. W. Grove, Seely also added: "We have about fifty bedrooms laid up, a good deal of plastering done, the steam heat is nearly all in, and the forms are nearly finished for the roofs of three of the buildings. We are not waiting for the roofs at all. Simply going along just as fast as we can, and if you could pay us a visit and see the way things are moving around here, not to think of the way the steam shovel I rented is eating the hill out below here, I think you would have some idea that we were building a hotel."

In January of 1913, Fred Seely designed and ordered the hotel's first stationary bearing a drawing of the Grove Park Inn across the top with the caption, "To Open July 1st, 1913." On the back he included the following:

*We are building the finest resort hotel in the world and will open it July 1st, 1913. It will be absolutely fireproof, and is being built of the great boulders of Sunset Mountain, at whose foot it sits. It is being built by hand in the old-fashioned way. Full of rest and comfort and wholesomeness.*

*The Inn is located on the side of Sunset Mountain, about a mile from the top, and is not only cool enough in the Summer to make a blanket necessary at night, but is protected and mild enough in the Winter to make life enjoyable without enervation.*

*The front lawn is the hundred-acre eighteen-hole golf links of the Asheville Country Club, and with it sixty acres of our own lawn.*

*We own eight hundred acres around the Inn (consumptives not taken) and are glad to be able to offer the finest combination of climate, of comfort and of happiness in surroundings that we believe has ever been made possible.*

*The purist water obtainable anywhere, piped seventeen miles, from the slopes of Mount Mitchell, over 6,000 feet altitude. Biltmore cream and milk exclusively, supplied from 200 registered Jerseys on the estate of Mr. George W. Vanderbilt. It is doubtful if this famous dairy is equaled in the world. Four hundred one-piece rugs are being made at Aubusson, France. Seven hundred pieces of the furniture are being made by hand by the Roycrofters. The silver will be hand-hammered.*

One of the greatest fears travelers faced during the early years of the twentieth century was being trapped in a deadly hotel fire. Prior to an era of building inspections, smoke alarms and fire escapes, older wooden hotels and boarding houses were often hastily wired by inexperienced workmen totally untrained to calculate the number of lights a set of wires could handle before overheating.

To allay their fears, Fred Seely and Edwin Grove, both seasoned travelers, agreed that the design of the Grove Park Inn should make it virtually fireproof. Improvements in the formula for concrete, most notably the invention of Portland cement and the addition of steel reinforcing bars to improve its strength and resistance to cracking, had led to increased use of concrete in commercial construction at that time.

As a result of their concerns and recent innovations, a minimal amount of wood was incorporated into the Grove Park Inn. The vertical columns and foundations were composed of poured concrete, upon which the masons laid up walls of hollow concrete blocks that were quickly covered with granite boulders on either side. Floors were also formed of poured concrete, twelve inches thick, upon which a layer of grey tiles were later set and grouted. High above the Great Hall, concrete beams laced with tons of steel reinforcing bars stretched from column to column without a single crack, a credit to the ability of the unsung hero of the Grove Park Inn, the architect and structural engineer G. W. McKibbin.

One hundred years later, it is interesting to note how Fred Seely had nearly allowed the name of G. W. McKibbin to slip into obscurity. In 1917 Seely wrote and published the first booklet on the Grove Park Inn, noting such details as which firms provided the brass piping and bathroom fixtures, who had woven the rugs and built the furniture, how many inches of concrete were in the floor, how many tons of boulders were in the fireplaces, even which brand of mattress he had selected.

What he somehow failed to mention was the name of the architect who had turned his crude sketch and E. W. Grove's vision into page after page after page of detailed blueprints, the man who had calculated the strength of each of the pillars and concrete beams in the Great Hall, the man who had laid out the rooms, designed the undulating roof line, and who had determined the height of the Palm Court and the depth of the foundation.

G. W. McKibbin, architect.

The unsung hero of the building of the Grove Park Inn.

In 1922, upon a request for a letter of reference for McKibbin, who was being considered for a hotel project in Cordele, Georgia, Fred Seely did write in a personal letter, "I am very glad to say that Mr. McKibbin had charge of the entire detail work in connection with the planning of the Grove Park Inn, and that he is thoroughly capable of planning and supervising the construction in your job. This work here involved about one million dollars and after ten years time we fail to find a crack or settlement on any wall. We have tile floors 120 feet long in a straight sheet without a single crack."

McKibbin undoubtedly spent much of 1912 and 1913 in Asheville, where later in his career he briefly operated an architectural office, as he conferred with Oscar Mills and Fred Seely in their wooden shanty. Little he had done in Atlanta could have totally prepared McKibbin for the challenges he faced in engineering a six-story resort hotel built of boulders perched on a mountain ledge, not to mention satisfying both Fred Seely and E. W. Grove. Hiding elevators inside fireplaces, calculating poured concrete beams for the Great Hall, designing an indoor swimming pool for the basement, as well as an invisible, elaborate web of pipes for water, steam and waste, must have kept the architect working late into the night trying to stay ahead of the workmen relying on his instructions.

Undoubtedly McKibbin's greatest challenge in the project was the design for the roof, which E. W. Grove and Fred Seely had decided would be the first continually poured concrete roof in the region. As Fred Seely described in his 1917 brochure, "The roofs of the Inn form an excellent illustration of its massiveness and the care in construction. First there was poured a roof five inches thick of Portland cement concrete, reinforced with 90,000 pounds of steel rods. On this was laid five layers of Trinidad Asphalt interposed between three layers of asbestos felt. On this fifteen carloads of fireproof tile, held on with one and one-half tons of coppered steel nails and twenty tons of Tucker's fireproof roof cement."

What Seely did not have space to explain in the promotional brochure was that before the concrete could be poured, his workmen had to build a complete wooden roof capable of supporting hundreds of tons of steel and concrete without collapsing. Once the wooden forms had been built, the men began hoisting up and lacing together the 90,000 pounds of half-inch steel reinforcing rod, creating a virtual spider web stretching across the entire roof to provide the concrete with additional strength.

In 1913, however, pouring a concrete roof six stories above the ground was not as simple as it sounds today. No equipment existed that would enable the workmen to pump a slurry of wet concrete that high into the sky. Instead, the workmen had to construct a temporary elevator shaft inside what is now the chimney for the south fireplace. The elevator car, however, could only hold one man with one wheelbarrow of wet concrete at a time.

The slow process started with one man and a wheelbarrow of heavy concrete entering the makeshift elevator for the slow ascent to the top of the roof. Once he reached the peak, more than eighty feet above the ground, the workman had to concentrate on keeping the wheelbarrow perfectly balanced as he pushed it across a narrow walkway running the length of the peak of the roof. As he did, the elevator returned to the ground floor, where the next man and his wheelbarrow of concrete stood waiting their turn. As the second man rode toward the top, the first would have been dumping his wheelbarrow of concrete down the slope of the roof, where a team of men used steel rakes and shovels to spread an even layer of concrete throughout the roof.

The concrete had to be mixed to the perfect consistency. Had it been too thin, it would not have clung to the forms creating the gentle curves around the edge of the roof and the dormers. Too thick and they would not be able to move it before it began to harden. As a local newspaper had reported after an interview with Fred Seely, "There will be no angles anywhere in the roof. There will be only lazy, graceful slopes and the effect will be something unique for this section of the country."

Once begun, the pouring of the roof continued non-stop from one end to the other on each section. Crude strings of electric lights were strung across the roof to guide the men as they wrestled with the wet concrete and steel reinforcing bars in the middle of the night for weeks on end. The pouring started in March of 1913, when nighttime temperatures routinely dropped near freezing.

We can only imagine the conditions under which the men had to work each night, illustrated by a letter foreman Oscar Mills wrote on March 24 to his family back in Georgia, "I had to come back to the hotel tonight. They are pouring the concrete roof on and are working sometimes all night. I came down off the roof and taken these few minutes to write You all; the wind is blowing up on the roof like fury. I can see all over Asheville, but Good Lord how one peep of Dear Old Atlanta would stir the latent blood in my veins."

With five separate sections of roof to build and pour, plus the covered outdoor terraces, the work had to be carefully scheduled, but, then, that was Fred Seely's greatest asset. While one crew continued to weave reinforcing bars together, another was pouring concrete on a separate section of roof; meanwhile yet another crew was covering the dried concrete with three layers of asphalt roofing material, sandwiched between five applications of hot tar, to ensure that the roof would remain waterproof.

But while waterproof, the concrete roof was far from finished. Even as the men were still lacing bars, pouring concrete and mopping on hot asphalt, the first of fifteen railroad cars of red clay tile from the Murray Roofing Tile Company in Cloverport, Kentucky, was being stacked beside the hotel. Attaching tens of thousands of clay tiles to cured concrete, however, posed a challenge for Seely and Mills. In some places their solution was to spread yet another inch of wet concrete, into which the men placed long, narrow boards.

Once the concrete had dried, firmly gripping the boards, the men returned to begin attaching the six-inch wide tiles, each of which had been molded with two nail holes at the top. The tiles were secured to the boards with copper-coated steel roofing nails. In other places the concrete remained soft enough to allow the copper-coated steel nails to be driven directly into it.

The combination of concrete, asphalt and red clay tile, while time-consuming and expensive to install, emerged as one of the most noteworthy features of the hotel, and served the Grove Park Inn for nearly ninety years before the tile had to be replaced.

And, as winter gave way to spring, and spring to Fred Seely's deadline for the grand opening, Oscar Mills knew he would soon be able to pack his bags and head back to his home and family in Atlanta.

*Workmen shovel concrete over a sixth-floor dormer laced with a spiderweb of steel reinforcing bar. Once begun, the concrete was poured and shoveled non-stop, so as to avoid having any seams in the roof.*

*Room 262 as it appeared in July of 1913. Note the Roycroft ceiling light and the burlap wall covering, framed in oak boards.*

# Chapter 6

# "An Arts and Crafts Hotel"

*The Grove Park Inn could never be complete in its fulfillment of purpose without the assistance of The Roycrofters. And so it is that the dining room will be entirely furnished with Roycroft furniture -- plain, simple, straight-lined pieces, genuinely handmade and with the quality the first and last endeavor.*

Elbert Hubbard, 1912

In 1895, in the small town of East Aurora, New York, 22 miles southeast of Buffalo, a young writer by the name of Elbert Hubbard (1856-1915) began publishing his own work under the name of the Roycroft Press. Hubbard had one distinct advantage over most frustrated writers:  he had money. His skills as a marketing genius and talented copywriter had carried him to the top management level of the nationally known Larkin Soap Company. Then, at age 36 and nearing the peak of his corporate career, Hubbard had done what millions only dream of doing.

He quit.

With the equivalent today of nearly $250,000, Elbert Hubbard left Buffalo, bought out a small printer in nearby East Aurora and began training some of the local townspeople. He soon was publishing booklets, books and magazines, all printed by hand in the Arts and Crafts style inspired by William Morris. Within a few years the enterprising entrepreneur had begun expanding his business, buying, moving and constructing buildings in East Aurora for what would eventually become the Roycroft print shop, the Roycroft blacksmith shop, the Roycroft copper shop, the Roycroft leather shop, the Roycroft furniture shop and the Roycroft Inn.

Arts and Crafts furniture had become one of the later additions to the Roycroft line. Years afterwards, Hubbard enjoyed telling audiences the story of how in 1902 he began hiring local carpenters to make simple, straight-lined furniture for his new Roycroft Inn, only to discover that his guests began requesting pieces for their own homes. By 1904, sales of Roycroft Arts and Crafts furniture prompted Hubbard to build a new three-story, wooden building on the growing Roycroft Campus for his woodworkers.

Like each shop on the Roycroft Campus, the furniture shop epitomized the Arts and Crafts ideals of hand-craftsmanship, simple, yet elegant designs and honest use of materials. As Hubbard wrote in 1912, "There is a distinctiveness about Roycroft Furniture that places it in a class by itself. The simplicity of design and the intent are strictly Mission -- made to use and to last. Roycroft Furniture resembles that made by the old monks, in its simple beauty, its strength and its excellent workmanship. We use no nails -- but are generous in the use of pegs, pins, mortises and tenons."

In 1901, a friend had given to Fred Seely, then working for his father-in-law in St. Louis, a subscription to *The Philistine: A Magazine of Protest,* that was published, edited and written by Hubbard.

# "An Arts and Crafts Hotel"

Elbert Hubbard's folksy, often sarcastic commentaries on life, politics, society, law and business, as well as his clever advertisements and promotions for everything Roycroft, captured the attention of Fred Seely, who began ordering Roycroft books, pamphlets and mottoes. In 1904, he placed an order for his first piece of Roycroft furniture -- a 60-inch oak magazine stand.

Ironically, it was a problem with his Roycroft furniture that cemented his lifelong friendship with Elbert "Bert" Hubbard II (1882-1970).

Just eleven years younger than Fred Seely and far more modest than his flamboyant father, Bert Hubbard learned the Roycroft operation from the ground up, rotating through the various departments and working alongside the blacksmiths, illustrators, printers and woodworkers employed by his father. In 1905, Bert Hubbard was handed a letter from Fred Seely complaining about the joinery in his most recent order. That letter, along with Bert's reply, inspired a friendship that grew even stronger as the two men later found they shared similar circumstances: each worked in the shadow of a famous man, each had become innkeepers and each eventually managed an Arts and Crafts enterprise.

While Fred Seely undoubtedly had great respect for the business that Elbert Hubbard had created, the senior Hubbard's personal life and his liberal stand on politics and social issues of the day may have prevented them from becoming intimate friends. Ten years earlier, Hubbard, already a husband and father of three sons, publicly confessed to having had a secret affair with feminist Alice Moore, who had given birth to his daughter in 1894. Torn between his love for Alice and his devotion to his wife, Bertha, who gave birth to their own daughter in 1896, Hubbard fled to England for two months. He returned with yet a third love -- the Arts and Crafts movement.

Hubbard continued to see both women until Alice threatened him with a child support lawsuit, and Bertha, embarrassed by newspaper reports of her husband's affair and illegitimate child, filed for divorce. She eventually moved to Buffalo with their younger children, while Alice and her daughter moved into Hubbard's home in East Aurora. Eldest son Bert elected to stay with his father and work as a Roycrofter.

In 1908, a bank panic spawned a nationwide recession, prompting Elbert and Bert Hubbard to all but close their small furniture shop. By 1910, however, the economy had recovered to the point where the workmen in the Roycroft Furniture Shop could again start producing a modest line of furniture.

Having lived with Roycroft furniture since 1904, Fred Seely certainly had been thinking about his friends in East Aurora as he discussed plans for the Grove Park Inn with his father-in-law. Shortly after the July 9, 1912, groundbreaking, Seely wrote Bert Hubbard, asking for drawings of their current line of Arts and Crafts furniture. As good fortune would have it, the Hubbards had just recently published their largest furniture catalog, illustrated not with their former rudimentary line drawings, but with professional photographs.

Within a matter of weeks Fred Seely had composed a list of the furniture the hotel would require. Each of the 150 guest rooms would have either one or two beds and nightstands, a vanity and chair, a desk and chair, a rocking chair and either one or two dressers, for a total of approximately 1,200 pieces of bedroom furniture. In addition, the hotel's dining room would require an additional 400 chairs, six corner servers, two massive sideboards and more than two dozen tray stands. Additional Arts and Crafts furniture would be required for the ladies' lounge, the writing room, the recreation area and several offices.

All in less than one year.

Fred Seely's choice of the Roycroft Furniture Shop to provide much of the furniture for the Grove Park Inn does seem a bit curious. While he had been both a client and a friend of the two Hubbards for nearly a decade, he also knew the limited capabilities of their small workshop. He could have easily approached any of a number of larger Arts and Crafts firms, from Gustav Stickley or L. & J. G. Stickley to Charles Limbert or Stickley Brothers, in addition to several well-known furniture companies, all of which had true furniture factories and employed hundreds of craftsmen.

In 1912, the recently reopened Roycroft Furniture Shop still remained more of a custom workshop than a furniture factory, with fewer than twelve craftsmen typically employed there. In contrast, ninety miles away in Syracuse, Gustav Stickley had built a true furniture factory, where more than 100 men worked six days a week producing a complete line of Arts and Crafts furniture for national distribution. Each of Stickley's four brothers had similar large furniture factories where they also produced extensive lines of Arts and Crafts furniture. Any of them would have been far better equipped than the small Roycroft Furniture Shop to handle the commission for a 150-room resort hotel.

Nevertheless, Fred Seely seemed intent on giving the Hubbards the opportunity to provide the furnishings for the Grove Park Inn. He invited Bert Hubbard to travel to Asheville in October of 1912, where they walked amid the steadily rising walls of the hotel and stood on the tower of scaffolding, taking in the view of downtown Asheville and the French Broad River valley in the distance. As the two men stood in the construction shanty erected on the site, flipping through pages of blueprints prepared by G. W. McKibbin, the scope of the project -- along with Seely's daunting deadline, a mere nine months away -- must have nearly overwhelmed the 32-year-old Bert Hubbard.

Before leaving, Bert Hubbard admitted that his band of woodworkers would be unable to produce Seely's entire order in the time allotted. It would appear that the two men agreed that the Roycrofters would furnish the dining room and other first floor public areas, excluding the Great Hall, which was to be filled with wicker furniture. In addition, based on surviving examples, Bert Hubbard must have offered to ship to North Carolina enough Roycroft furniture for approximately three of the sleeping rooms. This furniture then served as the models for the remaining bedroom furniture, all of which was manufactured in time for the July opening by the White Furniture Company in Mebane, N.C.

As Bert Hubbard was traveling back to East Aurora with his order in hand, Fred Seely was preparing a press release to appear on October 30 in the *Asheville Citizen* and the *Asheville Gazette-News*. It read, in part:

*Through Elbert Hubbard Jr., who spent yesterday here, the management of the Grove Park Inn yesterday closed a deal with the Roycrofters for 700 pieces of furniture which will be used in furnishing a portion of the hotel when it is completed.*

*The order is one of the largest which has ever been given in this city and the furniture is very expensive. The plant of the Roycrofters at East Aurora, N.Y., has furnished some of the most magnificent hotels in the world and the company has an international reputation.*

*The furniture will be shipped on a date which will allow it to reach Asheville in time for installing it before July 1, when the Inn will be opened. The order requires that all of the furniture be made according to the specifications of the buyer and no pains or expense will be spared to furnish the inn in the most elaborate, although unique style.*

*Mr. Hubbard, who has visited all parts of the nation and who has figured with owners of the most famous hotels in the country, was greatly pleased with Asheville and the new inn. He spent the greater part of yesterday in conference with W. F. Randolph and F. L. Seely, and, after completing the business transaction, was shown over the city.*

It should be noted that the newspaper article did contain a few inaccuracies and slight exaggerations. The Roycroft furniture "plant" was in truth a modest, three-story wooden structure more apt to be called a workshop than either a plant or even a factory. And while the Roycrofters could claim an "international reputation," it would more likely have been attributed to their magazines, their hand-bound books or their hand-hammered metalware than to their modest output of Arts and Crafts furniture.

As for other commissions, the Roycroft Furniture Shop did not furnish any "magnificent hotels" -- other than the 1904 sixty-room Roycroft Inn -- before or after the Grove Park Inn project. Finally, the Mr. Hubbard, "who has visited all parts of the nation and who has figured with owners of the most famous hotels in the country," was the senior Elbert Hubbard, who spent a great deal of his time delivering speeches across the country on the Chautauqua circuit. Prior to his father's untimely death in 1915, young Bert Hubbard rarely traveled outside the state of New York, for he was typically left in charge of the Roycrofters during the extended trips often taken by Alice and Elbert Hubbard.

In his typical style, a few months after the contract had been signed Elbert Hubbard wrote:

*Down in Asheville, North Carolina, there is being built a ho-tel. It will be known as the Grove Park Inn. Asheville will double its renown as a resort because of the Inn. This will be the finest resort hotel in the world -- no exceptions. It is minus the bizarre, the tawdry, the flashily foolish. The Grove Park Inn could never be complete in its fulfillment of purpose without the assistance of The Roycrofters. And so it is that the dining room will be entirely furnished with Roycroft furniture -- plain, simple, straight-lined pieces, genuinely handmade and with the quality the first and last endeavor.*

The Roycroft furniture that arrived in Asheville in time for the official opening was, in Hubbard's pronouncement, "made to use and to last," as much of it still remains in the Grove Park Inn. Spotting the original Roycroft furniture is made easier by the practice of carving into each piece the Roycroft shopmark: the letter "R" within a circle topped by a double-tiered cross. Stories as to the origin of the mark varied, often with each retelling by Elbert Hubbard himself. It may well have been inspired by a 15th-century Venetian printer who used a similar mark, but, as Hubbard once declared, "I am often asked what it means. I do not know what it means, and if I ever find out, I'll change it to something else."

While the Roycroft mark did vary slightly over the years, neither Elbert nor Bert Hubbard ever saw fit to change it, making it perhaps the most recognizable shopmark of the Arts and Crafts movement. Within the walls of the Grove Park Inn it can be found on several pieces of original furniture, ranging from the dining room chairs with the letters "G P I" carved across their top rail to the massive sideboards and corner servers in the dining room to the two magnificent grandfather clocks on display. Additional pieces of Roycroft furniture can be seen in the small museum on the grounds of

Biltmore Industries adjacent to the Grove Park Inn. After purchasing Biltmore Industries from Edith Vanderbilt in 1917, Fred Seely ordered new Arts and Crafts furniture from the Roycrofters for his office, much of which still survives.

With the Roycrofters taking responsibility for the dining room furnishings and other first-floor rooms, in 1912 Fred Seely was still in need of approximately 1,200 pieces of bedroom furniture. At the far end of the state, the owners of a small but respectable company by the name of the White Furniture Company in Mebane, not far from Durham, heard of the hotel being built in Asheville. As one of the family members recounted later:

*Arthur [White] did most of the selling, especially the sales of furniture for fine resort hotels. White Furniture Company shipped a sample dresser to Asheville to be shown as a typical piece of our quality. The gentleman [Fred Seely] who was in charge of buying furniture 'pooh-poohed' the idea of any furniture made in a little country town in North Carolina being even close to the standards which were wanted for the Grove Park Inn.*

*So, my Uncle Arthur uncrated the dresser and asked [Fred Seely] to select one of the drawers from the dresser and he would give a demonstration, which would prove that White Furniture Company produced furniture which would stand the use and abuse to which it would be subjected. A drawer was selected and taken from the dresser and laid down on the floor upside down. Then Uncle Arthur jumped on the drawer -- and there was no sign of the abuse to which it was subjected.*

*Arthur brought the order home in his pocket.*

Fred Seely had been so impressed with the quality of Arts and Crafts furniture which the White Furniture Company produced, modeled after Roycroft designs, that he also contracted them to make the oak doors for all of the 150 guest rooms, plus offices, closets and other various rooms throughout the hotel. In 1927, in response to a letter written by J. S. White, Fred Seely wrote, "Instead of deteriorating with age and wear, it seems to get better, and I can say frankly that the furniture which you supplied us when the Grove Park Inn was built is practically in the same condition it was the day we received it – perfect."

Much of the furniture that the White Furniture Company produced for the Grove Park Inn can still be found in the original guest rooms and on display in the hallways. They, too, had their own shopmark: a one-inch circular metal tag on the inside of one of the drawers. One stipulation that Fred Seely made, however, has caused some confusion today. As noted, the Roycrofters did produce approximately three sets of bedroom furniture for the White Furniture Company to use as models. In addition, Fred Seely ordered from the Roycroft Copper Shop approximately 2,500 hammered copper drawer pulls for all of the dressers, desks and vanities produced by the White Furniture Company. Each of the copper pulls bears the Roycroft shopmark, leading many collectors to assume that what in truth is a White Furniture Company product was made in the Roycroft Furniture Shop. The distinction is significant, for while a White Furniture Company library table might be worth $800, the same design of a Roycroft library table could easily bring $2,800 in today's market.

The combination of the original Roycroft furniture for the public areas, the White Furniture Company's guest room furniture, and the antique furniture purchased in 1984 and 1988 for the halls of the Sammons and Vanderbilt wings has catapulted the Grove Park Inn from being a footnote in the history of the Arts and Crafts movement to having the distinction of having the world's largest collection of American Arts and Crafts furniture.

Since 1988, the Grove Park Inn has also served as the site for the national Arts and Crafts Conference and Antiques Show on the third weekend in February. Each year more than 100 antiques dealers, craftsmen and craftswomen bring to the Grove Park Inn the finest assemblage of Arts and Crafts furniture, art pottery, metalware, art, textiles, rugs and jewelry for a three-day show attended by more than 3,000 collectors. Together with noted seminar speakers, discussion groups, tours, displays and demonstrations, this event has become known, as declared by the *New York Times*, as "the most important weekend of the year for Arts and Crafts collectors." Information on the next national Arts and Crafts Conference can be found at www.Arts-CraftsConference.com.

And while the Grove Park Inn may no longer claim the title that it had in 1913 as "the finest resort hotel in the world," it still stands today as the undisputed "finest Arts and Crafts resort hotel in the world."

*Note: For a more detailed account of the Roycroft and Arts and Crafts furniture in the Grove Park Inn's collection, please see Bruce Johnson's book* Grove Park Inn Arts & Crafts Furniture *(F+W Media, Cincinnati, OH, 2009).*

*Some of the 400 men who attended the opening banquet on July 12th, 1913.*

# Chapter 7

# "A Banquet Fit for a King"

*Today we stand in this wonderful hotel, not built for a few,*
*but for the multitudes that will come and go. Is it not better*
*to build such a monument than a tomb? I congratulate*
*these men. They have built for the ages.*

William Jennings Bryan,
Secretary of State

As Fred Seely's self-imposed deadline of July 1 drew closer, work on the interior of the Grove Park Inn increased to a feverish pitch. Tile layers, plumbers and trim carpenters stepped gingerly around each other, as the electricians, supervised by Roycroft metalsmith Victor Toothaker, wrestled the twelve enormous chandeliers out of their wooden shipping crates in preparation for hanging them from hooks embedded in the concrete ceiling nearly thirty feet overhead. A photograph taken of the Great Hall in June shows a stack of Arts and Crafts furniture temporarily stored behind the front desk, waiting to be carried to the guest rooms upstairs.

On June 13, 1913, E. W. Grove wrote a long letter to Fred Seely from his office in St. Louis. Near the end he reminded his son-in-law, "You know I have always argued about not overworking yourself to get the hotel open July 1st, or any specified time, and I wish to tell you again that your health is worth more to all of us than the completion of the hotel at any given date, and realizing the immense amount of work necessary to get all the furnishings placed, I want you to bear in mind the importance of taking whatever time is necessary."

It appears that Fred Seely had been thinking along those same lines, for Grove's letter also reveals something about the present state of plans for the formal opening. "I have never heard anything from you or Evelyn telling what the plans are or will be for the opening," Grove wrote, "whether or not there is to be a banquet for the citizens of Asheville and invited guests outside of the city. I will probably leave here about the 25th and, if you are too busy to write, get Evelyn to do so."

At some point in time in late June, Fred Seely realized that he would not be able to meet his own deadline of July 1, so he began making preparations for an opening on either July 5 or July 12, with July 15 being his third choice. Even so, he had to decide what portions of the hotel simply would not be ready, in order to pull workmen away from those areas to use them where needed more urgently. On his list of delayed completions he placed the sixteen guest rooms on the sixth floor, the landscaping around the building and the lower level indoor swimming pool area.

With those dates in mind, he began sending telegrams and letters to prominent politicians to check on their availability to attend the opening night banquet. He began quite optimistically with President Woodrow Wilson, whose candidacy Seely had earlier enthusiastically endorsed while still publisher of the *Atlanta Georgian*. He also contacted Secretary of State William Jennings Bryan. The two men had met in Atlanta in 1906 and had remained good friends ever since. Also on his list was North Carolina Governor Locke Craig, himself a former Asheville attorney, who Seely had also come to know through Democratic political circles, as well as Senator Luke Lea from Grove's home state of Tennessee. Lea, like Seely, was a former newspaper editor and publisher.

It was Senator Lea who wired Seely on June 26 explaining, "The President wishes me to express to you his appreciation of your most cordial invitation to be present at the opening of the Grove Park Inn. He tells me he will write you personally expressing his pleasure at the invitation and his regrets at his inability to accept it on account of Congress being in session."

In regards to Secretary of State Bryan's availability, Lea also included, "The secretary of state advises me that he is leaving [Washington] on the 16th to be gone a month and that it would not be possible for him to be present on the 15th. He thinks it would be possible for him to attend a banquet on Saturday night July 5. Suggest your wiring me whether you could have banquet that time. The secretary further states that Mrs. Bryan cannot visit you and Mrs. Seely now, but she might be able to do so in the early fall."

Both Governor Craig and Senator Lea, however, did indicate that they could also attend a banquet held on July 5, which, by that time, was only nine days away. Obviously worried about whether or not the hotel could be ready, Seely was still considering sending out invitations when Secretary Bryan wired, "Meeting changed to July 13. Can attend banquet Saturday night 12th. Answer."

Given the opportunity to have an additional seven days in which to print and mail invitations, plus prepare a hastily assembled banquet and housekeeping staff, Fred Seely pushed the opening date back to Saturday, July 12. As he later discovered, the change prevented Governor Craig from attending, but secured the appearance of Secretary of State Bryan and the legion of national reporters who would be sure to follow him.

The printer and Fred Seely's new office staff undoubtedly worked late into the night to print, address and mail several hundred invitations that read:

*Dear Friend --*

*On the night of Saturday, July 12th, we expect to hold our opening banquet -- opening the Grove Park Inn to the public.*

*We have built what we believe we can honestly claim is the finest resort hotel in the world, and on that night we shall be honored by the presence of the Secretary of State, William Jennings Bryan, who will make the principal address.*

*United States Senator Lea of Tennessee, my native State, the Mayor of Asheville, and the Governor of North Carolina will be the other speakers.*

*We invite you to be present. Please let us know on the enclosed postal if you will be here.*

*I believe it is generally known that this enterprise was not born of purely commercial motives, but was the outgrowth of a movement set on foot by Mayor Rankin and a number of prominent business men of this section who finally called on me at Saint Louis and placed the matter before me. After deciding to act on their suggestion, I did what I could to build a hotel worthy of these wonderful mountains.*

*That Asheville now has such a building as the Grove Park Inn is a source of great personal satisfaction to me. That it has come largely as the result of a common desire gives me greater pleasure.*

*That our efforts are honored to the extent of having so great and so busy a man as Mr. Bryan with us is a compliment not assumed by us, but to this incident, in the upbuilding of the South.*

*I sincerely trust, therefore, that you may be present at seven p.m., Saturday, July 12th, to view the building before the banquet, which is to be at eight o'clock.*

*Very sincerely,*
*E. W. Grove*

A newspaper reporter who had the opportunity to tour the Grove Park Inn shortly before the opening night banquet prepared this story for the July 13, 1913, edition of the *Asheville Citizen*:

*At Asheville, where the Appalachian Mountains culminate in the highest peaks east of the Rockies, on a table-land high elevated in the center of the Sunny South, latitude making for warmer in winter and altitude for coolness in summer, is the Grove Park Inn, the finest resort hotel in the world.*

*The pre-eminence of the inn among other hotels is not due so much in difference in degree of fineness as it is to the character of con-struction and as unrivaled is its location. It was its surroundings, in-deed, which inspired its building. High placed on the slopes of Sunset Mountain, 2,600 feet above sea level, the portal of its eastern approach looks up the forest-clad heights of its 800-acre park through which winds its exclusive automobile road to a breeze-swept summit. To the westward, its terrace descending to it, is the 100-acre green lawn of the Asheville Country Club, and a little further on the city of Asheville. The distance from the inn to the center of Asheville is 2 ½ miles.*

*Beyond and in the trail of the sun is the gorge of the French Broad River, and then the mountains, rising range on range with giant steps to the high spire of Mount Pisgah and the crouching 'Rat' on which is the hunting lodge of George W. Vanderbilt. To the southwest the Biltmore House, the white-walled replica of the Chateau of Blois, is commandingly viewed. Still further west are the mighty domes of the Balsams, their clouded summits higher than Mount Washington.*

## Construction

*The inn was made to fit these surroundings. Great boulders rose from their beds and formed walls rugged like those of New England pastures, and massive and strong as Roman ramparts. Hued with age, soft-tinted by the sun and rains of ages, their composite color attunes to the ensemble of forested heights in the background. Its tile-thatched, broad-eaved roof is matches the coloring of autumn.*

*Nature herself might have been the architect, so well does it harmonize with its setting; almost it seems a gigantic lichen-covered rock, firm planted in its rightful place. Its rugged exterior shows nothing of the cement which binds the boulders into cyclopean masonry, nor does one see under the tiling and velvet rugs the thousands of tons of concrete which in roof and floors make the structure one unaffected by fire or the elements. Its strength is superlative; it was designed to last as long as any handiwork of man might exist, and well-paid day labor gave its honest quota of toil.*

## The Interior

*Outside is this adornment of nature; within is the ultimate of comfort and the refinement of elegance. The command that this hotel* be the finest of its kind in the world has provided the utmost in luxury in fittings and furnishings, and this without ostentation. The perfection of this magical house lies in the simplicity of its beauty. Soft light illumines, but its source is invisible; there is heat, but no source to indicate whence it comes. Its furniture is the handiwork of master craftsmen and its rugs were woven by the looms of Aubusson.

The 140 baths are molded from pure porcelain and the pipes that carry water are high-grade brass. Fashioned from ingots handhammered is the silverware, and the napery is Ireland's linen of natural shade. Esse quam videri, "To be rather than seem," might appropriately be the motto of this inn, for there is no sham in it. Its atmosphere of friendship and good cheer is heartily genuine. The superbly proportioned great room on the main floor is intended to draw all the guests together in a congenial company, where twelve-foot logs will flame in the giant double-faced chimneys.

### Architecture

As seen from the golf club, the Grove Park Inn appears to be five separate but connected structures extending in a long and irregular line north and south. The central portion, of six stories, is the highest because it occupies the most elevated site and because of the high ceiling lobby. It is also the widest. Its narrower flanking wings do not extend to the line of its front, and to the north the roofs of the three wings step successively downward. An elevated cement portico, uncovered, projects [west] from the central portion and joins similar porticos of the wings, the latter being roofed. Entrances under the portico lead to the high ceiling, well lighted basement or ground floor. A great terrace descends to the 60-acre lawn, which joins the golf links.

*On the east a vast excavation has provided a level plaza to provide an approach and parking space for automobiles and carriages. The wide macadam road, which connects with Charlotte Street, is continued past the hotel to the top of the mountain, and from it a loop circles the front of the hotel. The infinite attention to detail, which characterizes Mr. Seely's work, has provided a high-grassed bank for the road as it nears the hotel to prevent the noise of automobiles from reaching it, and to the same end the road is made to descend to the entrance so that cars arrive with silent motors under the porte cochere.*

*Around the principal sections of the building are great porches, 24 feet in width, which look out over the beautiful green 100-acre golf course of the Asheville Country Club. Across the course lies the Asheville plateau, and beyond the great ranges of mountains pile up on the horizon, culminating with the majesty of Mount Pisgah's six thousand feet.*

*Under the great front porch and floor of the 'Big Room,' are located pool and billiard rooms, from the windows of which there is the same view of the mountains as from the porch itself. In the basement also are lockers for golfers, a bowling alley and a great swimming pool, 25 by 40 feet, around which are located shower baths and steel lockers for the benefit of guests.*

*The roof itself is one of the chief features of interest. It is a 5 ½ inch reinforced concrete slab, in which over 90,000 pounds of 7/8th inch square twisted steel was used, on top of which is a five-ply treatment of filler sheet fiber and Trinidad asphalt, all of which is covered with red tile shingles thirteen inches long and 3/8th inch thick, fastened on by copper clad nails through the shingles and into the sand finish of the cement slab.*

*There is not an angle in the entire roof, the whole thing being in graceful, lazy flowing curves. The base of the roof extends nearly five*

*feet below the top of the main wall, and a distance of nearly six feet
from the main wall. The peek of the roof is rounded and covered with
No. 14 spun sheet copper, so that from the ground it will have the same
appearance as the balance of the red tiled roof.*

## The Lobby

*The approach portal leads into the great lobby -- a room of
imposing and magnificent proportions. Its inside measurements are 80
by 120 feet and its ceiling is two stories in height. The walls are rugged boulders, as are the giant pillars that carry the weight of the floor
above, which was cast of concrete in a solid block. At each end is a
chimney the like of which is not to be found elsewhere -- titanic stacks
of mighty stones forming cavernous fireplaces capable of holding logs
twelve feet long. And in the jambs of each chimney are shafts for two
elevators. Suspended from the ceiling are twelve pans of copper, hammered by the Roycrofters and in each are electric lights of 1000- candle
power, sending soft rays from invisible sources.*

*The desk is formed of flint rocks, harmonizing with the other
construction. Connecting and in the south wing are the offices of the
manager. In this wing and opening into the Big Room is the ladies
reception room, and a large apartment which is to be occupied by a
dealer in women's furnishings and millinery. Stairways to the upper
floors reach a series of [second floor] rooms somewhat detached from
the others, suites desirable for those wishing a strict degree of privacy.*

## The Dining Room

*In the north wing and opening from the lobby is the beautiful
dining room, with floors of two levels, its windows looking east and*

*west. Its tables are legless, mushroom-shaped iron forms supporting the polished wood tops. The silverware is hand-hammered and the china the product of the most artistic designers. The dining room connects with the adjoining yet separate kitchen, this Gothic ceiling structure having an elevator serving the four floors used for storage and refrigeration.*

*The dining room will be conducted on the American plan [all meals included] and in the basement is a grill room always open, with services a la carte. The water supplied at the inn is the celebrated city water, piped 17 miles from the forest slopes of Mount Mitchell, a watershed above which no one lives or is allowed to pass.*

## The Rooms

*Designed to be comparatively narrow, the wings achieve their purpose of providing that each room be an outside room. The wider central portion gave opportunity for a striking architectural effect. An interior [Palm Court] for three stories above the main lobby ceiling is encircled by parapeted galleries, serving a group of 60 rooms, each of which is an outside room, a skylight surmounting the [Palm Court].*

As the reporter concluded,

*All the beds are arranged in suites, it being possible to provide a dozen in conjunction. Each of the 160 rooms is served by a bath, and each has a spacious closet with lighting automatic on the opening of its doors. All the doors are Indiana white oak and the furniture is also oak. Beds are singled, with mattresses that cost $50 each. Telephones are on movable stands. The heating of the rooms, as elsewhere, comes from radiators concealed in the walls under the windowsills.*

"A Banquet Fit for a King"

On the appointed day of July 12, after an afternoon shower washed away any remaining remnants of masonry dust from the driveway, a stream of automobiles began their ascent of Sunset Mountain. Car after car -- Model T's, Pierce Arrows, Cross Country Ramblers and Stuz Bearcats -- pulled to a stop in front of the east entrance of the Grove Park Inn, where their occupants, each dressed in formal attire, stepped out to absorb their first view of the massive stone structure.

As their cars were whisked away by their drivers or one of the Grove Park Inn attendants, each man strode beneath the covered entry, passed through one of the matched pairs of oak doors and stepped into the Great Hall. There against the first pillar stood a magnificent eight-foot tall Roycroft clock, its hand-hammered copper face and hands showing them the precise time. In the background a small orchestra provided soothing music as they stepped forward to be greeted by E. W. Grove and Fred Seely, their hosts for the evening.

And the women?

Well, they were not invited to the actual banquet, but those who were staying overnight with their husbands were allowed to tour the hotel. They did have, however, the option of gathering in the Ladies' Lounge located off the opposite end of the spacious lobby, where they could converse with Evelyn Grove Seely and Gertrude Grove or, safely out of sight of anyone in the Great Hall, light up one of their Sweet Caporal or American Beauty cigarettes.

By eight o'clock the men had all completed their tour and had made their way to the dining room located in the north wing, just past the fireplace with one of the two elevators hidden within its rock façade. What then transpired that evening appeared the following morning on the front page of the *Asheville Sunday Citizen*:

# SECRETARY BRYAN IS GUEST OF HONOR AT GREAT BANQUET THAT DEDICATES GROVE PARK INN

## SENATOR LUKE LEA AMONG THE SPEAKERS OF THE EVENING

Gastronomical and Intellectual Feast Characterizes Opening of New Hotel, Finest in the World Secretary Bryan Speaker

With Secretary of State William Jennings Bryan and Senator Luke Lea, senior senator from Tennessee, as guests of honor, four hundred representative Southern men, including notables from Asheville, Western North Carolina and parts of the two Carolinas, sat down to a veritable gastronomical and intellectual feast last night at the new Grove Park Inn, the most unique and finest tourist hotel in the world, the occasion being the formal opening of the new hostelry.

The opening banquet was strictly a 'stag' event. Served in the immense dining room of the new hotel, on the unique mushroom-based tables, with the exclusive Grove Park Inn design of china and sparkling cut-glass setting on the genuine Irish linen napery, every delicacy of the season was temporarily arranged to tempt the appetites of the guests present. Under the scintillating lights the formal black and white attire of the men formed a pleasing contrast to the sparkling glass and the exquisite decorations, which embraced every product of the horticulturist, and converted the immense room into a huge bower of flowers.

Out in the spacious lobby a first-class orchestra discoursed sweet music during the banquet, which added much to the enjoyment of the occasion. And when the last dish had been cleared away, the diners settled back in their seats to prepare for the rich oratorical feast in store. Every speaker received the most earnest and careful attention.

The four hundred guests who were greeted by an army of gray-coated attendants as they entered the great doorways noted the obliteration of all marks of the builders and mechanics. The great hostelry looked as if it had been completed for a year; not one person could realize that two weeks ago chaos and disorder reigned on every side. While some portions of the hotel and the surrounding grounds have yet to receive the finishing touches, it stands today as it will stand for all time -- a marvel of the builders' art, a triumph of architectural skill.

There was no confusion in the reception or in the allotment of guests, and the elaborate menu was served with perfect precision.

Seldom has a more representative gathering assembled in this immediate section. With a cabinet officer, senators and congressmen, men high in the various professions, men whose total wealth would run up into the millions, last night's gathering was an auspicious one in every way, and will be long remembered.

# Mr. Seely Toastmaster

Fred L. Seely acted as toastmaster and before introducing Mayor Rankin said that he had no speech prepared, for he felt that those who would address the guests would meet all demands. He said that it was scarcely a year ago since the first shovelful of dirt was turned. The hotel was rushed to completion so that it would open for the summer season. He said that he had no words to express his appreciation of Secretary Bryan's coming to aid him in opening Grove Park Inn.

"Mr. Bryan has been a great inspiration to me," said Mr. Seely, "as he has been to many young men. Nothing could give me more happiness than his presence here tonight."

Mr. Seely read a letter from Governor Craig in which the governor expressed his deep regret for his inability to attend. In expressing his appreciation of the invitation to be present, the governor said that the people of the whole state, and indeed the South, fully appreciated the work which Messrs. Grove and Seely had accomplished, the work which will contribute to the prosperity, not only of the immediate section, but of North Carolina. The governor said that he would have liked to have been present to introduce Mr. Bryan for whom he has expressed the warmest admiration.

# E. W. Grove

Mr. Seely then introduced E. W. Grove, who spoke as follows:

"A man never grows too old to build castles and dream dreams. Standing here tonight in the midst of my friends and invited guests, I find a dream realized and a castle materialized.

"After a long mountain walk one evening, at the sunset hour, I sat down here to rest, and while almost entranced by the panoramic view of these encircling mountains and a restful outlook upon green fields, the dream of an old-time inn came to me -- an inn whose exterior, and interior as well, should present a home-like and wholesome simplicity, whose hospitable doors should ever be open wide, inviting the traveler to rest awhile, shut in from the busy world outside.

"It affords me far more gratification than I can express in having in my immediate family an architect and builder who, by his artistic conception, by his untiring zeal, has studied out the minutest details, making my dream a reality indeed and accomplishing what in so short a time seems almost beyond human endurance.

"That which a man builds, that which a man creates, is a true index of his character, and these massive boulders, placed by skill and endurance into this wonderful structure, fittingly represent the sturdy character of the architect and the builder; and in his untiring efforts to build a monument to me and mine, to loved ones gone before me -- to me and my wife, to me and my children, to me and my grandchildren, to me and my friends, he has built an even greater monument to himself.

"Money is only the means to an end. The value of money cannot be compared to a mind capable of the wonderful conception necessary to create this most unique structure, which is unlike any other building in the world.

"To the men who have labored and endured shoulder to shoulder with him, I am deeply grateful for their faithfulness, working with cheerfulness early and late.

"To the city fathers and the citizens who have given encouragement, praise and appreciation we express gratitude.

"My dream did not reach to the great expectation of having as our guest of honor William Jennings Bryan, secretary of state.

"Since Mr. Bryan's first entrance into the public eye I have followed without wavering his beacon light, finding him magnificent in what some men call defeat and glorious in what all men call victory.

"We are highly honored in having him in our old-fashioned inn tonight."

## Mayor Rankin

Mr. Grove was followed by Mayor Rankin, who paid rare tribute to the builders of the new hostelry. Mayor Rankin said:

"I am grateful for the privilege of being in so distinguished a presence tonight.

"This occasion has assembled here representatives of every walk of life. Perhaps in the history of the South there has never been a gathering, under similar circumstances, which was featured by the attendance of so intellectual personages as the secretary of state and members of both branches of the congress.

"Tonight must always be for us a memorable occasion. Genius and talent have converted the wilds of a mountainside into a Garden of Eden and have built here the greatest hostelry in the world.

"Only a few years ago Dr. E. W. Grove came to Western North Carolina. By his brilliant fellowship, his broad enlightenment and gracious hospitality he has endeared himself to our population and is enshrined in the hearts of our people.

"In the great developments he has wrought he has become a benefactor to Asheville. The successful completion of this handsome and magnificent structure, not only now symbolizes the great public spirit of Dr. Grove, but it will be a monument to remind those who follow him of his foresight and beneficent accomplishment.

"Splendid as are his qualities as a philanthropist and benefactor, they do not obscure his usefulness as an active business man. Successful in many temporal pursuits, his name is linked with the nation's industries. But the greatest achievement which his sagacity and enterprise has obtained is the building of the hostelry, which we dedicate tonight.

"The opening of the Grove Park Inn marks an epoch in the modern history of the 'Land of the Sky.'

"Upon this auspicious occasion I am prompted to feeling of pleasure and regret. It is indeed a pleasure to be a member of this representative company, and yet I regret my poverty of expression, which does not permit me to fully portray the appreciation I have for the hour.

"The invitation which brings us to this festal board assigns me in part the credit of conceiving the building of a palatial tourist home in Asheville. I modestly acknowledge that for many years I have cherished the hope that a structure such as this might be built.

"In the construction of the Grove Park Inn is to be found a natural beauty and art coupled with the ingenuity of man.

"This magnificent hotel typifies and embodies the acme of perfection in architectural design and is equipped with every convenience which lends to the comfort of its guests.

"For fifty years I have watched the growth of Asheville. Step by step the progress of the town has been noted, completing a remarkable march from an obscure hamlet to a thriving metropolis. Not in wealth alone has the advance been signal; the proud position of our city today can also be traced back to the initial efforts of a loyal and devoted band of determined citizens.

"Each decade in the structural development of Asheville recorded its own achievements, until today we view this magnificent pile which must ever remain a monument to its founders. Here we see the triumph of architectural skill mingled with a scenic splendor of nature's handiwork, the whole blending in one great harmony never before equaled in the annals of the builder's craft.

"It is fitting and proper that in conclusion I should be mindful of the impetus behind this vast undertaking carried to successful completion. In Messrs. Grove and Seely we have witnessed a combination of remarkable foresight and constructive genius.

"Speaking for the citizenship of Asheville, we appreciate and are profoundly grateful for their splendid addition to our enterprises, and trust that their work will be crowned with a reward so richly deserved."

## Senator Luke Lea

Toastmaster Seely then introduced Senator Luke Lea, of Tennessee. Senator Lea said, in part:

"There is only one thing more miserable than to have to speak at all and that is to have to speak before Secretary Bryan. I am sure that I voice Tennessee's appreciation of Mr. Grove's magnificent enterprise and, when I pay tribute to Mr. Grove, I, of course, express my deepest appreciation of Mr. Seely's splendid genius.

"When he declared a year ago that he would open his hotel this month, I doubted the claim very much.

Now I feel that Mr. Seely can do anything; he is a man of rare accomplishments. I fully believe that if he said he would produce the sultan of Turkey at the Southern Railway station tomorrow, I would go down to see the sultan come in.

"Tennessee joins North Carolina in congratulating the entire South on this magnificent enterprise. I may say that Asheville is the twilight zone between the North and the South"

The speaker then paid glowing tributes to Mr. Grove, saying that he is a man who always remembers his friends, and he detailed an incident wherein Mr. Grove once received a loan for $5,000 when many other banks had refused him. "But this little bank," said the speaker, "had great confidence in Mr. Grove and that bank is now the largest bank in St. Louis, a position it has reached through the influence of Mr. Grove, who is now one of its directors. He has proven his loyalty to the South by erecting this magnificent structure, and Tennessee is proud of the man she has given to North Carolina."

Senator Lea then offered glowing praise of Secretary of the Navy Daniels, a North Carolinian, said the speaker, who is doing great work. "But I think the greatest work that Secretary Daniels has done is his order to 'desk heroes' to go to sea. North Carolina is proud of him.

"Nothing gives me greater pleasure than to sit at the same board with Secretary Bryan for whom I have the greatest love and admiration." Senator Lea then introduced Secretary of State William Jennings Bryan, who was greeted with cheers, the entire assembly rising to its feet and cheering for several minutes.

## Secretary Bryan

"I am grateful for the kind words which have been uttered here tonight. I am sorry your governor is not here, but I hope that I can come again when he is here, for I have always found him a man of the most charming personality. I promised Governor Craig that I would come later in the fall, and when I again visit your beautiful city I will bring Mrs. Bryan with me to share the enjoyment of these beautiful environments.

"Another North Carolinian of whom you should be proud is Josephus Daniels, Secretary of the Navy. When I heard that I was to be in the cabinet, I was extremely anxious that he should be there with me, and when his term of office has expired it can be said that the country never had a better Secretary of the Navy than Mr. Daniels. I will never be afraid for any ship under his charge, nor do I fear that he will ever neglect his duties. He has the highest regard for the men behind the guns, and when he retires the mothers of the country may feel that they had a friend in the Secretary of the Navy who is deeply interested in their boys.

"Friendship alone brings me here. Friendship for both men who have combined in the erection of this magnificent building. There were few men in 1896 who felt that they could trust me, and I will go a long way to show my appreciation of one who was not afraid in those dark days. Messrs. Grove and Seely had confidence in me and I have the utmost confidence in them. They have been loyal supporters of the ideas I advocated.

"I am going to speak tonight on Friendship and Faith. The faith of Mr. Grove and Mr. Seely made it possible for us to be here tonight. I admire the genius of a man who can see a boulder on the mountainside and know how it will look over a fireplace. Mr. Seely has that genius. It is the faith of the sculptor, and such faith as this marks the great minds of the world. Such thoughts of these have often entered my mind as I have stood before some of the world's greatest structures. I thought of this wonderful faith when I looked at the Panama Canal and admired the great minds that conceived it.

"My chief thought tonight or, I might say, my subject for tonight, is 'Building for the Age.' I have never seen any structure to equal this. I have looked through it and marvel at the triumph of the builder's art; and as I gazed, the thought impressed me that these men are not building for this generation or century, but for the age. It will stand forever. Why should not this hotel stand for all time, for it has none of the elements of decay? It will be here an eloquent monument to its founders in the centuries to come. It was built not for the dead, as were the tombs of kings, but for living human beings that they might find delight here. The sentiment of the present age is to build for others, not for themselves.

"It is pleasant to testify by our presence here tonight our appreciation for what they have accomplished. The thought that I would leave with you tonight is that just as these men have built for the ages, so are we building in our daily lives. We build temporarily or permanently; if we live for pleasure, we build for a day. But if we build our lives on high ideals, if we have the truest and high conception of what we put into this world, and measure up to our responsibilities, then we build for the ages.

"The characteristics of the heart are greater than the characteristics of the mind or brain. Let us not be discouraged that we have no part in this. Let us not be envious that we can claim none of the credit for such wonderful achievement. The characteristics of the heart of the founders of this structure have touched the people about them, and their names will live in the love and esteem of mankind when they are no more.

"Today we stand in this wonderful hotel, not built for a few, but for the multitudes that will come and go. Is it not better to build such a monument than a tomb? I congratulate these men.

"They have built for the ages."

*Heywood-Wakefield wicker rockers ring the six rock pillars in Great Hall in 1913.*

# Chapter 8

# "Fred Seely Takes Charge"

*I think sometimes I made a mistake in ever undertaking to build the hotel and now I am practically taking it on for life and making myself responsible for its success. I shall do the best I can. I have worked against many obstacles, and can do it again.*

Fred Loring Seely

On the Sunday morning after the opening banquet, as the last of E. W. Grove's illustrious guests were driven away in their cars, the Grove Park Inn must have seemed eerily quiet to Fred Seely. After more than twelve months of feverish noise and uproar, from the diesel-powered steam shovel and teams of braying mules to men shouting down from the roof and two-ton boulders being grunted into position, the Great Hall was, for the first time, suddenly still.

Although the hotel was now officially open for business, Seely still had a few weeks of work to oversee, from the completion of the sixteen rooms on the sixth floor to the landscaping around the building. After a series of extensive interviews, he had hand-selected

William S. Kenney, formerly of the prestigious Mount Washington Hotel, to serve as general manager for E. W. Grove, who was already anxious to return to his offices back at the Paris Medicine Company in St. Louis. Mr. Kenney had arrived from Bretton Woods, New Hampshire, in time to start training his front desk staff and to be on hand for the Saturday evening banquet.

In the weeks that followed, it must have seemed to Mr. Kenney that he was working not for Edwin Wiley Grove, but for Fred Seely. To someone who had just arrived at the Grove Park Inn, Seely must have appeared to be a general contractor unwilling to leave his pet project. Seely continued to come to the Grove Park Inn nearly every single day, and took it upon himself to begin handling the marketing and advertising for the hotel, starting with a full page ad placed in the prestigious *National Geographic* magazine.

Throughout the remainder of 1913 and into the early months of 1914, Fred Seely remained in Asheville, overseeing the gradual completion of the Grove Park Inn, taking a more active role in Grove's other real estate projects in the area, and continuing to represent the interests of E. W. Grove in persuading Asheville's policy makers to invoke and enforce stricter bans on sanitariums catering to people stricken with tuberculosis. Grove, however, was under the impression that his son-in-law would soon be accepting a position in the State Department under his friend William Jennings Bryan. In January, Seely wired his father-in-law, announcing, "We are not going to Washington. The place had to be filled at once and I could not do that. It was third offer and there will be others and better opportunities if at a future time it seems best."

Unable or at least unwilling to leave the management of the Grove Park Inn in the hands of general manager William Kenney, Fred Seely returned to the hotel each day, offering suggestions as to how the staff should be handled and the affairs of the hotel managed. Friction between Kenney and Seely mounted steadily, until sparks flew and Kenney tendered his resignation. In a move reminiscent of his days at the *Atlanta Georgian*, when as publisher Fred Seely forced his own editor to resign, then assumed his daily responsibilities, Fred Seely began serving as general manager while supposedly looking for a replacement. Along the way Seely must have reached a decision about his future, however, as an article in the May 23, 1914, edition of the *Asheville Citizen* reported, "work on the stone castle which Fred L. Seely is building on the brow of Overlook mountain has been resumed within the past few days and a force of thirty workmen is now engaged in erecting the walls of what is expected to be one of the finest residences in North Carolina, if not in the entire South."

In words that could only have come directly from Fred Seely himself, the writer observed, "Mr. Seely's new home, designed after his own ideas, follows closely the design of Forde Abbey, in England, a stone castle of the year 1520. It is to be 170 feet long, and, standing as it will on the brow of the mountain, will present very much the appearance of the old feudal castles of the fourteenth century. Mr. Seely is contemplating some walnut paneling of an exclusive design, to be made by the boys at the Biltmore Industries. The whole building will be thoroughly fire-proof and, aside from the antique designs, will be modern in every respect, so far as conveniences are concerned."

Fred Seely's plans, although unannounced, suffered a setback when, on June 18, 1914, the assassination of Archduke Franz Ferdinand of Austria set in motion a series of declarations that catapulted neighboring European countries into a world war. While the United States attempted to remain neutral, the conflict soon pitted England, France and Russia against Germany and Austria-Hungary. Political observers predicted that it would only be a matter of time before the

United States would feel compelled to stand alongside its allies. News of the bloody conflict sent shock waves across the country, compelling people to cancel their vacations. Even the new Grove Park Inn was not immune to the impact of the war in Europe, as cancellations outnumbered reservations that summer, prompting owner E. W. Grove to announce in September that he was temporarily closing the hotel.

Seely was both shocked and outraged by his father-in-law's decision, feeling Grove had overreacted to the situation and was being pressured by his bankers in St. Louis. He urged Grove to reconsider, but Grove responded by stating, "I am going to stand by our decision about closing on [October] fifteenth if conditions do not warrant remaining open. There is no use for us to deceive ourselves by thinking that the people are going to come because we are so anxious for them to come."

Seely, however, was not so easily deterred. He countered by proposing to his father-in-law that he would, in fact, lease the Grove Park Inn from Grove, provided he could then manage the hotel as he deemed appropriate. In exchange for paying Grove a percentage of the hotel's gross revenues, Fred Seely received a long-term lease placing control over the inn in his hands through the year 1927. Negotiations between the two men over the precise terms of the lease, which was officially re-written no fewer than three times between 1914 and 1917, resulted in the first public signs of their strained relationship.

In a letter revealing the extent of his frustration, Fred Seely wrote to Grove in 1914, "You have stated all along that you expected it to lose money for three years. I am now undertaking it to make money for you and for myself inside of two years. I think sometimes I made a mistake in ever undertaking to build the hotel and now I am practically taking it on for life and making myself responsible for its success. I shall do the best I can. I have worked against many obstacles, and can do it again."

With the approach of a new year, the 44-year-old Fred Seely found himself about to embark on yet another new career. After fourteen years working for the Paris Medicine Company and nearly six years as publisher and editor of the *Atlanta Georgian*, he was about to become president of The Grove Park Inn, Inc. With no first-hand experience in hotel management and war clouds drifting across the Atlantic Ocean toward the United States, he knew his task would be daunting.

Yet he hoped that, with his father-in-law presumably out of the picture, he could finally have the opportunity to manage a business just as he envisioned it should be run -- without his famous father-in-law looking over his shoulder.

*Early guests enjoying the Old Hickory rocking chairs on the front terrace.*

# Chapter 9

# "A Day at the Grove Park Inn"

*If you are a Big Business Man and feel the need of rest after these years of strain, you should come to Grove Park Inn, Asheville, N.C., where rest is made possible.*

*The Grove Park Inn is not a sanitarium, a hospital, or a health resort, but is operated on the highest plane that a home-like resort hotel can be operated. It is a resting place for tired people who are not sick, who want good food well-cooked and digestible, with luxurious, though sanitary, surroundings.*

Early Advertisements

From the first time that Fred Seely and E. W. Grove spoke of building a hotel on Sunset Mountain, they agreed that it should be "the finest resort hotel in the world." As both men were well aware, most hotels and boarding houses of their era were frequented by traveling salesmen. At a time when neither telephones nor automobiles were common, most businesses, including E. W. Grove's own pharmaceutical giant, the Paris Medicine Company, depended on traveling salesmen to generate revenues. These weary journeymen spent their days napping in railway cars, walking from store to store around courthouse squares, carrying their suitcases of salesman samples they unpacked on countless store counters until they arrived -- exhausted, dusty and sometimes ready for more than just a nip of Jack Daniels -- at the local hotel.

Seely and Grove had both stood shoulder to shoulder with many of these traveling men, and made the decision early in their planning that they were not the clientele the Grove Park Inn would encourage. Instead, they designed the hotel specifically for wealthy business owners in Chicago, Cincinnati and New York, wealthy retirees living in Miami and St. Petersburg, and influential politicians in Washington, all just an overnight train ride from Asheville.

Their formula met with success, as among their early guests were Charles Schwab, Henry Ford, Thomas Edison, H. J. Heinz, Harvey Firestone, Sir John and Lady Eaton, Charles Mayo, George F. Baker, Louis Swift, John Rockefeller Jr., William Jennings Bryan, and President Woodrow Wilson.

What, then, was it like to stay at the Grove Park Inn during those early years when guests came not for an overnight stay, but to spend several days -- perhaps even weeks -- at the famed resort?

Your first day begins nestled in comfort and in silence.

Each of the beds, as Fred Seely described them in an early brochure, "are six-feet, four-inches long, and are the finest and most comfortable money could produce. The springs are of the best double box type, upholstered with heavy pads on top, and the mattresses are the Sealy tuftless 'DeLuxe. The bed linens are of imported Oxford twill, and the pillows are of pure down. Spreads, curtains, pillow mantles and scarves are of the finest quality, pure brown linen."

"A Day at the Grove Park Inn"

Your room is outfitted with Arts and Crafts furniture, designed by the Roycrofters and manufactured from solid oak by the White Furniture Company. You would have either one or two beds in your room, each with a nightstand and Roycroft lamp, a mirrored vanity, a built-in dresser, a small desk and a rocking chair. The walls are trimmed in oak, with natural burlap as a wall covering. The white-tiled bathroom is outfitted with solid porcelain fixtures produced by Haines, Jones & Cadbury of Philadelphia. Your closet light comes on automatically when you open the door. As you slip out of bed, your feet feel a hand woven rug from Aubusson, France.

Those guests on the east side of the hotel awake to the sun streaming through the towering pines on the hillside above the hotel, while those across the open Palm Court face to the west, overlooking the golf course beside the tennis courts and the Blue Ridge Mountains in the distance. No one hears the sound of any delivery trucks or automobiles, as none are allowed around the hotel before nine o'clock each morning.

Outside your room, in the Palm Court area, housekeepers dressed in matching smocks and each wearing rubber-soled shoes, sit quietly on their chairs. They are ready to answer your questions and to help in any way needed, but are under strict instructions not begin cleaning any rooms until after nine o'clock.

Had you come to the Grove Park Inn with a child and nanny, they would have been assigned a room down the hallway in one of the wings off the Palm Court. Private servants and chauffeurs spent their nights in Sunset Hall, a three-story, stuccoed dormitory that once stood down the hill from the hotel, near the former livery stable and garage. Had you requested it, you could also have arranged for the room adjoining yours to have the bedroom furniture replaced with couches and chairs, so that you could have a two-room suite with connecting doors during your stay. Larger families also had the option of staying in one of the cottages built a short distance from the hotel.

"We prefer not to entertain children under ten years of age," Seely warned prospective guests. "We do so, however, except during February, March and April. Not that we dislike children ourselves, but that we wish to maintain a place where tired busy people may get away from excitement and all annoyances and rest their nerves."

Once you had dressed, you would have walked down the corridor to one of the elevators located at either end of the Palm Court. The elevator operator would greet you with the daily weather report and news of any special activities taking place that day. Once in the Great Hall you would stroll past the front desk, the eight-foot tall Roycroft clock and the gift shop on your way to the dining room located in the north wing. Outside the double doors to the Plantation Dining Room is the narrow door and stairway leading downstairs to a separate dining area for children and their nannies.

Waiters in the Plantation Dining Room had each been personally interviewed and selected by Fred Seely, who noted, "we dress all our waiters in freshly laundered white suits, with the sleeves buttoned around the wrist -- not dragging in your food. Every waiter is placed in line at lecture each day and inspected as to his personal cleanliness, even to the examination of his finger nails."

On your first arrival at the Grove Park Inn's dining room you would be assigned your own waiter and table, each of which would remain yours for the duration of your stay. Large windows flanking the walls of the dining room afforded guests panoramic views of Sunset Mountain above them or the distant Blue Ridge Mountains to the west. Your menu, printed the previous night, did not contain prices, as meals were included in the cost of your room.

## "A Day at the Grove Park Inn"

Fred Seely took great pride and care in how his staff prepared each meal, starting with breakfast. It began with Richelieu coffee, "prepared by a vacuum process, which renders it more nearly free from the acid properties which injure the stomach, than any real coffee ever discovered. But it is real coffee -- contains its caffeine -- and we believe it is as fine in flavor as coffee can be made. We simply sought the coffee which is the least injurious."

In addition to offering you eggs, pancakes and French toast, as well as oatmeal, "that we steam in dry, high-pressure steam chests twelve hours before we serve it," Fred Seely also passed out advice on proper eating.

"Nearly everyone should eat fruit of some kind," he wrote in the menu, "and most people want it for breakfast. Many people should never eat raw fruit. Their stomachs cannot stand the acids and the uncooked fiber. Prunes, however, can be eaten, but not all prunes are palatable. We supply the finest preserved prunes packed anywhere in the world -- they are preserved at the orchards in California and are not the usual dried prune. We serve them every morning year round."

After breakfast on your first day, you undoubtedly would want to familiarize yourself with all that the Grove Park Inn has to offer. Your tour would begin in the Big Room, as it was then called, a massive lobby Fred Seely described as "one of the most wonderful rooms in the world. It is 120 feet long by 80 feet wide and can comfortably entertain 1,000 people. The two great fireplaces in it burn eight-foot logs, and each required 120 tons of boulders to build." The room was furnished with Heywood-Wakefield wicker chairs and rockers with plush red leather cushions, inviting you to sit, rock and relax.

From the Big Room, now known as the Great Hall, you could stroll out onto the Sunset Terrace, which was then an unroofed porch lined with rustic rockers made by the Old Hickory Furniture Company. The rocking chairs became so popular that many guests, including Henry Ford, ordered them from Fred Seely for their homes. Here you could stand or sit while watching tennis players on the court below and golfers on the links bordering the grounds of the Grove Park Inn. You could then continue walking along the open terrace around the south end of the building, where an outdoor fireplace, only slightly smaller than those inside the Big Room, offered a means of warming yourself on chilly days or evenings.

You might have even seen Mr. Grove himself, as he enjoyed coming to the hotel in the early years. "He was the sweetest most gentleman you ever saw," one Asheville resident, whose father was a friend of Grove's, reported. "He was a small man in size, but he had a big heart. Dr. Grove would come to our house and he loved our kitchen. He and my father would try to make waffles, but they made such a mess! Dr. Grove was ahead of his time. He had great ideas of how Asheville should be built up. He felt the whole town should have grown toward the north and not the east, because of the huge mountains in the way in the east."

Your morning activities might also include a guided tour of the building and grounds; a hike up one of the many wooded trails maintained by the staff; a round of golf on the adjacent Asheville Country Club eighteen-hole course; archery and tennis on the court directly below the steps leading down from the Sunset Terrace; horseback rides up Sunset Mountain or in the riding ring next to the stables, or automobile tours to Mount Mitchell, Mount Pisgah, Chimney Rock or, beginning in 1930, to the Biltmore Estate.

"A Day at the Grove Park Inn"

Fred Seely had also planned activities for those days when the weather might keep you indoors. Stairways next to each of the elevators lead down to the lower level Recreation Room, where you could play either a game of pool or of billiards, or could bowl a few frames on one of three bowling lanes. Ping-pong tables, along with tables for bridge parties and other card games, were also arranged by the staff. Not far away, but also on the lower level, you could set up an appointment at either the Barber Shop or the Beauty Parlor.

When designing the Recreation Room, Fred Seely also included an indoor swimming pool, along with tiled changing rooms for both men and women. Later, as the hotel announced, "the Grove Park Baths have been added to the equipment, in order that our guests may have the advantage of health building facilities without the inconvenience and expense of hospital treatments." The brochure was quick to note, however, "the Grove Park Inn is not a sanitarium and we do not invite the patronage of sick people."

The Grove Park Baths were modeled after those designed by Dr. John Harvey Kellogg, founder of the famed Battle Creek Sanitarium and an early advocate of holistic medicine, good nutrition, daily exercise, vegetarianism and, naturally, of his own Corn Flakes breakfast cereal. Dr. Kellogg, a friend of Fred Seely and a regular guest at the Grove Park Inn, was a controversial figure in his time. He established the Battle Creek Sanitarium on the principles of the Seventh-Day Adventist Church, with whom he later broke. He believed in a vegetarian diet, abstinence from alcohol and tobacco, regular yogurt enemas and hydrotherapy. He felt that eating, in particular red meat, increased the sexual appetite. As an advocate of sexual abstinence, Kellogg recommended that people eat only two meals a day and that they avoid stimulating food and drink to reduce their sexual appetite.

The Grove Park Baths adopted "methods which have been the most successful in correcting deficiencies resulting from improper habits of eating and exercise, nerve strain, overwork and similar difficulties. Absolutely no medical treatments are given except under the personal supervision of a competent physician. Our service is designed to promote health and to prevent physical decline. We do not attempt to cure ailments which have reached advanced stages."

Treatments offered to guests at the Grove Park Inn included massages, mild workouts, hydro-baths, salt baths, medical gymnastics and an early form of tanning booths called "sunarc baths." Borrowing from the writings of Dr. Kellogg, the inn's literature declared, "there is nothing better than massage and vibration to tone up the general vitality, strengthen the muscular system and improve the functions of the internal organs. Improved circulation, increased muscle tone and a spirit of good health and well-being seem naturally to follow this delightful and beneficial method of treatment."

Lunch was served beginning at 1:00 p.m. each day, after which you could find a seat in the Big Room to enjoy an afternoon organ recital. "I remember the organ recitals very well," recalled one early guest when interviewed. "The grand Skinner organ was located in the back right corner as you come into the Grove Park Inn. The recitals were complimentary to hotel guests; however, to come in from the outside you had to be invited. And you had to dress properly to come. Guests were not allowed to smoke during a recital. If you talked too loudly during the recital, they brought you a card telling you to be quiet, or you would have to leave."

The staff would serve you tea from 4:30-5:30 p.m. before you would return to your room to prepare for dinner and the evening's entertainment. As Fred Seely also wrote, "Inasmuch as we are so frequently asked if it is customary at the Inn to wear evening dress at dinner, we desire to state that, as a rule, dinner coats are worn. This is merely given as information, and we wish it distinctly understood that we do not desire to suggest what our guests shall eat, drink or wear."

At seven o'clock guests would begin arriving at the Plantation Dining Room, where an attendant would direct you to your customary table and assigned waiter. Dinner would typically begin with a soup, such as Consommé Douglas, Consommé Vermicelli or Consommé Neapolitan, English Beef Barley or Puree of Tomato, perhaps accompanied by a Chesapeake Bay Oyster Cocktail. Entrees often would include your choice of either Broiled Shad or Red Snapper ("Received by Express this Morning Packed in Ice"), Roast Prime Rib, Roast Tennessee Turkey ("Prepared by a Formula of Our Own by Which the Turkeys are Steamed and Baked"), Fillet Mignon ("Sautéed in Butter and Served with a Rich Brown Sauce with Truffles and Fresh Mushrooms") or Fresh Milk-Fed Chicken on Toast, along with an assortment of fresh vegetables, potatoes and salads.

Dessert selections often included chocolate ice cream ("Made of Cream Containing 40% Butterfat and Sweetened almost entirely with Saccharine"), apple or cherry pie, pound cake, peach tarts, Boston cream pie, raisin cookies, apples, oranges, bananas and crystallized ginger -- dried ginger coated with sugar and believed to help alleviate any indigestion you might experience!

Fred Seely and his staff prided themselves on accommodating the requests of any of their guests, regardless how unusual. Former Asheville resident Noah Stewart, who as a young man worked at the Grove Park Inn, recalled, "One of the odd jobs I did was to take care of the little deer they kept. They were in the lot on the west side, next to the golf links. My job was to see that they had enough feed and water. They also had a lot where they kept possums, and I had to take care of them, too. There was this man whose job it was to remove all the scrap and waste foods from the kitchen. His name was Lyda Jordan. He would save me all the chicken heads and turkey heads, so I could feed them to the possums. Well, whenever William Jennings Bryan would come to the hotel, the cooks would bake him a 'big fat possum' to eat."

In addition to handling special requests and the delicate question of permitting children at the inn, Grove and Seely also had to deal with the challenge of alcohol consumption. Neither Grove nor Seely appear to have developed a personal taste for alcohol, but they could not expect you and their other guests to so readily follow their lead.

What you may not have realized before arriving at the Grove Park Inn was that the city of Asheville had banned the sale of alcoholic beverages since 1908. The law made it illegal for Fred Seely to sell any alcohol to his guests, but did not prohibit his waiters from serving any alcohol that you had brought. When pressed for a clarification, attorney James Britt explained to Seely, "I suggest that you be careful not to put the hotel in the attitude or even the appearance of receiving, holding or serving the liquors for itself. Offenses against our liquor laws are not, of course, in the use of the liquors, but in the mode of supply. Your relation to your guests must be strictly that of serving for them, without charge, that which they have supplied for themselves."

In a section of the country where local farmers had for generations taken pride in the production of their private blend of moonshine, called everything from White Lightning, Rotgut, and Mule Kick to Radiator Whiskey, Skull Cracker and Mountain Dew, supplying tourists with their own jug or Mason jar seemed a natural extension of their famed Southern hospitality. While never publicly acknowledged, descendents of early twentieth century moonshiners recalled stories of late night deliveries made to the employees' rear entrance at the Grove Park Inn. The repeal of prohibition in 1933 effectively signaled the demise of public demand for home-brewed corn whiskey, and enabled the staff at the Grove Park Inn to begin selling it openly to their guests for the first time.

In addition to the activities offered in the Recreation Room, Fred Seely also provided additional after-dinner entertainment for you and your fellow guests in the Great Hall. On Monday, Wednesday and Saturday nights his staff hung a screen over the north fireplace where movies were then shown. Seely took great care in selecting each film, often previewing it in his office. Evidence of his discretion is revealed in a memo dated January 24, 1927, to the company which provided movies for the Grove Park Inn: "Could not use *The Great Gatsby* as too risqué, so want to ask you to please cancel *Stranded in Paris,* as afraid to book any more pictures we have not seen." When asked, Seely proclaimed their most popular movies were "of travel and comedy."

On alternative nights, you could find a comfortable chair in the Great Hall to listen to Maurice Longhurst's organ recital from 8:30-10:00 p.m., after which those who were still awake could often listen to a presentation by a noted artist or lecturer. The Sunday night organ concerts became so popular that Asheville residents began dropping in, prompting Fred Seely to announce in 1923 that people were permitted, as long as seats were available, to attend the Sunday organ recitals, but, as he warned in the Asheville newspapers, "We do not admit children under sixteen to these concerts and we request that no children be brought to the Inn, for we would have to refuse them."

Despite his popularity, not even famed organist Maurice Longhurst could avoid Fred Seely's often scathing reviews, including this one written in a memo to him on November 22, 1918:

*We are spending a great deal of money in advertising the Inn as a place to rest from war weariness, and after the long tedious years of poor business and financial losses, I cannot help desiring to make the Inn a place where the public finds rest and recreation and a spirit of harmony and music. I must ask you, therefore, to come to the realization of the fact that the war is over and that the victory could not have been more glorious than it was.*

*If we intend to succeed, it would be no more than fair to ask you to throw your soul more into your work and not go about it in quite such a matter of fact manner as you have been accustomed to have for some time past. I have also noticed that for several evenings lately you have not worn formal dress. I feel that it is quite important for a man in your position to appear in keeping with your work and I sincerely trust that you will pay special attention to this duty.*

After the evening concert, movie or lecture, you might pull your wicker chair or rocker a little closer to one of the fireplaces where, on chilly nights, the bellmen would keep a fire burning. As one guest wrote to friends back home, "A wagon was loaded with wood for the big fireplaces, and a donkey pulled that wagon right into the Great Hall." After the evening's presentation, you would see bellmen making their way through the room, following a tradition that E. W. Grove had started years earlier in Paris, Tennessee.

Soon after endowing his hometown with its first public high school, E. W. Grove provided the board of education with money to keep a barrel of apples in the hallway for any student to eat at any time. It was his way, he explained, of making sure no student ever went hungry. Years later, the board elected to use the apple money for something else, but as soon as word of the change reached Grove in St. Louis, the checks stopped coming.

The apples were returned to the hallway the next week.

At the Grove Park Inn, Grove requested that each evening the bellmen walk through the Great Hall offering an apple to anyone who wanted one. Along with each apple, you also would receive a waxed paper wrapper, onto which Fred Seely had the following printed: "You will find it convenient to place the core in this wrapper until the boy comes round to collect it. If an apple does not agree with you before going to bed, try following it with a glass of water."

When the time finally came for you to retire to your room at the end of a long and event-filled day, you would have found the following printed on a pull-down window shade hanging in each of the elevators:

*Please be quiet in going to your room --*
*other guests may be asleep.*
*No objections to being in the Big Room as late as you like,*
*but we greatly desire quiet in the bedrooms and corridors*
*from 10:30 p.m. to 8:00 a.m.*

To ensure that no one missed the point of his message, Fred Seely had the following printed on each of the daily menus (the capital letters are his):

*We do, however, make one request and insist very positively upon compliance with it -- THAT GUESTS REFRAIN FROM UNNECESSARY NOISE IN THEIR ROOMS AFTER 10:30 P.M. WE MUST INSIST*

ON PROTECTING THE RIGHTS OF GUESTS WHO MAY HAVE RETIRED, AND AS THE INN WAS LOCATED PURPOSELY AWAY FROM RAILROADS, STREET CARS AND OTHER OUTSIDE ANNOYANCES, CONVERSATIONS, SLAMMING OF DOORS, THROWING SHOES ON THE FLOOR AND SIMILAR UNNECES-SARY NOISES ARE LIABLE TO ANNOY GUESTS IN ADJOINING ROOMS.

In addition to sending everyone off to their rooms feeling well-nourished, Fred Seely also provided the following assurance for anyone who feared they might have over-indulged, stating that:

*You need only telephone for the night steward. We keep an old-fashioned medicine chest at the Inn. It contains everything from Paregoric [for diarrhea] to Veronal [a low-dosage barbiturate sleeping pill or powder made by Bayer]. We try to have every convenience and comfort you could possibly have at your home. He will bring you any remedy you may need, usually two doses in an envelop or bottle, put up and sealed by our druggist, and labeled by him, so there would not be any risk of a mistake. We make no charge for these things except where full packages of proprietary articles might be asked for.*

Although Fred Seely had taken the helm of the Grove Park Inn without any prior experience in hotel management, he certainly understood what his elite clientele wished to find when they traveled away from home. And while some guests understandably may have bristled at a few of his restrictions, for nearly two decades his management of the Grove Park Inn left no doubt in anyone's mind that, indeed, it did deserve to be called "the finest resort hotel in the world."

*The pull-down shade in the elevator asking guests to be quiet after 10:30 p.m.*

*The elevator hidden inside the south fireplace in the Great Hall.*

# Chapter 10

# "The Elevators in the Fireplaces"

*One of the curses of the ordinary hotel is the lack of consideration for guests who need rest, or care to retire before midnight. At the Grove Park Inn it is different.*

Fred Loring Seely

If you didn't know where to look, you might not find them.

Tucked inside each of the two mammoth twin fireplaces flanking either end of the Great Hall is one of the trademark and totally unique features of the Grove Park Inn: a hidden elevator.

Classic Fred Loring Seely.

Like Edwin Wiley Grove, his famous father-in-law, Fred Seely traveled a great deal on behalf of the Paris Medicine Company. And when he did, he often stayed in hotels where guests had to listen to the clanking of the machinery or the closing of the metal doors all night long. When given the opportunity to design and supervise the construction of the Grove Park Inn, Seely devised a unique means of silencing nearly all of the sounds that elevators typically make.

While both the concept and early versions of the elevator date back several centuries, one of the earliest and most famous lifts was constructed inside the Palace of Versailles in the 18th century. There the notoriously promiscuous King Louis XV (1710-1774) wanted easy and private access to the second floor apartment his mistress, Marie Anne de Mailly (Madame de Chateauroux), described as the "youngest and prettiest of the five famous sisters, four of whom would become the mistress of King Louis XV." His private elevator was powered by a counterweight tailored specifically for him.

Remembered for more noble reasons, Elisha Otis (1811-1861) first designed a freight elevator for a New York furniture maker before turning his attention to passenger elevators for department stores and hotels. To demonstrate the effectiveness of one of his most important inventions, the elevator safety brake, in 1854 his firm constructed an elevator inside the New York Crystal Palace during the Industry of All Nations exhibition. While the crowd watched in awe, Elisha Otis stepped inside his elevator and signaled he was ready to be hoisted to the top of the building. Once there, to the horror of the assembled spectators, his assistant sliced the hoisting ropes. Instead of sending the elevator and Otis plunging down the shaft to a gruesome death, the teeth on his patented brake slipped securely into the notches on the guide-rail and held the car safely aloft.

Three years later, Otis Brothers built the first public elevator inside a five-story Manhattan department store. The elevator company quickly rose to become the leader in its field and never looked back. Over the course of the remainder of the 19th century, the elevator industry witnessed an explosion of improvements and patents, including faster hydraulic, electric and steam powered elevators, automatic doors, push button controls, better safety features and increased weight capacities.

The stellar reputation of the Otis Brothers firm prompted Fred Seely to contact them when it came time to order elevators for the Grove Park Inn. Unfortunately, none of the earliest correspondence between the Otis Elevator Company and Fred Seely has surfaced, but it is doubtful if Seely and Grove would have seriously considered any firm other than Otis for the elevators in their six-story hotel.

For anyone who has seen them, the two public elevators in the Great Hall appear unlike any others, for these elevators are located inside each of the twin fireplaces. For Fred Seely, this was not a public relations stunt or a novelty idea. He had one goal in mind and only one: to prevent any sound of the machinery from escaping the elevator shaft and reaching any of the guest rooms.

To Seely, the solution seemed obvious: put them inside the fireplaces.

In truth, Seely's request did not pose any special challenges to the Otis Brothers Elevator Company, for the elevators are, in fact, located inside a standard concrete block shaft that was then encased in boulders.

What may have first had them scratching their heads back in the New York offices, however, was yet another unique feature of the Grove Park Inn: each elevator had to have three doors.

Guests stepping into the elevator from the first floor lobby might have then expected to step out through the same main door, as is generally the practice in most buildings. Because of the way the rooms were laid out, however, the only time guests step in or out of the main elevator door is when they are on the ground floor.

As Fred Seely designed it, guests assigned a room on the second floor wing would have to exit through a door located in the side of the elevator. Those continuing up to the third, fourth, five or sixth floors would exit out the opposite side, leading onto the spacious parapets looking down into the Palm Court.

One, two, three sets of doors -- all in one elevator.

All inside a gigantic fireplace.

Never one to let anything go to waste, Fred Seely found a novel use for the fourth wall -- the only one without a door -- inside each elevator. Printed on a retractable window shade he had installed on the back wall was the following notice:

*Please be quiet in going to your room --*
*other guests may be asleep.*
*No objections to being in the Big Room as late as you like,*
*but we greatly desire quiet in the bedrooms and corridors*
*from 10:30 p.m. to 8:00 a.m.*

The greatest challenge the Otis Elevator Company may have faced at the Grove Park Inn, however, most likely began after the July 1913 deadline Fred Seely had set for them. Even with the elevators tucked away behind the massive boulders and the electric machinery encased in a separate room in the basement, Fred Seely remained notoriously sensitive to any sounds emitting from them. Indicative of his long stream of correspondence with the Otis Elevator Company is this letter, dated the tenth of March in 1925:

*Gentlemen:*

*Your Mr. Gray is quite familiar with the worry we have had over the noise caused in the operation of our Otis Elevators. They still hammer about as badly as ever and are very unsatisfactory. We have been compelled to prevent the operation of the elevators as much as possible until the guests begin to get up in the morning, for these switches pound loud enough to wake up nearly anyone with a room near the elevator.*

*We are going to be compelled to either sell these elevator motors or put in some other equipment. We cannot be annoyed by the noise and hammering indefinitely.*

*Very truly yours,*
*F. L. Seely*
*President*

Despite Fred Seely's personal dissatisfaction with the distant, muted sounds barely seeping out of the elevator shafts, guests at the Grove Park Inn have always found them fascinating. One guest went so far as to send a description of the elevators to the nationally syndicated newspaper column, "Ripley's Believe It Or Not," where a sketch of the towering fireplace soon appeared with the following notation:

*THE GROVE PARK INN*

*in Asheville, N.C. built in 1913 has two huge fireplaces*

*in its lobby each some 34 feet wide and over 19 feet high*

*WITH ELEVATORS LOCATED INSIDE THEIR ROCKWORK !*

Believe it or not, it was classic Fred Seely.

*An inspirational motto selected by Fred Seely and still visible in the Great Hall.*

# Chapter 11

# "Perhaps Walls Can Talk"

*Take from this hearth its warmth,*
*From this room its charm,*
*From this Inn its amity,*
*Return them not -- but return.*

Fireplace Motto

One of Fred Seely's early role models was the charismatic Elbert Hubbard, the founder of the Roycroft community of craftsmen
in East Aurora, New York.

Elbert Hubbard (1856-1915) was first and foremost a writer
who, in 1895, after his earliest novels had been rejected by main-
stream publishers, established his own small print shop and publishing offices. The men and women who worked for him were soon
printing, binding and distributing a monthly magazine called *The
Fra*, as well as Hubbard's books and his popular series of pamphlets
entitled *Little Journeys*.

Were he alive today, Elbert Hubbard would also be known
as an inspirational speaker, for he often traveled the Chautauqua

circuit, appearing along with vaudeville acts on a makeshift stage beneath an enormous canvas tent. The long haired, always smiling Hubbard was a popular headliner, who reportedly could make more money in one summer giving inspirational speeches than his Roycrofters could in an entire year back in East Aurora.

In addition to everything else that he was writing, Hubbard enjoyed dashing off epigrams for his typesetters to insert into empty spaces in his magazines and booklets. Some were original, while others were either adopted -- or adapted -- from other writers, ranging from Shakespeare to John Ruskin. Always frugal and ever alert to fresh opportunities, Hubbard instructed his employees to print some of his mottoes on leftover stock, which he then inserted into envelopes alongside letters to friends and clients. Typical of the style and content of Elbert Hubbard's mottoes are these:

*Blessed is that man who has found his work.*
*Be gentle and keep your voice low.*
*Do unto others as though you were the others.*
*A bad compromise is better than a good lawsuit.*

In 1905, while living in Atlanta and corresponding with the Roycrofters regarding furniture for his new home, Fred Seely received one of Hubbard's printed mottoes, writing back, "I so much want a few of all the kinds you have. I really hope I am not asking for something that you wish to remain exclusive with the [Roycroft] Shop. What better missionary work can be done than to sell these little things to businessmen who may spread the gospel of friendship without other motive than the good feeling within his heart? Would not this, while carrying its message of hope and love, take the Roycroft mark around the earth, and do a good turn for the Shop?"

While Hubbard's son Bert explained, "that we have never printed them except for our own use," the Roycrofters soon added packets of mottoes to their inventory of gift items for sale in their shop.

And one day in 1913, when Fred Seely was standing amidst the chaos of workmen hoisting boulders in place above the twelve-foot firebox, pushing wheelbarrows of rocks up long sloping ramps and tamping mortar deep within the crevices so that it would scarcely be seen, an idea occurred to him: have an artist hand-letter inspirational mottoes on some of the rocks.

While some of the mottoes were destroyed or covered during subsequent remodeling projects at the Grove Park Inn, many still survive. Several have since been repainted, but even those that are somewhat faded are still legible. Here, then, is a compilation of some of the original Grove Park Inn mottoes selected by Fred Seely, many of which can still be found on the walls of the Great Hall:

*The sun will shine after every storm. - Emerson*
*Burdens become lighter when cheerfully bourne. - Ovid*
*It is a sure sign of rain when it is black all around and pouring out in the middle - Indian Saying*
*How much pain have cost us, the evil that have never happened - Thomas Jefferson*

*The gem cannot be polished without friction or man perfected without trials - Dutch Proverb*
*Be not simply good -- be good for something. - Thoreau*
*Take things always by their smooth handle - Thomas Jefferson*
*Little words make or mar men.*

*Think of your own faults the first part of the night*
*when you are awake,*
*and the faults of others when you are asleep. - Chinese Proverb*
*Nisi Utile est quod facimus stulta est Gloria.*
*(Unless what we do is useful, glory is foolish.) - Phaedous*
*Every book is a quotation: every house is a quotation out*
*of all forests and mines and stone quarries,*
*and every man is a quotation from all his ancestors. - Emerson*
*Little men want big titles, big men refuse them. - Hawthorne*
*Small strokes fell large oaks.*
*Tongues in trees, Books in the running brook, Sermons in stones*
*and Good in everything. - Shakespeare*
*If a man can write a better speech, preach a better sermon or make*
*a better rat trap than his neighbor, though he builds his house in the*
*woods, the World will make a beaten path to his door.*

*This old world we're livin' in*
*Is mighty hard to beat;*
*We get a thorn with every rose,*
*But ain't the roses sweet.          - Stanton*

*Confide ye aye in Providence,*
*For Providence is kind;*
*And bear ye a life's changes*
*Wi' a calm and tranquil mind.*
*Tho' pressed and hemmed on every side,*
*Have faith and ye'll win through,*
*For like blade o' grass*
*Keeps its own drop o' dew.*

Among those mottoes believed to have once appeared on rocks which have been removed or covered are the following:

*The only reward for real service to humanity*
*is an opportunity to do more. - Henry Ford*
*Pearls unpolished shine not. - Japanese Proverb*
*If you wish another to keep your secret, first keep it yourself. - Seneca*
*Live with the wolves and you will soon*
*learn to howl. - Persian Proverb*
*Let thy discontent be secret. - Franklin*
*An empty bag cannot stand upright. - Franklin*
*He hath no leisure who uses it not.*
*The eagle does not catch flies. - Latin Proverb*
*The empty vessel makes the greatest sound. - Shakespeare*
*Let none falter who think he is right. - Lincoln*
*It is easy to be at the helm in fine weather. - From the Danish*
*Failures are but pillars of success. - Welsh Proverb*
*Honesty is the first chapter in the book of wisdom. - Jefferson*
*When money speaks, truth keeps silent. - Russian Proverb*
*To do a common thing uncommonly well often brings success. - Heinz*
*People do not lack strength, they lack will. - Victor Hugo*
*Genius is the art of taking infinite pain. - Carlyle*

So enraptured was Fred Seely with these inspirational mottoes that he selected verses for the two oak Roycroft clocks he commissioned for the hotel. While we still do not know whether the anonymous woodcarver given the task of carving the poems into the front panels worked in East Aurora for Elbert Hubbard or in Asheville for Fred Seely, the two clocks and their epigrams still remain inside the Grove Park Inn.

On the eight-foot clock that greeted each guest arriving through the double front doors can be found the following carved verse:

*Not enjoyment and not sorrow -*
*To our destined end or way -*
*But to act that each tomorrow -*
*Find us farther than today -*

On the six-foot Roycroft clock, believed to have been commissioned by Fred Seely for his private office, we find yet another verse:

*Tis a mistake, time flies not,*
*It only hovers on the wing,*
*Once born the moment dies not,*
*Tis an immortal thing.*

*- Montgomery*

Fred Seely continued his practice by painting inspirational verses on the walls surrounding his weavers and woodworkers inside the adjacent Biltmore Industries buildings. Built between 1917-1920, the five buildings still remain, and many of their original mottoes are still visible, having been spared the paintbrush several times over the course of nearly one hundred years. Viewed together, they serve as a reflection of Fred Seely's philosophy of life, friendship, money -- and work.

## "Perhaps Walls Can Talk"

Among those which can still be found are the following:

*You can't believe everything you hear -- but you can repeat it.*
*He profits most who serves best.*
*The feller that agrees with everything you say is either a nut*
*or gittin' ready to skin you.*
*Keep thy shop and thy shop will keep thee. - Poor Richard's Almanac*
*Life without industry is guilt; industry without art is brutality.*
*Quality is never an accident; it is always the result*
*of intelligent effort. - John Ruskin*
*God gave man five senses -- touch, taste, sight, smell, and hearing --*
*the successful man has two more -- horse and common.*
*Our greatest glory is not in never falling, but in rising*
*every time we fall. - Confucius*
*I will study and get ready, and maybe*
*my chance will come. - Abraham Lincoln*
*Every oak was once an acorn.*

*There is hardly anything in the world that some man cannot make a*
*little worse and sell a little cheaper. -- John Ruskin*
*A still tongue makes no enemies. -- Mexican Proverb*
*One way to cover up a bad past is to build a big future over it.*
*A man full of words shall not prosper upon this earth. - Proverbs*
*Except ye utter words easy to be understood,*
*how shall it be known what is spoken. - St. Paul*
*A man's first duty is to mind his own business. - Lorimer*
*It ain't so much the things that people don't know*
*that makes trouble in this world, as it is the things people*
*know that ain't so. - Mark Twain*
*Quitters never win -- winners never quit.*

*No man has a good enough memory*
*to be a successful liar. - Abraham Lincoln*
*The man who gives up and says "I can't"*
*is usually right about it. - Barkslee*
*Careful attention to one thing often proves superior to genius. - Cicero*
*Give every man thy ear, but few thy voice. - Shakespeare*
*One generation passeth away, and another generation cometh;*
*but the world abideth forever. - Eccl. 1:4*
*This day we sailed west because it was our course. - Columbus*
*There is nothing so fatal to character than half finished tasks.*
*Love the little trade which thou hast learned,*
*and be content therewith. - Marcus Aurelius*

*Opportunity is often lost through delay. - Publius Syrus (B.C. 42)*
*Success comes in cans -- failure in can'ts.*
*It is the peculiarity of knowledge that those who*
*really thirst for it always get it.*
*The Strength of the Hills is His also.*
*What is dishonorably got is dishonorably squandered. - Cicero*
*He who would gather roses must not fear thorns.*
*Flattery is nothing but "soft soap," and soft soap is 90 percent lye.*
*Sin has many tools, but a lie is the handle that fits them all. - Holmes*
*How prone to doubt, how cautious are the wise. - Homer*
*Judge not that ye be not judged.*
*People who are not up on a thing are usually down on it.*
*The borrower is servant to the lender. - Proverbs*
*Put all your eggs in one basket and*
*watch that basket. - Pudd'nhead Wilson*
*Credit and friends are good when not used. - Van Linge*
*Creditors have better memories than debtors. - Benjamin Franklin*

## "Perhaps Walls Can Talk"

*The night cometh when no man can work. - Psalm 101*
*I do the very best I know how; and I mean to keep on doing so*
*until the end. If the end brings me out all right, what is said*
*against me won't amount to anything. - Abraham Lincoln*

Noah Stewart, one of the young men who helped build the Grove Park Inn, stayed on to work at the hotel after it opened. Later, he went to work for Fred Seely at Biltmore Industries, where he carded wool and learned to weave homespun cloth on the looms, all the while exposed to Fred Seely's mottoes hand lettered on the walls. When interviewed in 1984 at the age of 86, Noah Stewart concluded his recollection by remarking to the reporter, "I have often said to myself, 'Whatever you do, or whatever you love to do, do it good.'"

Classic Fred Seely.

Words to live -- and work -- by.

*Famed automaker Henry Ford (center) poses with host Fred Loring Seely (right) and editor Horatio Seymour on Tuesday, August 27, 1918, during a break from Ford's highly publicized camping trip with Thomas Edison, John Burroughs and Harvey Firestone.*

# Chapter 12

# "Four Famous Campers"

*Ladies of Mars Hill College: I write books and Mr. Ford makes cars. I hope you will read my books, and ride in nothing but Ford cars.*

John Burroughs

On August 20, 1918, one of the most famous -- and unlikely -- group of celebrated campers pulled out of Pittsburg and headed into the Appalachian Mountains for nearly two weeks of respite from their hectic daily schedules.

Lead by automobile manufacturer Henry Ford, then 55 years old, the group of campers included tire maker Harvey Firestone, age 50; inventor Thomas Edison, age 71; and naturalist and author John Burroughs, the elder statesman at age 82.

But they had no intention, it seems, of living off the land -- or sleeping on it the entire time.

Their entourage also included Sato, Henry Ford's Japanese cook, in charge of the truck Edison scoffed at as "our Waldorf-Astoria on wheels that followed us everywhere." In addition to Kato at the wheel of his heavily laden truck, the caravan also included a carload of newspaper reporters and photographers anxious to record every minute of their journey. One of them was quick to note that despite his criticism of Ford's provisions, Edison did not seem ready to sacrifice his "munching on chocolate-nut bars and drinking pop."

As Harvey Firestone explained to one of the reporters assigned to them, "We were all head over heals in war work, but we decided that a couple of weeks off would freshen us all a bit and make us better able to go on with our work."

Like the organized individuals they were, the group first assigned tasks to each of their members. Thomas Edison immediately appointed himself navigator for the group, prompting Firestone to quip, "It was Mr. Edison's route, for the rest of us didn't know where we were going. He writes us giving the route, then he writes again, giving another route and when we actually start, he commonly selects a third route. We never know where we are going, and I suspect he does not either."

The others agreed, noting that, "Edison never chose a comfortable line of march if a crude one were available. [We typically] argued at length on how to proceed, then followed Edison's orders down still another rough route." The elderly inventor, they soon discovered, was so nearly deaf that their objections to his hazardous routes often never registered with him.

Had he read it, Firestone might have become a little nervous at Edison's statement that the men were going "to revert back to nature and get away from fictitious civilization." Reportedly, that included exploring the depths of West Virginia's treacherous mountain terrain.

Edison began the journey by directing the caravan of six bulging vehicles -- three trucks, plus a Simplex, a Packard and a

Ford -- south out of Pittsburg toward the wilds of West Virginia. The caravan had just gotten started when a fan blade on a Packard truck broke, puncturing the radiator and causing the engine to over-heat. After what surely must have been a few pointed remarks, Henry Ford removed his jacket and proceeded to wire the errant blade back in place and patch the offending hole in the Packard. In short order the group was back on board and headed south, soon crossing the border into West Virginia.

The campers were left to their own devices when it came to finding a campsite their second night. As darkness was descending, they found a spot near the banks of a stream near Horseshoe Run. As Burroughs recalled, "I got the reluctant consent of the widow who owned it to pitch our camp there, though her patch of roasting-ears [of sweet corn] nearby made her hesitate; she probably had experience with gipsy parties, and the two magic names which I gave her of the men in our party did not impress her."

Upon his return to the group, Burroughs discovered that Edison had decided they would pitch their tents not in the open field Burroughs had secured for them, but among the boulders nestled beside the creek. While Sato supervised setting up the dining tent, and the reporters began struggling with their own equipment, Edison was stringing electric lights from tent to tent and tree to tree before powering them with a truck battery. Even so, one reporter described their site as having "all the wildness, roughness, and loneliness of a Jesse James hideout."

As word spread through Tucker County of the famous group of campers, several local farmers and their families began dropping in to observe the well-dressed campers, much to the consternation of more than a few of the city-bred reporters. As the group watched, the celebrated campers hiked to a nearby abandoned grist mill to have their picture taken while perched on a gigantic over-shot water-wheel. The next morning a lumberman even fired up his locomotive and engineered it along a set of logging rails, much to the delight of Edison and Ford, who posed for pictures on the panting steam engine before heading toward Elkins, their planned mid-day stop.

After a warm reception in the town of some 8,000 residents, the campers continued on their journey, until interrupted by a broken bracket on one of the car's rear springs. Unperturbed, Henry Ford again came to the rescue, this time borrowing a needed bolt from a threshing machine in an adjoining field to make the repair. Their destination that night was the Cheat Club House in Tygart's Valley. After a late dinner, the majority of the campers accepted their host's invitation to sleep in real beds, but the two eldest, namely Edison and Burroughs, scoffed at the idea. They returned to their folding cots inside their tents for the night, despite the fact that temperatures dropped below freezing just before dawn.

Ford's mechanical training also helped a Virginian out of a jam a few days later. The campers came upon a fellow with a stalled luxury car of a make other than a Ford. Without identifying himself, Ford stepped out of his own car, once again rolled up his sleeves, opened the hood and soon had the man's car running again.

"How much do I owe you, stranger?" the Virginian asked, reaching for his wallet.

Ford shook his head. "Not a cent, friend. I really don't need the money."

The Virginian looked over at Ford's car, then exclaimed, "My good man, I insist on paying you for this work. Whether you say you need the money or not, I don't agree with you. No man would be riding in one of those little Fords if he had all the money he needed."

The campers spent the rest of the week, as Firestone recalled, "crossing many times the border between the two states, now in one, then the other, all the time among the mountains, with a succession of glorious views from mountain tops and along broad, fertile valleys, [becoming] pretty intimate with the backbone of the continent."

According to the reporters following the campers, they each soon fell into their own nightly routine. Ford was always the first to grab an axe and split enough firewood for the evening campfire, while continuing to make any necessary repairs to the six vehicles. Harvey Firestone, who was accompanied by one of his sons, Harvey Jr., taking time off from Princeton, enjoyed reading one of the books he had brought along. John Burroughs frequently went off by himself, searching for examples of unusual flowers and birds. He also set an example for the group by insisting that every meal be cooked and consumed outdoors.

Their navigator, Thomas Edison, was believed to have enjoyed the trip more than anyone, having soon become a "vagabond very easily, going with his hair uncombed and his clothes unattended for long periods." After setting up camp, it became his habit to retire to his car to read.

As John Burroughs noted in his recollections of their 1918 summer adventure, "It was a great pleasure to see Edison relax and turn vagabond, sleeping in his clothes, curling up at lunch time under a tree and dropping off to sleep like a baby, getting up to replenish the campfire at daylight or before, [washing] at the wayside pool or creek. He can rough it week in and week out and be happy."

Burroughs' age, however, and his gradually declining health combined with the rigors of sleeping outdoors on a cot, contributed to what he described as his own "sulkiness and ungraciousness."

"The night was chilly," he wrote of their adventure, "and I got more of the bitter than the sweet. But I had been a prophet of evil from the start, and it was fit that I should justify myself the first night. Folding camp cots are very poor conservers of one's bodily warmth, and until you get the hang of them and equip yourself with plenty of blankets, sleep enters your tent very reluctantly. She tarried with me but briefly, and at three or four in the morning I got up, replenished the fire, and in the camp chair beside it indulged in the long, long thoughts which belong to age more than to youth. Youth was soundly and audibly sleeping in the tents with no thoughts at all."

Burroughs, it should be noted, passed away just three years later at the age of 84.

The campers awoke in Bristol, Tennessee, on the morning of August 27 to even more newspaper reporters anxious to get a quote from Henry Ford on the senate primary contest being held that very day in Michigan. Earlier that year, upon the urging of President Woodrow Wilson, Ford had agreed to run for the post of United States senator, but refused to commit to either party or to make any speeches. As a result, both the Republicans and the Democrats decided to place his name on their primary ballots.

While voters in Michigan were marking their ballots, the caravan of Ford, Edison, Burroughs and Firestone was slowly making its way through the mountains down Highway 23. Although Fred Seely and his staff at the Grove Park Inn had expected them to arrive that afternoon in plenty of time for the special dinner being prepared on their behalf, the crush of crowds along the way brought their cars to a halt several times.

At Mars Hill College the campers were met by the college president and a group of coeds who presented Thomas Edison with a large bouquet of flowers. As John Burroughs recounted, "An octogenarian has no business to go a-gypsying up and down the Appalachian range, and when a man of letters like myself goes a-junketing with three such well-known men as Thomas Edison, Harvey Firestone and Henry Ford, he shines mainly by reflected light, for he is in famous company.

"The public is eager to press the hand and hear the voices of these three men, but a writer of books excites interest only now and then. School teachers, editors, doctors, clergymen, lawyers and nature lovers frequently gravitate to my side of the car, while the main crowd of working and business men go to the other side. A big band of college girls at Mars Hill swarmed up to our car and the president of the college was with them. He turned to his pupils and said, 'Ladies of the college, this is Henry Ford,' and Mr. Ford stood up and made his best bow.

"I sat there smiling and expectant, but the 'ladies of the college' will never know by what a close shave I missed fame at that moment. I was in total eclipse. I had my little speech ready on my tongue. I was going to say, 'Ladies of Mars Hill College, I write books and Mr. Ford makes cars. I hope you will read my books and ride in nothing but Ford cars.'"

Students at the nearby all-black Long Ridge School were also present to meet the distinguished group, and were amply rewarded when Ford announced to the crowd that he would donate to their school the funds needed to build an art room onto their one-story school house.

A few miles later, unbeknownst to the campers, a delegation of civic leaders from Asheville had assembled in Weaverville, ten miles north of the city, to join the crowd waiting to greet them. Among them was a reporter from the *Asheville Citizen,* who observed:

*The first car that appeared on the road from Tennessee was a Packard with Harvey Firestone Jr. driving at a speedy gait on the asphalt-surfaced highway, Mr. Burroughs being seated with him in the front. The second car, a Simplex, carried Mr. Edison on the front seat next to the driver, [with] Mr. Firestone and Mr. Cline riding on the rear seats. It may be remarked that all the cars were equipped with Firestone tires and also that Mr. Firestone's business, when he is not camping out, is making tires. There was no tire trouble en route, it was stated.*

*The Fords came later, bearing the cooking and dining room equipment and the tents. "We had less trouble with the Fords than with any car on the trip," remarked Mr. Ford, with one of his frequent smiles.*

*Mr. Edison came in for a big share of the attention at Weaverville. The progress of the party was blocked by a big crowd, attractive school girls forming a large proportion, and calls were made on Mr. Edison for a speech, but he smilingly declined. Presented by Dr. Blake of Weaver College, Mr. Firestone then made a brief and well-worded talk which caught the fancy of the people, especially his reference to Mr. Edison as "the greatest man in the scientific world, the man who has done the most for humanity."*

Afterwards, when asked by a newspaper reporter about the war, Mr. Edison shook his head. "Man's foolishness," he said. "That's all you can make out of it. Man is a fool."

All of the talks and presentations had to have been driving Fred Seely crazy back at the hotel, where his chef had undoubtedly prepared a special meal for the four famous campers and their entourage of national reporters. By the time they broke away from the admiring crowd and drove the remaining ten miles to the front entrance of the hotel, it was already 8:30 that night.

By that time, the preliminary reports telegraphed to Fred Seely from Michigan indicated that while Henry Ford had failed to win the Republican nomination, he would be the Democratic candidate for the U.S. Senate. That fall, however, the millionaire industrialist and roadside auto mechanic fell just 4,500 votes short of becoming a United States senator.

The swarm of reporters waiting in the lobby of the Grove Park Inn that evening surrounded the car of Henry Ford, peppering the lean, tanned candidate with questions about the war, President Wilson's proposed League of Nations and plans for his campaign. Relieved to have finally arrived and ready for a good night's sleep in a soft bed, Firestone, Burroughs and Edison gladly slipped away, guided by Fred Seely through the throng and into the Great Hall. Shaking hands with the uniformed staff and admiring guests along the way, the trio followed Fred Seely into the dining room.

While no record survives of what delectable dishes the chef had prepared for them, an original menu dated just a few weeks later may provide some indication of what they ate that evening.

After a bowl of Consommé' Vermicelli or English Beef Soup with Barley, they may have had their choice of either Boiled Sea Trout with Hollandaise Potatoes, Fresh Shrimp a la Newburg, Roast Prime Ribs of Beef, or Broiled Milk-Fed Chicken on Toast.

Grove Park Inn side dishes would have included mashed and baked potatoes, hominy grits, corn on the cob and fresh local spinach. Their choice of salads might have included "Asparagus Tips with Russian Dressing" or "Lettuce and Sliced Tomatoes with Mayonnaise." The dessert list at the inn that summer generally offered diners their choice of chocolate ice cream, custard pie, peach tarts, pound cake, raisin cookies, Bell's Fork-Dip Chocolates, apples, apple sauce, honey dew melon and crystallized ginger.

Needless to say, after a hearty meal that may have lasted until nearly midnight, the weary campers were ready to retire to their sleeping quarters, most likely rooms on the third floor opening onto the Palm Court and offering a panoramic view of the Great Smoky Mountains from which they had just descended.

Henry Ford reportedly stayed up late that night preparing a statement for the press anxious to hear his reaction to the Michigan primary results. Both he and Edison slept late the following morning, exhausted, no doubt, from their ten days on the road and enjoying their comfortable beds and warm showers. In all likelihood, Fred Seely had chosen to remain at the hotel as well. Known as an early riser anyway, he undoubtedly was up at dawn inspecting the hotel and making sure breakfast preparations were well underway.

After meeting in the Great Hall and chatting with the reporters who had assembled there, the campers were led into the dining room for breakfast. Part of the conversation may have been directed at young Harvey Firestone Jr., who prior to enrolling at Princeton had attended Asheville School, a private boys' school set on 300 acres of land west of the city. Both he and his father had visited the hotel prior to their arrival the previous day. Although Henry Ford and his wife had vacationed at the Grove Park Inn two years earlier, this was the first visit by Edison and Burroughs, so at the conclusion of their meal, Fred Seely led the group on a tour of the hotel.

Afterwards, since none seemed anxious to hit the open road quite yet and since two of their supply trucks, slowed by a heavy downpour, had spent the night several miles north of Asheville, Fred Seely offered to take them to his home, Overlook Castle. As a portion of his compensation for serving as designer and contractor for the Grove Park Inn, E. W. Grove had given Seely thirteen acres of prime real estate located on the summit of Sunset Mountain. The spot had for years been a popular viewing point, where a wooden observation tower topped by an American flag in Overlook Park gave visitors a distant view of mountain peaks in Tennessee, South Carolina and Georgia.

Spurred by his success in designing and building the Grove Park Inn, by 1915 Fred Seely had begun construction on a 20,000 square-foot castle inspired by the medieval Forde Castle (c.1278) in the Northumberland district of England. Although one wing remained unfinished for several decades, by 1918 Seely, his wife Evelyn and their five children had moved in and undoubtedly were on hand that morning to greet the famous party. As a collector of rare, first edition books and autographs of famous musical composers, Seely must have been bursting with pride as he led the men into his bookcase-lined library with its towering twenty-foot ceiling and a wall of windows affording a view down over the sprawling Swannanoa River valley.

After driving back down to the Grove Park Inn, the group disembarked amid a swarm of reporters. "If Mr. Ford was in the least bit interested in the results of the Michigan primaries," one wrote that day, "he cleverly concealed the fact. Mr. Ford will accept the [Democratic] nomination, but does not want it and, as he remarked the day before, would give a million dollars to be out of politics into which President Wilson's request precipitated him."

Stymied in his attempt to get any additional information out of the canny automaker, an Asheville reporter turned his attention to Thomas Edison, who explained, "in his own good time, what part his new inventions are playing in the war."

"Mr. Edison," he wrote of his interview, "is somewhat stouter than the current pictures of him show, is more ruddy and vigorous than might be expected of one who works twenty hours a day." Then the writer added, explaining, perhaps, his brief report, "He is handicapped somewhat in conversation by impaired hearing." Another reporter referred to Edison and Ford as "human dynamos, [who] arose late and therefore speeded in action when they did get started. The 'Wizard' set the pace even for Mr. Ford and it was a case of 'go here' and 'go there.' Return from one place was the signal to go to another place."

Ultimately the group gathered in front of the hotel for a series of now-familiar photographs. Orchestrated, undoubtedly, by Fred Seely, the campers obligingly stood first beside one of their touring cars, then before a low rock wall and hitching post beneath the open portico. In each photograph a crowd of curious onlookers can be seen in the background, straining to get a look at the famous troupe.

With waves to everyone assembled around the porch that morning, as well to those guests leaning out the windows above, the campers boarded their cars and continued on their journey, headed east that day toward their final destination in Maryland.

By the end of the week prints of the photographs taken that morning were appearing in newspapers across the country, exactly as Fred Seely had hoped when weeks earlier he had extended an invitation for Henry Ford to bring his friends to the Grove Park Inn.

And in all likelihood, as was Fred Seely's practice, the celebrities, despite their collective wealth measured in the millions of dollars, would have discovered that morning that Fred Seely had waived any charges for their meals or lodging.

The publicity they brought to the Grove Park Inn, he reasoned, was worth a hundred times the cost.

Before leaving his room that morning, one of the campers, most likely John Burroughs or Thomas Edison, penned the following letter on hotel stationary, which they each then signed:

*August 28th, 1918*

*Dear Mr. Seely -*
*After a ten day camping trip through the mountains of West Virginia*
*and your own Land of the Sky, we felt when we arrived at Grove Park*
*Inn, the Finest Resort Hotel in the World, that possibly we were not*
*quite presentable enough to expect a welcome. We not only received the*
*welcome, but the warmest hospitality we have ever had extended to us.*
*May you live long and be a blessing to many other travelers.*

The four men, however, left behind more than just a thank-you note.

They left behind a small mystery, more aptly described as a case of mistaken identity.

In what may well be the most famous photograph ever taken at the Grove Park Inn, we see a number of familiar faces.

In the trio to the far left is Harvey Firestone, standing beside Thomas Edison and Harvey Firestone Jr. In the trio on the far right stands the familiar Henry Ford, leaning comfortably on the hitching post, flanked by Fred L. Seely in his all-white suit, and a man who has for years been captioned as being Edwin W. Grove *(see pg. 162)*.

But is it?

At first glance it certainly would appear so, and it might seem quite likely that the owner of the Grove Park Inn and the Paris Medicine Company, who typically vacationed in Asheville during the summer, would be on hand that morning to meet such an illustrious group of manufacturing legends.

When this photograph appeared in more than one million copies of the September 22 edition of the *New York World*, Harvey

Firestone had been cropped out and the caption read, "Thomas A. Edison, H. S. Firestone Jr., Horatio Seymour and Henry Ford photographed at Grove Park Inn, Asheville, after a week of 'roughing it.' "

Horatio Seymour?

Not Edwin Wiley Grove?

Horatio Winslow Seymour (1854-1920) was a well-respected newspaper reporter and editor who had worked at the *Milwaukee News*, the *Chicago Times*, the *Chicago Herald*, the *Chicago Chronicle* and the *St. Louis Republic* before being named editorial supervisor for the *New York World*. As such, he could easily have been tapped to travel to Asheville to cover the arrival of Henry Ford and his heralded band of campers at the Grove Park Inn.

Seymour did, in fact, bear an uncanny resemblance to Edwin Wiley Grove, as only four years separated them in age. Close examination of this photograph and a comparison to documented photographs of Grove taken around this same time period do reveal subtle, but distinctive differences between the two men. In addition, E. W. Grove seems to have never been photographed in anything other than his trademark formal three-piece suit and narrow, conservative tie. It would have been totally out of character for him to arrive at the Grove Park Inn on this highly publicized morning -- with scores of civic leaders, national reporters and newspaper photographers on hand -- wearing no vest and with the rumpled traveling jacket and the wide, short tie seen on the man in this photograph *(see pg. 180)*.

Added to this is the fact that in August of 1918, Fred L. Seely and Edwin Wiley Grove were barely on speaking terms. Their once close relationship had by now disintegrated during the previous year's contentious negotiations over Fred Seely's lease on the Grove Park Inn. It would be difficult to imagine Grove appearing at the Grove Park Inn during Fred Seely's greatest moment of triumph, let alone consenting to having their picture taken together.

Confirming this theory is a letter written on September 2, 1918, by Fred Seely to Frank D. Caruthers, business manager at the *New York World*, where their mutual friend Horatio Seymour also worked.

*Dear Frank:*

*I am enclosing a rather unusual photograph with a very familiar face in it, which may make it interesting for your Sunday supplement. I have an idea that it wouldn't reach the supplement if Mr. Seymour knew you were going to do it, for we have found him to be very modest.*

*It is such a good picture, however, and with one exception such an interesting group, that I thought possibly you would like to have it. If you don't want to use it, suppose you send it back to me, as I am going to send Mr. Seymour a good sepia print just as soon as it comes.*

*Very sincerely yours,*
*Fred Loring Seely*

Case closed. Mr. Seymour it is.

As a postscript to the visit of the four famous campers those two days in August of 1918, was this following report, published after Henry Ford had left Asheville in one of the local newspapers:

*Out of deference to Mr. Ford's feelings, no reference was made until after it was too late for him to hear of it, was the unaccountable misbehavior of the Ford of [Asheville's] secretary of the Board of Trade Neptune Buckner while it was engaged in piloting the visitors [the final few miles] to the Grove Park Inn.*

*Instead of showing off its good qualities before its master, this censurable machine "lay down" on Beaverdam Road and "went dead," quitting as the other cars swept by. After filling the radiator, which lacked only a pint of being full, and saying it looked like rain, the inexpert companions boarded the car of a passing Samaritan and basely deserted Mr. Buckner.*

*This car can no longer be called a "typical Ford" machine after the way it behaved on the trip. Whether from excitement at meeting Ford, Edison and Burroughs all at once or from other causes, the reputation and the gas of the car both failed, and it was ignominiously towed home after its maker had swept by.*

The party is greeted by Mr. Seely at Grove Park Inn, Asheville, N. C., where they broke camp August 27. Mr. Burroughs and Prof. DeLoach left the party at this point and returned by train. Mr. Edison, Mr. Ford, Mr. Firestone and Harvey, Jr., returned by motor.

*The campers prepare to depart: Henry Ford, Harvey Firestone Junior, host Fred Seely, Thomas Edison, author John Burroughs and Harvey Firestone Senior.*

*E. W. Grove with his grandson Edwin W. Grove III and son Edwin W. Grove Jr.*

*Gertrude and E. W. Grove near their winter home in St. Petersburg, Florida.*

# Chapter 13

# "A Family Feud"

*While I have not been able to agree with you in some*
*of your business ideas, I have always admired your high*
*ideals and strong moral character, and I have never*
*doubted your correct living, devotion to your family, and*
*high purpose to be helpful to others. The best thing for us*
*to do to get the family trouble out of the way is to Forgive*
*and Forget! Not to give any explanation and not to ask*
*for any.*

E. W. Grove to Fred L. Seely

No one is quite sure just when the feud began.

But there was no doubt with how it ended.

Tragically.

Some felt it began simmering as far back as 1902, not long after the 31-year-old Fred Seely had gone to work for his father-in-law,
Edwin Wiley Grove, at the Paris Medicine Company in St. Louis.
Grove, who was then 52 and a multi-millionaire, had spent nearly
a year in Asheville, recuperating from the stress of managing his

pharmaceutical business. His list of products had grown to include no fewer than six different brands, ranging from his world-famous Grove's Tasteless Chill Tonic to his most recent invention, the first cold tablet.

Fred Seely, fresh from his rapid rise through the ranks of Parke, Davis & Company in Detroit, had then been anxious to prove his worth both to his father-in-law and to his new wife, Evelyn. While Grove rested in Asheville, Fred had begun instituting major changes in every department, from accounting and marketing to production and sales. Those who could not adjust to Seely's new methods soon found truth in the old adage "My way -- or the highway." Complaints from employees, including many whom Grove had hired from his hometown of Paris, Tennessee, eventually prompted Grove's return to the offices and factory in St. Louis.

Two men, two different generations, two different styles of management.

And Fred Seely should have known -- or did know -- that even at age 52 Edwin Grove was not yet ready to retire to a rocking chair on the front porch of his Liberty Street home in Asheville.

Or give up control of the multi-million dollar business he had created nearly thirty years earlier in the back room of a small pharmacy in Paris.

Other people believed the feud started as far back as Fred Seely's wedding on October 24, 1898, when he married Edwin Grove's only surviving daughter, the daughter Grove had raised after the love of his life, the beautiful Mary Louisa Moore, had died in their Paris home. Evelyn was only seven when her mother, weakened by childbirth, is thought to have succumbed to yellow fever, and, as Grove later wrote, "for a long time I had to act as both mother and father to her, and no one knows but myself how dear she is to me, and the interest I feel in any change affecting her future."

Concerned, perhaps, that his daughter had only known Fred Seely for a few months, Grove nevertheless seemed pleased to welcome the ambitious, serious and self-disciplined young man into his family -- as much as he could be pleased with any man who was about to share his daughter's bed.

And while Fred Seely later learned that E. W. Grove, so long as he was alive, would always need to have control of the Paris Medicine Company, Fred could control the one woman Grove would always love, but could never have -- Evelyn. Both blinded, perhaps, by their pride, by their egos, by their reputations, Fred Seely and E. W. Grove each made fatal mistakes that hot summer of 1902 in St. Louis. Mistakes that would alter the course of the rest of their lives.

Four years later, in 1906, Grove and Seely did attempt to patch things up. Against his better judgment, but anxious to have Evelyn and Fred settled in Atlanta rather than in California near Fred's brother, E. W. Grove provided hundreds of thousands of dollars to become Fred's silent partner in the *Atlanta Georgian*. Grove even went so far as to buy Evelyn and Fred their first house on Peachtree Avenue. Grove, in fact, liked Atlanta. He found the summers no hotter than what he suffered through in St. Louis, and the winters far milder. He had invested money in Atlanta real estate, starting two subdivisions, Atkins Park and Fortified Hills, on the edge of the city. So attached was he to his daughter that he even went so far as to consider moving the Paris Medicine Company from St. Louis to Atlanta.

The Recession of 1908 may have derailed his plans, or perhaps he soon realized that Fred's newspaper would never succeed against the well-established *Atlanta Evening News,* the *Atlanta Journal* and the *Atlanta Constitution.* He may have sensed that Atlanta businessmen, civic leaders and powerful politicians would always consider Fred Seely an outsider, a Yankee from New Jersey, and a constant reminder that just 42 years earlier the victorious and vicious Union General William T. Sherman had stood on a hill overlooking their once beautiful city, now "smoldering and in ruins, the black smoke rising high in the air, and hanging like a pall over the ruined city," as his troops marched on toward Charleston.

Perhaps, too, he discovered that Atlanta was but an overnight train ride from any of his three homes located in St. Louis, Asheville and St. Petersburg. And if there was anything E. W. Grove loved, it was to board a train bound for one of his many investments: his coal fields in West Virginia, his cattle lands in Texas and Mexico, his stands of timber in Arkansas or his real estate properties in Florida, Atlanta and Asheville. He loved his temporary escapes from his daily responsibilities both at the factory and at home, where his second wife, Gertrude, always seemed to be complaining about her latest medical condition, problems with their household help, the humid summer heat or their son's troubles with his teachers. E. W. Grove had become a father again, this time at the age of 41, but not even a son, his namesake, could diminish his devotion to Evelyn, especially a son who soon proved to be insolent, disrespectful and lazy.

And, so, he might have thought, as he stared out the window of the plush Southern Railway dining car with its white linen tablecloths and attentive staff, speeding across his home state of Tennessee, that having Evelyn and his grandchildren living in Atlanta might not be such a bad thing after all. As much as he disliked sending checks every month to Fred and disagreed with how he was running the newspaper -- refusing to take ads from businesses he did not like, attempting to reform their deep-rooted Southern traditions -- being able to see Evelyn and his grandchildren without having Fred Seely underfoot back at his offices was palatable.

## "A Family Feud"

But then Fred got restless.

After six years of working six days a week and never showing a profit, Fred Seely was ready to leave the newspaper business and their home in Atlanta. He was about to turn forty and now had to provide for their four children. He had too much pride to go crawling back to his father-in-law at the Paris Medicine Company, where he knew he would soon be locking horns not just with E. W. Grove, but with junior as well. At age nineteen, Edwin Grove Jr. was just old enough to begin realizing how much money was rolling into his father's company -- and what that money could buy.

Fred had listened, both in their Peachtree Avenue home and on their trips up to Asheville, to his father-in-law singing the praises of Asheville's future, of how George Vanderbilt and his sprawling Biltmore Estate had brought national attention to this mountaintop oasis, how the banks were willing to lend him whatever money he wanted to develop even more property, and how Asheville was about to break free from the bonds of being a haven for the ill and infirm, destined to become one of the South's most famous resort cities.

Fred Seely had grown tired of the newspaper business, just as he had grown tired of the Paris Medicine Company, but as much as he also recognized the advantages of living in Asheville, he really had no idea of what he could do there.

Until talk turned to building a hotel.

Fred had dabbled in construction while in Atlanta, building a few rental houses and serving as contractor for a mid-sized church. With several sets of blueprints which Grove had received from architects across the country spread out before him, Seely began to sketch a six-story, 150-room hotel built of boulders hauled from Grove's nearly 1,000 acres of surrounding land to a site on Sunset Mountain.

Anxious to both have Evelyn living in Asheville and to save what money he could building a unique resort hotel bearing his name, Grove jumped at Seely's proposal that they sell the *Atlanta Georgian* to William Randolph Hearst and use that money to build the hotel together. Grove offered to pay his son-in-law $7,500 to serve as contractor and, to further encourage Fred to remain in Asheville afterwards, gave him and Evelyn thirteen acres of prime real estate on the summit of Sunset Mountain for them to build their next home.

Groundbreaking took place on July 9, 1912, and, as promised, Fred Seely completed the Grove Park Inn just twelve months later. Four hundred distinguished guests joined them on the evening of July 12, 1913, for the opening night banquet, where Secretary of State William Jennings Bryan stood before them and declared, "I congratulate these men. They have built for the ages."

That summer, while general manager William S. Kenny trained his staff and greeted their guests, Fred Seely oversaw the completion of the last of the sixth-floor guest rooms and the landscaping of the grounds around the hotel. As he later wrote to his father-in-law in St. Louis, "The landscaping is finished, the plantings are beautiful and the place is more beautiful it seems to me than any place I ever saw. Of course, you will grant me the privilege of feeling this way, for it seems like a child to me."

Despite his attachment to the hotel he had personally designed, built, furnished, decorated and staffed, the 42-year-old Seely, now a father of four, was fully aware that he no longer had a job. Returning to the Paris Medicine Company was not even an option, as 22-year-old Edwin Grove Jr. had assumed Seely's former position as heir to his father's office. Edwin made no attempt to hide his hatred for his brother-in-law. While a rebellious teenager, Edwin had been sent to Atlanta to live and work with Fred at the *Atlanta Georgian*. Seely's strict regimen only served to instill in Edwin a bitterness toward both Fred and E. W. Grove, who reluctantly allowed Edwin to come back to St. Louis, where Gertrude insisted that Grove begin training their son to someday take over the Paris Medicine Company.

Although his letters never indicated he was anxious to leave Asheville, in 1913 Fred Seely was considering a position in the State Department under his friend William Jennings Bryan. "I shall leave Asheville with no little regret," he confessed to Grove. "It is the most wonderful place to live and I am sure I will find my way back here in my old age, if I am blessed with one."

President Woodrow Wilson and Secretary of State Bryan had far more pressing matters to deal with, however, as simmering border disputes in Europe were threatening to boil over. When, on June 28, 1914, the Archduke of Austria was assassinated, the battle lines were quickly drawn, as England, France and Russia soon squared off against Germany and Austria-Hungary in the First World War. Despite Wilson's assurances that the United States would remain neutral, the American people responded by curtailing both their international and domestic travel, leaving the freshly finished rooms, restaurants and sunny terraces at the Grove Park Inn nearly empty.

Faced with a growing payroll and dwindling income, E. W. Grove announced in 1914 that he was laying off the staff and closing down the Grove Park Inn until the situation in Europe was resolved. Stung, perhaps, by Grove's failure to discuss the closure with him, Fred Seely publicly criticized the decision, urging Grove to stay the course. In October Grove responded, stating, "I am going to stand by our decision about closing on the fifteenth if conditions do not warrant remaining open. There is no use in us deceiving ourselves by thinking that the people are going to come because we are anxious for them to come."

Determined not to see the lights go out on the Grove Park Inn, Fred Seely approached his father-in-law with a proposal: he would lease the hotel from Grove for a fixed percentage of the gross revenues in exchange for being able to manage and operate it as if it were his own.

Buoyed by the prospect of having Evelyn and his grandchildren living permanently in Asheville, not to mention being relieved of the responsibilities of directing a hotel from his office in St. Louis, Grove accepted. While the hotel's revenues had been hurt by the European conflict, sales were soaring of Grove's latest invention, his Bromo Quinine tablets, brazenly advertised as "The Original One Day Cold Cure," bringing in profits of more than one million dollars per year for him.

And as a reminder, perhaps, of what Seely could have had back in St. Louis, Grove instructed Fred to make his lease payments out to Evelyn, compensating her for the money that her stepbrother Edwin was making at the Paris Medicine Company.

As it turned out, the border disputes in Europe were not the only thing simmering toward a boil.

Despite his nearly fanatical organizational skills, Fred Seely could not, as Grove had predicted, simply will people to come to the Grove Park Inn. The war in Europe was about to wrap its tentacles around the United States, especially after the sinking of the luxury liner the *Lusitania* on May 7, 1915, taking to their watery graves two of Fred Seely's friends, Alice and Elbert Hubbard of the Roycrofters. Fearful how the war would effect their economy, many Americans soon turned frugal, preferring to stay at home rather than booking a two-week stay at the Grove Park Inn.

## "A Family Feud"

The pressure began to take its toll on Fred Seely, who held himself to an even higher level of expectations than did his wife or father-in-law. Financially, the Seelys were secure, even with the cost of building their 30,000 square-foot home, Overlook Castle, atop the peak of Sunset Mountain, but that security came in the form of royalty checks made out to Evelyn from the Paris Medicine Company and lavish gifts from E. W. Grove.

Seely had been forced to ask Grove in each of the first three years of his lease to reduce the percentage of revenues that he would be paying as rent for the hotel. Grove obliged, reminding Fred each time that he didn't really need the money, as the Paris Medicine Company and his other various investments were generating more than enough money for the entire family.

On January 22, 1917, Fred Seely unleashed his pent-up fury in a five-page, single-spaced, typewritten letter to his father-in-law in which he wrote:

*I have thirty to fifty letters of yours assuring [Evelyn] you were trying to amass a fortune for her and the children. It seems not to have occurred to you that I may have had the ability and, when given half a chance, will take all the care necessary of my family. Your attitude toward me has been to get every service you have needed me for, and to keep your heel on my neck just as heavily as you dare, [since] you saw I would stand it for the sake of my home, over which you well knew you ruled. You have reached a point, however, where self-respect will not permit me to tolerate it any longer.*

*You not only have taken every opportunity to alienate confidence in me, but have prevented confidence she would have had. You write her, assuring her that you "love her better than any human being on earth," which possibly is to keep her mind occupied while you squeeze a little more life out of me. Any further direction to Evelyn as to my affairs will not only be unwelcome, but will not be permitted.*

*Your daughter is not in need of any fortune for her protection and I trust she will be confident of my ability to provide such a one as she may need. So please do not make any further effort along that line in her behalf.*

*The slavery we have all passed through these past ten years as part of your land purchasing efforts has resulted in far more unhappiness than all the lands can ever undo. Your mania for lands has broken up the happiness of everyone near you and has robbed our home of much of its happiness.*

At the close of his letter, Fred Seely presented E. W. Grove with a final demand:

*The records all show that I owned 51% of the stock of the Georgian Company... [but] I have said nothing of my share of the $200,000 in bonds [paid for the newspaper by William Randolph Hearst in 1912]. Seeing from your recent letters how amply able you are to take care of this matter now..., I am sure these bonds are released from security, and I ask you therefore to turn over my portion, which would be $102,000, and interest you have received since you have had them.*

Fred Seely's demand for more than $102,000 from his father-in-law set off a public firestorm among those who knew either Grove or Seely in Asheville, St. Louis and Atlanta. Grove hired former judge Junius Adams, who also had been serving as legal advisor to Edith Vanderbilt after the death of her husband in 1914, to represent him. Seely engaged the services of Clifford Anderson, a friend and attorney from Atlanta, to handle his side of the negotiations. After three months of haggling, during which time a number of past disagreements were brought up, Fred Seely agreed to accept $90,000 from E. W. Grove as his share of the proceeds from the sale of the *Atlanta Georgian.*

Needless to say, relations between the two men were never the same again.

That same year, Fred Seely purchased from Edith Vanderbilt the small weaving and woodworking business she had founded in 1905 called Biltmore Estate Industries. Since that time she and George Vanderbilt had paid the salaries of the two instructors, Eleanor Vance and Charlotte Yale, plus any shortages that the business incurred. Not long after the unexpected death of George Vanderbilt in 1914, as he was recuperating at their home in Washington, D.C., from an operation to remove his inflamed appendix, Vance and Yale tendered their resignations in order to move to Tryon, where they founded the Tryon Toy Makers. Burdened not only with the management of the 125,000-acre Biltmore Estate and 250-room mansion, but also with the raising of their teenage daughter by herself, Edith Vanderbilt elected to sell the small business to Seely.

Fred Seely, just prior to his provocative 1917 letter to E. W. Grove quoted here, had obtained from Grove a lease on several acres of land adjacent to the Grove Park Inn on which he built five quaint Arts and Crafts buildings for his woodworkers and weavers. He shortened the name to Biltmore Industries and operated it until his death in 1942. Judging by the tone of his letter to E. W. Grove, it seems apparent that Seely was anticipating or, at the least, preparing for the possibility that someday he might not be managing the Grove Park Inn.

For the next two years the two men seldom wrote or spoke to one another, with the exception of exchanging business accounting reports. With the signing of the armistice on November 11, 1918, and the subsequent return of the soldiers from combat, the American public and the American economy began the adjustment to peacetime. Business increased for both the Paris Medicine Company and for the Grove Park Inn, thawing the chilly relations between E. W. Grove and Fred Seely.

Temporarily.

In 1919 the two men began discussing an addition to the north end of the hotel, designed to increase the number of rooms and, hopefully, the resulting revenues for both Grove and Seely. Preliminary plans were drawn up, materials were being ordered and financing options discussed when Grove suddenly decided to cancel the addition. The move caught Fred Seely off-guard, as he had even gone to the expense of printing new stationary, postcards and souvenir plates showing people how the Grove Park Inn would appear once the new wing had been completed.

Grove, as it turned out, had decided to invest his money in not one, but two other hotels.

The first was the Manor Inn, built in 1898 and which also included several eclectic Arts and Crafts rental cottages on a steep hillside on Charlotte Street leading to the Grove Park Inn. The 32-acre tract bordered Grove's other holdings on Sunset Mountain and had long been of interest to him. It was not until Thomas Wadley Raoul, son of founder William Raoul, accepted Judge Junius Adams' invitation to become one of the original investors in a new subdivision called Biltmore Forest that Grove was able to purchase the Manor Inn, cottages and grounds in 1920.

That same year Grove took the unusual step of also buying what had long been the pride of downtown Asheville -- the stately Battery Park Hotel. Built in 1886 on the highest hill in the city, the

Battery Park Hotel had served as the social hub for Asheville for nearly four decades. Famous guests had included President Teddy Roosevelt, the John D. Rockefeller family and George Vanderbilt. The towering wooden hotel, built in the Victorian Queen Anne style, featured electric lighting and water-powered elevators, and had once been considered to be the finest hotel in the South.

By 1920, however, the grand dame of Asheville was beginning to show her age. In need of painting, upgrading, updating and a major facelift, the Battery Park Hotel was beginning to attract more traveling salesmen than wealthy tourists. Just as talk began to surface about a possible sale, E. W. Grove announced that he had purchased it.

His explanation to Fred Seely?

"The way I figured when I bought the Manor and Battery Park [Hotel] was that you and I were bringing this increased business to Asheville each year, so why not take advantage of the situation and reap the benefit of your work and my work rather than let someone else come in and buy Battery Park, tear it down and build a 500-room fireproof hotel? As the old building can never be a competitor of the Grove Park Inn, we can afford to hold it just as it is and not let someone get it who would build a real competitor."

As he concluded in his January 21, 1921, letter, "There is no reason in the world why all three hotels should not each cater to a different class, all get all the business they can handle and all work in harmony. I often wish you could realize my strong interest and friendship for you, but I realize that it is no fault of yours that you cannot understand me."

On November 28, 1922, the citizens of Asheville opened their morning paper to a banner headline announcing:

# GROVE TO BUILD HOTEL ON BATTERY PARK HILL

## New 200 Room Commercial Hotel
## To Replace The Battery Park;
## Begin Developments At Once

The lengthy article concluded with a statement that, "While Mr. Grove appreciates the sentiment that has existed for many years on the part of the patrons of the Battery Park Hotel and the residents of Asheville toward Battery Park Hill, the hotel is rapidly outgrowing its period of usefulness. However, it is pointed out, the new hotel will be desirable from a scenic standpoint and plenty of open space will be provided, with [Mount] Pisgah still visible in the distance."

Indicative of the tensions that existed between Fred Seely and E. W. Grove is this letter written that same year from Grove to Seely:

*For some time I have been trying to reach a decision as to what my duty is as regards our families, touching the state of mind which has existed for many months and which has become a source of great unhappiness and embarrassment to all. I am making the first advance in this matter because I have decided to do what I believe to be my duty to your wife, my only daughter, to your children and my grandchildren, to mama and to you.*

*I am going to speak to you and Evelyn and the children when-ever I meet them. If they are not permitted to speak to me, that will not change my decision to do my duty. This family estrangement causes tourists as well as Asheville people to talk about and magnify it, and it is a bad state of affairs for all of us. Some tourists at the Manor last summer went so far as to say that I would not permit my granddaugh-ters to come to the Manor. There are some fine people who go to the Manor and we should stop this kind of gossip.*

*As you know, I was in your home a great deal when the chil-dren were babies and they learned to love me next to their father and mother, and it will be bad for them in many ways if they grow up under the existing feeling between us. Because you and I can't see business matters in the same way is no reason why we should not be the best of friends. Some of the best men in the country will differ in matters of business; and while I have not been able to agree with you in some of your business ideas, I have always admired your high ideals and strong moral character and I have never doubted your correct living, devotion to your family, and high purpose to be helpful to others.*

*The best thing for us to do to get the family trouble out of the way is to Forgive and Forget! Not to give any explanation and not to ask for any. If these suggestions meet with your approval, you can let me know in your own way.*

In due time, Fred did just that.

In 1924 E. W. Grove, now 74 years old, began lengthy discus-sions with his family in regards to his intentions for his investments and his property, including the Grove Park Inn, upon his death. Whereas a few years earlier he had expressed an interest in buying back Fred Seely's lease on the hotel, now he was offering to extend the lease to Fred for another 25 years "and, as advised to you before, will direct that the entire rent be paid to Evelyn as long as she lives, and then to the children."

"And at my death," he outlined in a letter to Fred Seely dated March 25, 1925, "the Grove Park Inn and the land which goes with it is to be Evelyn's as long as she lives, and for the children as long as they live, and to be run by you for the benefit of all."

*To be run by you....*

This was not what Fred Seely expected to hear.

Fred Seely had been living for more than twenty years under the impression that, according to an Asheville newspaper, "Mr. Grove [had] agreed that, in consideration for certain valuable services performed for him by Mr. Seely, provision would be made in Dr. Grove's will giving his son-in-law choice between a controlling interest in the Paris Medicine Company, or else all of Dr. Grove's property outside of the Paris Medicine Company."

Those provisions, it was widely believed, dated back to their first few years working together from 1898 through 1902, when Fred Seely's tablet-making invention paved the way for the Paris Medicine Company to be the first to market a cold tablet. At that same time Fred Seely had assisted Grove in buying back enough of the original shares of stock which Grove had first sold to friends in Tennessee to give Grove complete control of his company.

Instead, in 1925, E. W. Grove announced that upon his death his entire estate, including the Grove Park Inn and the Paris Medicine Company, as well as his extensive land holdings, all valued at more than $10 million, would be placed into a trust to be administered by the St. Louis Union Trust Company. "I did not want Edwin or Fred L. Seely to have anything to do with the managing of my estate," he wrote to a friend. "Families always cause trouble, and I am sure that Edwin and Fred L. Seely would cause trouble if they would have anything to do with it."

The annual income from the trust would, according to Grove's wishes, be divided equally between three people: Gertrude Grove, Edwin Grove Jr. and Evelyn Grove Seely.

No mention was made of Fred Seely.

And then the trouble really started.

On July 25, 1925, E. W. Grove was served with a formal notice filed by Fred Seely that Grove had violated the terms of their lease agreement, most recently revised in 1917, when he began operation of the new Battery Park Hotel. His contract with Fred Seely clearly stated that Grove "agrees that if he should determine to erect another hotel on any property owned by him in or near Asheville, North Carolina, the character of hotels so erected by him will be such as will cater to the patronage of persons of moderate means and will in no respect compete with the Grove Park Inn."

"I shall prove," Seely stated in his complaint, "that the Battery Park Hotel was constructed for tourist business, advertised for it and that this summer they have entertained owners of jewelry stores and their families, owners of large coal mines with their families, owners of tile factories, and no end of well-to-do tourists."

Then, on December 29, 1925, Fred Seely filed a lawsuit in St. Louis circuit court for the amount of $5 million, claiming that E. W. Grove had also violated the terms of their 1900 agreement "to transfer, at his death, a controlling interest in the company to Seely, or, if Seely should so elect, to transfer to him all other property owned by Grove outside his holdings in the medicine company. Grove, it is alleged, made a will which provided for the carrying out of this agreement," according to the *St. Louis Post-Dispatch*.

"Recently," the newspaper reported, "Seely says he discovered that his father-in-law had destroyed or revoked the [1900] will made in accordance with the agreement, and had made another will containing no provision for the compensation which Seely was to receive after Grove's death. Seely says that in signing the 1917 contract, he had no intention of waiving his rights under the previous agreement, although he says Grove has sought to represent that Seely did so waive his rights. Seely alleges that the earlier [1900] agreement was entered into as an inducement to keep him in the company at a time when he was needed."

Nearly all of the following year was consumed by no fewer than five attorneys working on the lawsuit, as they tracked down and took lengthy depositions from witnesses who had worked with either E. W. Grove or Fred Seely around 1900 in both Asheville and St. Louis.

Late in 1926, however, E. W. Grove's behavior turned erratic, causing alarm for both sides. A Pinkerton detective hired by Fred Seely reported on September 24 that "Mr. Grove appeared to be somewhat absent minded and on several occasions during our conversation we would be talking and he would turn to me and ask what we were talking about. He appears more feeble than he was the last time I saw him and appears to be in considerable pain when he rises from the chair."

Edwin Grove Jr. also was concerned with his father's health and mental stability, as he likewise hired a private detective to follow Grove. When he learned that his father had suddenly left his winter home in St. Petersburg accompanied not by his wife, but by a young nurse, Miss Ruby Dellinger, and had checked into a Philadelphia hotel, he gathered up his mother and followed the pair.

Edwin checked into the room next to his father's and drilled a hole through the wall so that he could observe his father and his nurse. At midnight he and his two private detectives burst into Miss

Dellinger's room "only giving her time to put on a kimono," and threatened to have her arrested if she did not leave Philadelphia immediately. The next day Grove's doctor asked Edwin, "what he would have sent her to the penitentiary for, and he said because she was poisoning his father's mind and trying to keep him and his wife from getting any money." Later, when confronted by E. W. Grove's attorneys, Edwin and his mother quickly left the hotel. E. W. Grove insisted that Miss Dellinger be returned to Philadelphia to accompany him back to his suite at the Battery Park Hotel.

As Seely later described the journey to his children, "I think you understand that Mrs. Grove and Edwin tried to have a guardian appointed over him, and that he left Philadelphia and came here [Asheville], evidently to escape them. Naturally to get out of a sick bed in Philadelphia where he had lain for nearly six weeks and make the trip to Asheville in the middle of the winter was likely to result in pneumonia. In fact, Mr. Parker told me the doctor warned him of that very thing. However, there are too many complications to write about."

Little more than a year later, Ruby Dellinger sued young Edwin Grove Jr. for $100,000, claiming "she was mortified, humiliated, slandered and brutally treated at the hands of Mr. Grove while she was employed by a nurse attendant upon his father." The young woman, the newspaper report continued, "was constantly shadowed by detectives even after she had accompanied Dr. Grove to Asheville. It is alleged in the complaint that [Edwin Grove Jr.] charged her with attempting to rob his father of his properties and holdings, and that she had exerted a fraudulent and improper influence over him." The suit was settled out of court.

E. W. Grove arrived in Asheville on January 7, 1927, and remained in his suite atop the Battery Park Hotel, accompanied by

Ruby Dellinger. He continued to refuse to join Gertrude Grove at either their Chestnut Street home or in St. Petersburg. Shortly thereafter, Grove developed one of his severe and prolonged cases of hiccups, which he had battled at various times throughout his life, often not being able to sleep or eat for days at a time. This latest onslaught developed into pneumonia, which gradually sapped his remaining strength. His physician, Dr. William L. Dunn, immediately called in three other doctors, including Dr. Thomas Brown of Johns Hopkins Hospital, but little hope could be offered because of his frailty and advanced age. Grove lingered for five days before succumbing at 8:10 p.m. on Thursday evening, January 27. He was 77 years old.

With him at his time of death were his wife Gertrude, along with his son Edwin and his daughter-in-law Marguerite. His daughter Evelyn, who had been seriously ill herself, was unable to leave her bed, and was also advised by her physician not to attend her father's funeral held in Paris, Tennessee, a few days later.

Grove's final will was released the following month, with portions of it published in the St. Louis and Asheville newspapers. It was dated June 11, 1921, but had been edited three additional times, the last being one year prior to his death.

As expected, Grove had placed all of his properties and investments, including the Paris Medicine Company and the Grove Park Inn, into a trust to be administered by the St. Louis Union Trust Company and, to some surprise, by his son Edwin, who was also named president of the Paris Medicine Company. Income from the trust was to be dispersed equally to his wife, son and daughter. Included in a number of minor bequests was an allowance of $40 per month to Grove's servant, Wiley Gilmore, for his entire life.

Two codicils were included in E. W. Grove's will. First, "in the event of a contest during the life of this trust by any beneficiary or prospective beneficiary, the income or gift to him or her under this will is hereby revoked."

Second, his Asheville area properties were not to be "put on the market and sold in whole or in part, but be handled as during my lifetime."

Grove also stipulated that upon the death of his wife, Gertrude, her portion of the income from the trust would pass equally to Edwin and Evelyn. In the event of her death, Evelyn's portion was to pass directly to her children. No mention, reference or provisions were made for Fred L. Seely, whose lawsuit against E. W. Grove was still scheduled to be heard in St. Louis circuit court in 1927.

Called "one of the most unusual legal proceedings ever commended in any court," case #95218 with plaintiff Frederick Loring Seely versus the defendant, the Estate of the late Edwin Wiley Grove, opened on Tuesday, December 8, 1927, in the St. Louis courtroom of Judge Robert W. Hall. In lieu of a twelve-person jury, both sides had agreed that Judge Hall would render a verdict at the close of the trial.

"An interesting and very interested spectator at the trial," observed one reporter, "is the widow of the deceased Mr. Grove. [Gertrude] attended every session of the hearing, sitting at the very foot of the witness stand, due to the fact that she is almost deaf. By her facial expressions and her actions it is easily apparent that the aged lady is directly interested in the outcome of the trial."

The trial opened precisely at nine o'clock when the plaintiff's chief counsel, O. J. Mudd of St. Louis, called Fred Seely to the stand. As Mudd, once described as "veteran barrister and a former Southern gentleman himself," carefully guided his client through a series of questions, Fred Seely explained to the courtroom how, while employed by Parke, Davis & Company in 1898, he first met Edwin Wiley Grove, who was having difficulty at that time with his formula for a cold tablet. By June, Seely had not only solved Grove's problem with the formula, but had entered into his employment, working in the fledgling Tasteless Quinine Company warehouse in Asheville. A few months later, in October of 1898, Fred Seely and Evelyn Grove were married.

When the questioning that afternoon turned to the process Grove had instituted for developing new products at the Paris Medicine Company, including new formulas for his cold tablets and Tasteless Chill Tonic, Mr. Mudd asked Seely, "On whom did he try many of his experiments?"

"On anyone who would let him," came Seely's reply. "I had to take my share along with the others."

During the second day of the trial the strategy of each opposing side became clear. O. J. Mudd, working on behalf of Fred Seely, systematically introduced into evidence letter after letter, first showing it to Fred Seely and then asking him to identify it prior to it being entered into the records of the court. In each instance one of five the attorneys representing the estate of Edwin Wiley Grove would stand and object, "despite the fact," a reporter noted, "that each one bears the signature of Grove and were about or on some particular angle of the patent medicine business. The objection set up by the defense to each of these letters is to the effect that each one is irrelevant, immaterial and incompetent. These objections are without hesitation overruled by the Court and the letter is admitted as evidence and thus becomes a part of the record of the trial."

One reporter did take time to note that "a peculiar thing about this case, in its entirety for that matter, and which might indicate that neither Seely nor Grove at any time felt sure of the action of the other, is the fact that each one saved every single piece of correspondence that he received from the other."

"A Family Feud"

That afternoon, Fred Seely was asked by Mudd to provide the court with details on the trip he and Evelyn had taken to Java from 1900 into 1901 on behalf of the Paris Medicine Company. In addition to serving as their honeymoon, the trip had also enabled Seely to secure long term contracts guaranteeing an uninterrupted supply of quinine on which the company relied for many of its products. As the reporter noted,

*Seely again launched into a further narrative into his trip to Java, which was highly interesting and educational. During this time he was not interrupted once by counsel for either side and the entire courtroom was in rapt attention. Judge Hall, who all through the trial thus far has appeared very bored, sat up and listened attentively to Seely, who has a wonderful command of language and a vocabulary readily understood. He spoke in a calm, clear voice for more than an hour, telling just how he had secured the contract in Java, and what it was necessary for him to do, and the hardships he underwent to secure quinine for his firm back in America.*

Mudd closed the day by probing the relationship between E. W. Grove and Fred Seely during those early years when they worked together, first in Asheville and then in St. Louis at the main factory and offices. Mudd asked Fred Seely to describe what his relationship with E. W. Grove had been like around 1900. Seely's reply, as recorded by one of the St. Louis reporters at the trial, "was that it was much like father and son, saying that Mr. Grove often kissed him when he went on a trip and when he returned."

Before the court adjourned at the close of the second day, Mudd asked Seely about his reasons for leaving his lucrative position and promising career at the Paris Medicine Company in 1902. Seely explained that, in the words of a reporter, "some time later [after his return from Java] when the business was running along smoothly, he and Grove were walking home from the plant, and the former told him that he thought it best for him to go to some other city, preferably Atlanta. Seely gave as the reason the fact that there was some friction in the immediate family relations [between Gertrude Grove and her stepdaughter Evelyn]."

Observers attending the third day of the trial in hopes of hearing some additional personal insight into the Grove and Seely families were disappointed when the wrangling among the various attorneys slowed the legal process down to a painful crawl. After entering into the record scores of letters between Grove and Seely, all intended to show that, despite his absence from St. Louis, Fred Seely remained active in the affairs of the Paris Medicine Company and that Grove and his staff relied on him for advice, Mudd finally broached the subject of the Grove Park Inn. In describing the terms of the lease he and Grove signed in 1914, Seely stated that he "had always paid Grove from $35,000 to $40,000 annually as rent on the Grove Park Inn with a profit left for himself."

At one point in Seely's testimony, a question from Mudd "brought three of the defense attorneys to their feet before Judge Hall, vigorously shouting objections and making every effort to prevent Seely from answering either yes or no. [The judge] could not have heard if he had. The objection interposed by counsel for the defense was then made the basis for a short but heated argument on both sides, and the Court finally ruled that Seely could answer."

Mudd then changed his focus back to 1903 when, for a brief period of time after leaving St. Louis, they lived in Princeton, New Jersey. When pressed by his own attorney to explain what he did during that time, Fred Seely expressed reluctance, stating, "There were some things [I] do not like to tell."

As the crowd leaned forward in anticipation, "The attorney told him it did not matter whether he liked to tell it or not, that it was necessary that the court be fully advised, and the question was repeated."

*Seely then replied that he had gone to Princeton at the insistence of Mr. Grove, whose son E. W. Grove Jr. who is now in attendance at the trial here, was not doing very well in school. He said that young Grove at that time was about 15 years of age and that Grove Sr. had had quite a bit of trouble with him. "Mr. Grove asked me," Seely continued, "if I would take charge of him, Edwin. We sat up one night until after midnight talking it over. Mr. Grove said he could do nothing with the boy and that he would mind me better than he would him and he would like to see if I could get the boy to study. I told him I would. We then moved to Princeton, but the boy did not get along so well in school and I finally engaged a private tutor, Professor N. Lucien Knight, who since has become a very prominent figure in the education world. Professor Knight came to the house each day to give Edwin his lesson. Still he did not get along as I thought he should, and we again moved, to Atlanta, where I put Edwin in Georgia Tech, but I was unable to keep him there. I later engaged another private tutor for him in Georgia.*

Nothing in the record indicated how Edwin Grove Jr., who, like his mother, attended every session of the trial, reacted to Fred Seely's testimony.

The next morning, everyone in the courtroom settled in for what they expected to be a fourth full day of O. J. Mudd leading Fred Seely through another slow recitation of his career and relationship with E. W. Grove. After a few minutes of questioning, however, the counsel for Seely surprised everyone in the room by suddenly turning and advising the team of defense attorneys that they could now begin their cross-examination of the witness. Although momentarily caught off-guard and needing a few minutes "to get their bearings," the attorneys for the defense "promptly squared away and settled down to give Mr. Seely a grilling that will likely occupy the rest of the week and probably run over into next week."

The attorneys charged with disproving Fred Seely's claim that Grove had promised him in his will of 1900 his choice between controlling interest in the Paris Medicine Company or in Grove's other investments immediately cut to the heart of the matter.

"You testified," said Chief Counsel Green of the defense, "that attorney George H. Williams, now Senator George Williams, did draw up the will?"

"Yes," said Mr. Seely. "Williams did draw up the will. I had the notes given by Mr. Grove telling me how he wanted the will drafted and I took the notes to Mr. Williams."

"Do you have a copy of them?"

"No, sir."

"Were they typewritten?"

"No, sir, in pencil."

"How soon did Williams bring the will back to Dr. Grove for his signature?"

"It was several days after that."

"Where was Dr. Grove when the will was brought to him?"

"In his office, at the plant of the Paris Medicine Company, after office hours."

"Did you read the will?"

"Yes, sir, I did."

"Did Dr. Grove read it?"

"He did."

"Was the will and its terms satisfactory to you?"

"That's absurd, and I refuse to answer that question for it was not my will. It was Dr. Grove's and if it was satisfactory to him that was all that was necessary. It certainly was none of my business."

At this point Judge Hall interrupted the two men to ask for a clarification from Fred Seely. "Did the will embody terms carrying out the agreement [you] had had with the former medicine maker?" Those were the terms that served as the basis for the lawsuit.

Seely replied that it did.

Attorney Greene then casually asked Fred Seely if Dr. Grove had signed the will there in his office at the time that George Williams had brought it to him, and Seely replied in the affirmative.

According to newspaper reports, Green then turned and "fired" the next question at the witness.

"Is it not a fact that the will was signed in the office of attorneys Johnson and Richards [where George Williams then worked]?

Seely denied Green's statement, reiterating his recollection that Grove had signed the 1900 will in his office. "He said that as nearly as he recalled Senator Williams came up to Mr. Grove's office with the will and that there were a few minor details which Dr. Grove wanted changed, wherein Williams took a pen and scratched through two or three lines and then proceeded to write in the changes that [Grove] wanted. He said he supposed, too, that Williams had taken the documents back with him, as Grove was not much given to taking care of documents of any sort."

Green again asked Seely if the will had been typewritten and Seely replied, "it was a typewritten document." As a reporter observed, "Green seemed to seek to get the witness confused here, and again demanded if he was sure that it was typewritten, whereupon the witness replied again that the will was typewritten."

Unwilling to let the matter rest, Chief Counsel Green pressed the issue. "Now, is it not a fact that the will was written by Senator Williams in long hand?"

But Fred Seely remained adamant.

After a lengthy discussion of details included in the will, including an affirmation from Seely that, according to the 1900 will that he had read in Grove's office, "he was to receive control of the Paris Medicine Company at the death of Mr. Grove or, if he so desired in preference, a half interest in all the holdings Mr. Grove had."

Green then asked, "When did you learn that the will of 1900 had been destroyed?"

Seely replied that "Mrs. Williams [Seely's former secretary at the Paris Medicine Company] had intimated to him in 1911 that it had been changed and that he had not been mentioned."

When asked when Grove had informed him that the will of 1900 had been changed, reflecting Grove's desire to have all of his holdings placed into a trust, the income from which was to be divided equally each year among Gertrude, Edwin and Evelyn, Seely answered by stating that Grove told him in 1924 or 1925.

One reporter covering the trial also noted that on this day defense attorney Green "made an effort to confuse the witness, listing and calling off a lot of technical drug terms not readily understood by laymen, but perfectly well known to Seely, apparently, who told what each one was, how it was used and what it contained." When that tactic failed, Green attempted to portray Seely as "inexperienced at the time [1898] that he came into the employ of Mr. Grove, and also an attempt was made to discredit testimony he had already offered to the effect that he had designed and ordered most of the machinery used by the Paris Medicine Company."

"A Family Feud"

After establishing that Seely had been employed by Parke, Davis & Company prior to going to work for E. W. Grove in June of 1898, Defense Counsel Green asked, "Is that the time the Parke Davis Company had you arrested and put in jail?"

According to newspaper reports, "A bombshell dropped in the courtroom could have caused little more consternation. O. J. Mudd was on his feet shaking his fist and shouting an objection and denouncing the question in language not commonly used by attorneys toward one another, and Green was insisting the question be answered."

Fred Seely jumped to his feet, explaining above the uproar, "Sir, I resent that. That is absurd. The Parke Davis Company did not have me arrested, did not have me put in jail. I have never been arrested for anything in my life at any time."

As the courtroom quieted, Green responded, "I am sorry and will apologize."

"I should think you would," snapped Seely.

"I was merely laboring under a false impression," stated Green. "I had been told upon what I thought was reliable authority that you had been arrested [for stealing plans for tablet machinery]. I am sorry and will withdraw the question."

Seely's attorney, however, insisted that the question stand and that his client be allowed to answer it. "He related that when he attempted to go to the employ of Mr. Grove, the Parke Davis Company made every attempt to stop him, even to attempting to defame his character, and that for a time Grove believed them, but upon investigation found that their charges against him were false."

In an attempt, perhaps, to relieve the tension that had been building between the opposing sides over the course of four very intense days, Defense Counsel Green paused, then asked of Fred Seely,

"Now, how long did this 'kissing business' continue between you and Mr. Grove?"

"The question," a writer reported, "brought laughter from all the attorneys at the counsel table, which was joined with expressions of amusement from the spectators in the court. Seely replied that it had continued up until their relations had become more or less strained over the renewal of the lease on the Grove Park Inn [in 1917]."

The rigors of a fourth day of testifying had begun to take their toll on Fred Seely. As newspaper reports confirmed, "Seely showed plainly that the experience was a strain on him. He showed some signs of fatigue at the end of the third day and that was when he was still under direct examination, which, of course, was not nearly so strenuous as the ordeal of cross-examination. At the beginning of the trial and up until about the middle of the afternoon of the third day, Seely was prompt to reply to every question and his testimony was offered in a firm, sound voice that could be heard plainly in every part of the courtroom, and the evidence he gave was most interesting, for instance, when he told in detail of his trip to Java for the Paris Medicine Company, and again when he told in detail of the construction and operation of the Grove Park Inn at Asheville, which he claimed he designed and built himself.

"But it was plain to be seen that the strain was beginning to tell on him. Dressed in a plain dark suit of clothes, the cloth for which is manufactured by [Biltmore Industries] in Asheville, of which he is the head, Seely appeared late yesterday afternoon to be ill at ease. While at no time did he become 'rattled' at questions painfully and slowly intoned at him by counsel for defense, he could not remain still long at a time in his chair. He nervously crossed and uncrossed his legs and his answers to questions of counsel were much slower than they had been at any time during the trial."

Given the weekend in his St. Louis hotel room to rest and relax his voice, Fred Seely returned to the stand at precisely 9:00 a.m. on Monday morning, December 12, prepared for another round of battling with Defense Counsel Green. As the attorney began laying his groundwork by reviewing some of the testimony Seely had given the previous Friday, Judge Hall interrupted, informing all of the attorneys for both sides "that the court was fully informed and that it was not necessary to go over that part of the testimony again."

After finding little new material to discuss, O. J. Mudd asked his client why, given the animosity that had been growing between the two men, did Seely continue sending Grove letters of congratulation upon learning each time of the increased business being generated at the Paris Medicine Company?

"I was more than glad to see the business growing," Seely replied that morning, "realizing that someday it would be mine and therefore I was much interested in it."

A short while later, on redirect by Defense Counsel Green, Seely was asked, "When Mrs. Williams [Seely's former secretary] told you in 1911 that a new will had been drawn by Mr. Grove and that you were not mentioned, did you protest to him?"

"No, sir, I did not."

"When Dr. Grove told you in Atlanta that he had made a new will, did you protest then?"

"No, sir, I did not. He simply told me that he had made a new will, but he did not say that he had left me out."

"Was there ever a time when Dr. Grove so much as intimated to you that he had changed his will to leave you out and not keep his [1900] contract with you?"

"No, sir, there was never a word said about it."

And with that Fred Seely, after four-and-one-half days, stepped down from the witness stand.

The second witness to take the stand in the trial was Senator George H. Williams of St. Louis. A former judge and attorney, Senator Williams had served both Edwin Wiley Grove and Fred L. Seely early in all three of their careers. Fred Seely had testified the previous week that it was George Williams who, in 1900, had come to Edwin Grove's office with a typewritten text of E. W. Grove's will, based on notes he had earlier been presented by Fred Seely.

When asked by attorney O. J. Mudd if he "knew of the contract purporting to be an arrangement for the disposal of the stock of the Paris Medicine Company, the senator replied that he knew such an agreement was in existence."

When asked to affix a date to the drafting of that agreement in the form of a will, Senator Williams replied that it occurred in 1900, adding that "his firm [Johnson and Richards] had moved from one building to another, and said he had nothing in his files to show it, as they had been destroyed."

The attorney asked Senator Williams to share with the court what he could recall about the event. As recorded on the front page of the *Asheville Citizen* on December 13, 1927, "He said that the contract was already made at the drafting of the will, and that he had at several times discussed this agreement with Dr. Grove, and that Mr. Seely had been present sometimes and sometimes not. He said that [Fred Seely] had come to his office with notes that he had taken down at the dictation of Mr. Grove and wanted him to prepare a will.

"I discussed with Mr. Grove several times," Senator Williams continued, "the legal aspect of the will embodying the contract. Mr. Grove wanted to be sure that the will carried the contract and that it was legal and binding. I assured him that it was perfectly all right for the will to include the contract, and showed him how it was binding."

"What was the subject of that contract?" Mudd then asked.

"Both the contract and the will stipulated that Mr. Seely was to have control of the Paris Medicine Company or, at his election, a half interest in Mr. Grove's other holdings."

When then asked if he had drawn up the contract between E. W. Grove and Fred Seely under which Seely was to have the option of taking control of the Paris Medicine Company under Grove's death, Senator Williams confessed that he could not recall.

After Mudd announced that he had no additional questions, Defense Attorney Green then rose and asked Senator Williams to again describe for the court the will which he had prepared in 1900 for E. W. Grove, that being the will that also contained the contract which served as the basis for Fred Seely's lawsuit.

"The senator testified," the newspaper reported, "both in direct testimony and in cross-examination, that he had drawn the will for the deceased patent medicine maker, and that it had been typewritten and taken to the office of the Paris Medicine Company where, in the presence of Mr. Seely, himself, Dr. Grove and two employees of the company, the deceased medicine man had signed it."

Green then slowly walked back to the defense table, where he open a folder and slid out the contents before walking back to the witness stand.

"Senator Williams," he began, "I have before you a will dated May 25, 1900, and signed by Edwin Wiley Grove." He paused, as the courtroom grew silent. "However, it is written in long hand, not typewritten, and is signed, as you will see, by two witnesses who were, in fact, partners in your former law firm of Johnson and Richards -- not employees of the Paris Medicine Company. Is this, Senator Williams, the same will which you drew up for Edwin Wiley Grove in 1900?"

A newspaper reporter in the room stated that "the entire courtroom was breathless, and seemed hanging on what the senator would have to say as to whether or not he held in his hand the original 1900 will which he had drawn for Mr. Grove. The senator was completely taken aback, and said nothing for a period of at least one minute, which seemed like half an hour."

At last he said, "This is the will which I drew up for Mr. Grove."

The spectators gasped as Defense Counsel Green quickly moved in for the fatal blow to Fred Seely's case.

"Can you tell the court, Senator Williams -- in this will which you wrote -- is Fred Seely identified as a beneficiary upon the death of Edwin Wiley Grove of either controlling interest in the Paris Medicine Company or, if he so desired, half interest in all the other holdings Dr. Grove had?"

Senator Williams, who had continued to stare at the handwritten will he held in his hands, silently shook his head, then confirmed that Fred Seely was not listed as a beneficiary.

Recognizing that their case and all of the weeks spent preparing it suddenly had "the props knocked from under it," the attorneys representing Fred Seely quickly conferred, then made a formal request to the court for Judge Hall to dismiss their suit.

With the banging of Judge Hall's gavel, the case was suddenly over.

And without ever setting foot in the courtroom, Edwin Wiley Grove had won.

But the formal dismissal of the lawsuit did not answer many of the questions still buzzing around the courthouse that day.

Did Fred Seely knowingly fabricate his entire story of the writing of the will?

Was he hoping -- or thinking -- or bluffing -- that the original no longer existed?

And, if so, how did he convince a respected attorney, judge and United States senator to perjure himself in court? What would Senator Williams have to gain by doing so?

If Senator Williams was, in fact, correct that he had written, prepared and witnessed the signing by E. W. Grove of a typewritten will stipulating and asserting Fred Seely's claims, what happened to it?

Could it have once existed, but then E. W. Grove may suddenly have had second thoughts about what he was leaving to this young man from Detroit whom he had only known for two years? Or what the consequences might be should Evelyn divorce him? And what this arrangement would later mean for his 9-year-old son?

And, on the other side of the courtroom, where did the 1900 will come from?

Did the defense team and the Grove family have it the entire time, or was it suddenly discovered that weekend among E. W. Grove's papers?

And if the Grove family had it all along, why not produce it as early as 1925, when Fred Seely first filed his lawsuit?

Why wait and undergo all of the expense, scrutiny and unwanted publicity of a courtroom trial?

A portion of the answers did lie in the contract that had remained attached to the May 25, 1900, will the defense team produced that day in court. The separate contract, which had been prepared in 1900 a few weeks prior to the writing of Grove's will, did stipulate that upon Grove's death Fred Seely, while not owning either one, would have "control" of the shares of Paris Medicine Company stock which Grove had accumulated for himself and the good of his family, and would be the "trustee" of all of Grove's holdings outside the medicine company.

Grove's intent, it could be inferred, would have been that should he suddenly die, Fred Seely would be entrusted with managing the Paris Medicine Company and Grove's outside investments for the benefit of Gertrude, Edwin and Evelyn. It should be noted that Grove turned fifty in 1900 and had been in poor health for several months, both factors which may have contributed to his concern over his will and the fate of his company and his investments.

And when the relationship between Grove and Seely soured, Grove, had he known the agreement attached to his early will still existed, would not have wanted to bring it to light. Since Grove could not be completely sure if a copy existed in the files of Fred Seely, George Williams or the law firm of Johnson and Richards, Grove did not dare destroy his original, in the event he would ever need to produce it to prevent an outcome his family had narrowly avoided that day in court.

When pressed by reporters for a statement after the trial had concluded, Fred Seely replied, "The written contract which came to light was a change from the original agreement, and made it necessary immediately to dismiss the first suit and to proceed on a different basis. Demand is being made on the Paris Medicine Company to abide by the terms of the written contract of May 25, 1900."

In truth, however, no further legal action was taken by Fred Seely in an attempt to gain control or influence over the Paris Medicine Company, the Grove Park Inn or any of E. W. Grove's extensive investments.

Six months later, on June 21, 1928, Gertrude Grove died suddenly of a heart attack while in her home. Edwin was with her at the time. One week later, when Edwin, as her executor, filed her will in St. Louis probate court, it was disclosed that sometime after her husband's death in January of 1927 Gertrude Grove had invoked her legal right to her 'widow's dower.'

This obscure but legal statute enabled Gertrude Grove to renounce her husband's will, demanding instead her third of the contents of the trust outright, rather than accepting the annual income payments Grove had intended. Gertrude had then written her personal will, stipulating that upon her death her third of the $10 million dollar estate would go solely to her son Edwin.

Had she not renounced E. W. Grove's will, after her death Gertrude's income from the trust would have been divided equally between her son Edwin and her step-daughter Evelyn. Instead, Evelyn, Fred and their children were legally deprived of millions of dollars that her father had intended for her to inherit.

Ah, sweet revenge.

Years after the lawsuit between Fred Seely and Edwin Wiley Grove had been dismissed, the youngest son of Evelyn and Fred Seely revealed that Evelyn Grove Seely had refused to speak to her husband for nearly a year after the lawsuit had been filed. Fred and Evelyn remained married, however, living in Overlook Castle atop Sunset Mountain on the income he earned from Biltmore Industries and the monthly checks she received for the remainder of her life from her father's trust. Ironically, years later, when portions of the estate were being liquidated, Evelyn Grove Seely inherited the Battery Park Hotel, the very building that had kindled the fire that destroyed the relationship between her father and her husband.

On March 14, 1942, Fred Seely passed away at the age of 71, and was fondly remembered by the people of Asheville not for his lawsuit against his father-in-law, but for his decades of philanthropy in support of numerous charities and worthwhile causes in Western North Carolina.

And while his dream of owning the Grove Park Inn never materialized, it was Fred Loring Seely -- not Edwin Wiley Grove -- who had the greatest and longest lasting influence over the design, the construction and the character of the famous hotel.

Even without his name attached to any of it today.

*Fred Loring Seely*
*(1871 - 1942)*

*After 1928, a series of new owners attempted to modernize the hotel by bringing in oak 'paddlearm' furniture, adding new rugs, painting over the stenciling, and cutting out the bottoms of the Roycroft chandeliers to emit more light.*

# Chapter 14

# "Bankrupt!"

*As you remember, Mama Grove broke my father's will,*
*but that was perfectly all right, as I received far more*
*than I deserved, and I am certain it was never intended*
*for my children to have great wealth.*

Evelyn Grove Seely

With the death of owner Edwin Wiley Grove on January 27, 1927, and the departure of general manager Fred Seely at the conclusion of his lease that following December, the 15-year-old Grove Park Inn was about to begin a new era.

According to the stipulation in E. W. Grove's final will, the staff expected that the Grove family would hire a new general manager in 1928, but would retain ownership of the hotel, as Grove had insisted that neither the Grove Park Inn nor the Paris Medicine Company be sold. Instead, he had instructed the St. Louis Union Trust Company to oversee his estate in conjunction with his executor, Edwin W. Grove Jr. The annual income from all of his investments, properties and businesses was to be distributed equally among three people: his wife Gertrude, his son Edwin and his daughter Evelyn Grove Seely.

No mention had been made in E. W. Grove's will of his son-in-law Fred Seely.

Soon after her husband's funeral and burial in Paris, Tennessee, Gertrude and her son Edwin asked for a meeting with their attorneys and the officers at the St. Louis Union Trust Company. That day Gertrude Grove announced that she wished to invoke an obscure law, called the 'widow's dower,' which entitled her to immediate possession of one-third of her late husband's estate to provide "for her support and the nurture of her children." Despite the fact that everyone gathered in the room knew that Gertrude Grove and her son would be receiving nearly one million dollars a year as income from the E. W. Grove trust, no one could legally dispute her claim to her "widow's dower."

In order to raise the estimated three million dollars in cash that Gertrude Grove demanded, the bank officers and executor Edwin Grove Jr. began selling various assets in the family trust, including the Grove Park Inn. A few months later, on June 21, 1928, Gertrude Grove unexpectedly died of a heart attack. When her last will and testament was read, the family learned that she had left her entire estate, including her widow's dower of an estimated three million dollars, to her son Edwin, rather than splitting it between Edwin and Evelyn.

Years later, Evelyn Grove Seely remarked to a friend, "As you remember, Mama Grove broke my father's will, but that was perfectly all right, as I received far more than I deserved, and I am certain it was never intended for my children to have great wealth. It is far better for them to work and earn [and] possess sympathy with those who must balance the budget."

## "Bankrupt!"

On September 22, 1927, Edwin Grove Jr. publicly announced his intention to sell the Grove Park Inn. Initially, buyers were hesitant to step forward, as Fred Seely's lawsuit against the estate of Edwin Wiley Grove was still pending. The trial disputing ownership of the famed hotel finally opened in December of 1927, and on December 13, after a dramatic discovery and presentation of Grove's lost original will, the judge dismissed Fred Seely's case, ruling in favor of the Grove family.

With Fred Seely both literally and legally removed from the Grove Park Inn, real estate negotiations began in earnest. By May 1, 1928, the sale had been finalized to T. E. Hambleton and Donald McKnew, partners in a Baltimore-based brokerage firm representing "a corporation organized and existing under laws of Maryland and comprising Baltimore banking interests." The purchase price was reportedly one million dollars.

Made at a time when both stock market prices and real estate values were skyrocketing, seemingly with no end in sight, the new owners were heavily leveraged. They apparently paid approximately $225,000 themselves, then borrowed $300,000 from a bank in Baltimore and took out a mortgage with the St. Louis Union Trust Company, representing the Grove estate, for an additional $475,000.

The new owners retained Martin H. Burke as the inn's general manager, then embarked on a series of changes intended to update the Arts and Crafts hotel. Little more than one year later, however, the Stock Market Crash of 1929 signaled the abrupt end of the age of prosperity that had embraced the country for nearly a decade after World War I. As the number of guests at the inn plummeted as quickly as the Dow Jones average, the Grove Park Inn struggled to remain profitable.

On January 15, 1932, the new owners defaulted on both their first and second mortgages, prompting an Asheville judge to appoint an attorney to work with the owners in an attempt to refinance the purchase. Later that year, a group of the original stockholders reorganized the ownership of the hotel, hiring Albert N. Barnett as the inn's general manager.

Albert Barnett, though seldom recognized for his efforts, guided the Grove Park Inn through some of its most challenging times. Born in Ripley, Mississippi, as a young man he began working as a clerk in various hotels, rising up through the ranks and gaining valuable experience in Detroit and Atlanta. In 1923, he came to Asheville and served as Fred Seely's assistant, overseeing the operation of the hotel during Seely's extended travels. He remained with the Grove Park Inn after its sale by the Grove family in 1928 and was promoted to general manager in 1932, a position he held until leaving in 1940.

Although he held no official position at the Grove Park Inn, former president Fred Seely was never able to completely divorce himself from the hotel he had designed, built and guided for nearly fifteen years. Anticipating the day when he and the Grove family would find their differences insurmountable, in 1917 he had purchased from Edith Vanderbilt a small weaving and woodworking business called Biltmore Estate Industries. First organized in 1905 as a woodcarving club for the sons of employees on the Biltmore Estate, Edith and George Vanderbilt financed the hiring of two instructors, Eleanor Vance and Charlotte Yale. These two young women were Presbyterian missionaries from Chicago dedicated to improving the lives of young men and women in the Appalachian region.

Working in tandem with Edith Vanderbilt, Eleanor Vance and Charlotte Yale expanded the original club to include girls, and then modeled the Biltmore Estate Industries after the popular Arts and Crafts philosophy of quality hand-craftsmanship and designs inspired by nature. From a small store in Biltmore Village located outside the gates to the estate, the young men and women sold hand-woven fabric and hand-carved mahogany and walnut bowls, book-ends, picture frames, book racks and occasional pieces of furniture to Asheville residents and the growing number of tourists who vacationed in the area.

After the sudden death of George Vanderbilt in 1914, the departure of Vance and Yale the following year and a devastating and deadly flood in 1916, Edith Vanderbilt soon felt it necessary to begin divesting herself of additional responsibilities. Having known Fred Seely for several years and his affinity for the Arts and Crafts style, she felt comfortable entrusting him with the future of Biltmore Estate Industries.

Catching his father-in-law in one of his more generous moments, Fred Seely obtained from E. W. Grove a 99-year lease on approximately nineteen acres of land adjacent to the north end of the Grove Park Inn. In 1917, Seely began construction, at his own expense, on the first of five Arts and Crafts workshops for his company of woodworkers and weavers, now called simply Biltmore Industries. While they continued to make hand-carved items, under Fred Seely's management Biltmore Industries soon became known across the country for their fine hand-woven homespun cloth. At a time when tailored jackets were fashionable for both men and women, such luminaries as First Ladies Eleanor Roosevelt and Lou Hoover were often seen wearing jackets and skirts made from Biltmore Industries fabric.

After the sale of the Grove Park Inn in 1928, Fred Seely retreated to his office at Biltmore Industries, but kept a close eye on developments across the road. Since 1917 his Biltmore Industries staff had maintained the News Stand in one corner of the Great Hall, selling not only Biltmore Industries woodworking and homespun cloth, but also art pottery from such noted firms as Roseville, Weller and Newcomb College Pottery, plus Cherokee woven baskets and hand-hammered copper items from the Roycrofters in East Aurora, N.Y. Fred Seely quickly renewed his lease on the News Stand with the new owners from Baltimore, and was further able to watch what was happening in the hotel.

For Albert Barnett, having his former employer as his advisor undoubtedly was a double-edged sword. Never one to mince words, Fred Seely would have been open and direct with his advice as well as with his criticisms, but Fred Seely was also responsible for bringing some of the Grove Park Inn's most famous guests to the hotel. When President Hoover's son was in need of a place to recover from a bout with tuberculosis, it was Fred Seely who convinced the president and Mrs. Hoover that their son should come to Asheville. Subsequently, the Hoovers made several trips to Asheville, staying both at Fred Seely's home and at the Grove Park Inn. With each trip the Grove Park Inn basked in the glow of national publicity.

With the re-election in 1936 of President Franklin D. Roosevelt, who also had stayed at the Grove Park Inn, the country's economy slowly began to heal. The Baltimore-based owners, however, still struggled under the massive debt they had incurred in order to purchase the hotel. A second reorganization took place in 1938, but the Grove Park Inn was teetering on the verge of closure when on December 8, 1941, America was drawn into World War II.

Suddenly, the Grove Park Inn had a new client -- the United States government.

# "Bankrupt!"

*Although still serenely perched astride Sunset Mountain, inside the granite walls the staff struggled to keep the Grove Park Inn afloat during the Great Depression.*

*The Fitzgerald family -- Scott, Zelda and only daughter Scottie -- are seen celebrating Christmas ca. 1925, already nearing the peak of his literary career.*

# Chapter 15

# "Scott and Zelda:
# The Dark Side of Paradise"

*They were careless people, Tom and Daisy -- they smashed
up things and creatures and then retreated back into
their money or their vast carelessness, or whatever it was
that kept them together, and let other people clean up the
mess they had made.*

> *The Great Gatsby* (1925)
> F. Scott Fitzgerald

*Our love was one in a century. Life ended for me when
Zelda and I crashed. If she would get well, I would be
happy again and my soul would be released. Otherwise,
never.*

> F. Scott Fitzgerald, 1935
> The Grove Park Inn

They were the most famous literary couple of all time.

Scott and Zelda Fitzgerald.

The king and queen of The Jazz Age.

Prohibition and moonshine.

Flappers and bathtub gin.

Paris and Broadway.

At the tender age of just 24, Frances Scott Key Fitzgerald (1896-1940) burst onto the literary scene and the social pages of newspapers across the country with the popular success of *This Side of Paradise* (1920), a thinly veiled autobiography about young love, infidelity, wealth and loyalty.

A Princeton dropout and struggling Manhattan copywriter, young Fitzgerald's attempts to win the heart of Zelda Sayre (1900-1948), the golden girl of Montgomery, Alabama, had been rebuffed until the overnight success of his first novel. Wooed by his newfound glamour and sudden riches, the 20-year-old Zelda Sayre married F. Scott Fitzgerald that same year.

The Fitzgeralds entertained the country with their childish antics and brushes with the law as both New York celebrities and expatriates in Paris and the French Riviera: leaping off a hotel balcony into a swimming pool, turning cartwheels inside the Princeton Club, riding around Manhattan on the roof of a taxi and fighting with doormen and bouncers at the finest clubs.

On one of their trips aboard a luxury liner bound for Europe, an inebriated Zelda, staring at a storm building at sea, decided that they could scare "the gods of the tempest, and walked around the decks with a crowd after her, banging on all kinds of utensils they could find." She then announced that the gods demanded a sacrifice, so she tore off the diamond engagement ring Scott had given her and threw it overboard, encouraging others to follow suit.

Though easily lured away from his writing by Zelda and their constant stream of parties, in 1922 Fitzgerald managed to assemble a collection of his short stories in *Tales of the Jazz Age*, plus a second novel, *The Beautiful and the Damned*, providing the carefree couple with the cash they needed to sustain their extravagant lifestyle.

In 1925, shortly after publication of his third novel, *The Great Gatsby*, the Fitzgeralds met Ernest Hemingway in a bar in Paris. Fitzgerald immediately took a liking to Hemingway, who was then working on his first novel. Zelda, however, either out of a simmering jealousy or keen intuition, never trusted the brash and burley young writer. Fitzgerald used his influence with Scribner's to help Hemingway get *The Sun Also Rises* published in 1926, but their friendship slowly soured, as they soon became literary rivals. Later, Zelda's intuition proved accurate, as Hemingway turned on his friend, publicly mocking him, much to Fitzgerald's horror, in letters and one of his most popular short stories.

As Fitzgerald later wrote, "Too often literary men allow themselves to get into destructive quarrels and finish about as victoriously as most of the nations at the end of the World War. I consider it an example of approaching maturity on my part and am proud of my self-control. He is quite as nervously broken down as I am, but it manifests itself in different ways. His inclination is toward megalomania, and mine toward melancholy."

Although Fitzgerald had published three novels and more than two dozen short stories in just five years, the combination of their constant drinking and the pressure to satisfy his critics began to take their toll on Fitzgerald, on Zelda and on their marriage. It took nine years for him to complete his next novel, *Tender Is the Night*, which was published in 1934 to only lukewarm reviews and disappointing sales. It would be the fourth and final novel he would complete. At age 38, his literary career was in shambles.

The Fitzgeralds' private life fared no better. When sober, their marriage was wracked with insecurity, jealousy and intense competition, as Zelda also began writing fiction and selling short stories. Each of them often relied on the other for inspiration, at times basing characters and scenes on their real lives, much to the discomfort of the other. At just age 27, the first signs of Zelda's mental instability began to surface, as she became obsessed with becoming a professional ballerina. Injury, exhaustion and finally a mental breakdown ensued. She entered the first in a series of sanatoriums in 1930, where the doctors diagnosed her as schizophrenic. Nevertheless, in 1932 she completed her only novel, *Save Me the Dance,* but it sold only 1,392 copies. In a sense of true literary irony, Scott Fitzgerald berated Zelda for basing her novel on their crumbling marriage, despite the fact that Fitzgerald was doing the same in *Tender Is the Night.* Both novels were financial failures, as the American public, caught in the deadly grip of the Great Depression, had little empathy for the mess the young Fitzgeralds had made of their lives.

By this time Scott Fitzgerald was convinced that he had contracted tuberculosis, although many of his biographers suspect he was actually suffering from the affects of nearly two decades of destructive drinking. In 1935, with Zelda institutionalized in Baltimore, Fitzgerald climbed into his car and drove to North Carolina. As early as 1920 he had referenced Asheville in a short story he had written for *The Saturday Evening Post* entitled "The Ice Palace." He mentioned it a second time in 1925 in *The Great Gatsby,* both times characterizing it as a resort town for Southerners.

"I was just about up to the breaking point financially," he later wrote "when I came down here to Asheville. I had been seriously sick for a year and just barely recovered, and tried to set up a household in Baltimore, which I was ill equipped to sustain. I was planning to spend a fairly leisurely summer [in Asheville], keeping my debt in abeyance on money I had borrowed on my life insurance. But the more I worried, the less I could write. My nervous system is pretty well shot. You have probably guessed I have been doing a good deal of drinking to keep up what morale has been necessary."

In May of 1935, soon after he had settled into the Grove Park Inn, he wrote to a friend, "I am benefiting by my rest here, gaining weight, exuberance. But living alone leaves so many loopholes for brooding, and when I do face the whole tragedy of Zelda, it is simply a day lost. She seems so helpless and pitiful. Liquor used to help me put it out of my mind, and it was one of the many services my old friend Barleycorn did me."

He continued, "As to health, the body had been gradually sliding toward annihilation for two years, but the process didn't get acute until about six months ago, and when it did, it went fast. I was doing my stuff on gin, cigarettes, bromides and hope. Finally, the stuff itself was getting rather watery, so I decided to get away while I was still on my feet. I laid up, or rather down, in North Carolina, recuperated quickly, and decided to quit drinking for a few years [which he failed to do until 1937]." A few weeks later he wrote, "I am still swollen up like a barrel but have reduced my beer consumption to nine bottles today."

Fitzgerald remained at the Grove Park Inn throughout the summer of 1935, during which time he became embroiled in a torrid affair with an attractive, young married woman staying at the hotel with her sister. It was neither his first nor his last practice of infidelity. As his biographer Andrew Turnbull noted, "Since Zelda's breakdown Fitzgerald had drifted into affairs here and there -- not many, considering the opportunities. In July a young married woman from

Memphis, visiting Asheville, fell in love with him on sight. She was already enamored of his writings, and when she pursued him, they became lovers despite misgivings on his part. She was pretty and wealthy but not otherwise remarkable, and he resented wasting time on her -- that is, until her husband joined her [on July 15]. Then Fitzgerald decided he really did love her and was plunged into a misery which he prolonged and dramatized, continuing to meet her at grave risk of being found out. After the woman had gone, she wrote Fitzgerald heart-breaking letters which he was reluctant to answer, for by now he saw the affair for what it was -- an evasion, like his drinking."

"Don't women have anything more to do," Fitzgerald wrote after again falling prey to his emotions and spending a drunken weekend with her, "than to sit around and make love and drink beer? This time my emotions aren't even faintly involved and I'm such a wreck physically that I expect the heart, liver and lungs to collapse again at a moment's notice -- six weeks of late hours, beer and talk, talk, talk."

In August he described the affair in another of his many letters written from the Grove Park Inn. "I have just emerged, not totally unscathed, I'm afraid, from a short, violent love affair. It's no one I ever mentioned to you but it was in the bag when I came to Southern Pines and I [would] had done much better to let it alone, because this was scarcely a time in my life for one more emotion. Still it's done now and tied up in cellophane -- and maybe someday I'll get a chapter out of it. God, what a hell of a profession, to be a writer. One is one simply because one can't help it."

After the collapse of the Jazz Age and the Roaring Twenties, Fitzgerald's audience had quickly eroded. Sales of his novels dwindled, forcing him to churn out short stories for popular magazines, including *The Saturday Evening Post, Esquire, Vanity Fair* and *Colliers*. Over the course of his twenty-year career, F. Scott Fitzgerald wrote and published 164 short stories. Although his reputation could still command anywhere from two thousand to four thousand dollars per story, he soon fell behind with Zelda's hospital bills, their daughter's private schooling and his own daily expenses. "He is so very casual about money," an acquaintance wrote in 1935, "and spends so much that he never seems to have enough."

Many of his letters written from rooms 441 and 443 at the Grove Park Inn were to his agent, friends and publisher, asking for loans or advances on his next short story. Soon even his short stories began to suffer from his erratic behavior and his dependency on alcohol, as rejection slips began replacing royalty checks. In comparison to Hemingway, who had fought in World War I, reported from the front lines of the Spanish Civil War and led hunting safaris in Africa, Fitzgerald lamented that he had no real life experience on which to base any fresh plots or characters.

As Tony Buttitta, author of *After The Good Gay Times,* a chronicle of his summer spent with Fitzgerald in 1935, observed, "But now he had also run out of material. His personal experiences had served him well for years; he had used them over and over again, and he needed a new source."

The more depressed Fitzgerald became that summer of 1935 at the Grove Park Inn, the more he drank. Laura Guthrie, hired as his typist and secretary, and who escorted Fitzgerald around Asheville, generally to various hotel bars, kept a journal of their time together. After one of their late-night outings she wrote, "When Scott gets to drinking, then he sits and sits and it is almost impossible for him to go home. He was sorry that he was in [such] a state again and said so. 'Here I am just about as bad as when I left [Baltimore], have about twenty or more bottles a day now. And [I] only had four or five in the North.' "

As Miss Guthrie also wrote, "I think that if all the bottles of beer that he had were put end to end they would go to the moon! He is beginning to break out in welts that itch. This and the trembling are getting worse, and yet he keeps on with the beer. It is almost beyond my comprehension, for he seems in the grip of a force stronger than he is. It seems to me that he is an alcoholic already, whether he knows it or not."

"He is so alarmed over his health," she continued in her journal on July 14, "and yet he lives the most unnatural life of any man I know. If he ever eats a decent meal, it has not been since I have known him. And he lives on beer, as high as 37 bottles in one day. It seems incredible, but it is so, and on the floor of one of his closets march a whole regiment of empty bottles, ones that he has broken, that he thinks the hotel does not know about. He smokes all the time, too, Santo cigarettes, by preference, as he thinks they do not hurt him. And Beatrice [his married mistress] sends him three cartons at a time."

Tony Buttitta also noted that "insomnia had a firm hold on him; he was taking a combination of pills to get a few hours' sleep. He took Benzedrine (years before 'bennies' became fashionable) to wake up in the morning, so he could think and try to write. He needed a drink to stir his memory, heighten emotions and thoughts, and give his style brilliance. If he took one drink too many, he couldn't think or write, and another day was shot."

Laura Guthrie also commented on his writing habits. It was Fitzgerald's practice to re-write each short story as many as four times, each starting with her freshly-typed draft which he would then edit in pencil. She once asked him if, in his earlier years, he always wrote three or four drafts of each story. "Yes," he replied. "I always did the best I could at the time. Three revisions are always necessary. First, going over the first draft, the high inspiration points. Then, second, the cold going-over. And, third, putting both in their proper balance." She also added, "He told me that in [early] years hotels would keep him for nothing, because his name made good advertising for them. Also, ocean liners carried him for nothing! Not that he knew it usually, for he was drunk all the way over. First, he drank to keep from being seasick and, then, to keep other people company."

On those days at the Grove Park Inn when he was able to write, Laura Guthrie recalled that "for an hour [we] talked of inconsequential things, and then, suddenly realizing that we had any amount of work to get thru, sat down at my desk table which I had prepared for him and got to work. I got to work in the next room and we about kept pace with each other, though I was a little behind; in other words, he could correct a page sooner than I could type the whole thing. It wasn't until about two that we stopped to have some food, and then it was the remains of what he had bought last evening. And meanwhile he was going strong on ale and when the evening came (and we were still working) I had to phone for more ale. He had 14 ales altogether. Then I got him some soup in the evening and he only ate the juice part and left the vegetables. He ate absolutely nothing else. It was a terrible, terrible strain and I realized that now my nerves were getting strained to the breaking point, too. It wasn't until just on the stroke of midnight that I copied the last word, so [the story] had gotten completed today as he wanted."

She described a day in September as Fitzgerald dictating "to me while he had beer. And walked around the two rooms [441 and 443] in his dressing gown, most unkempt. Drink makes a person not care at all how he looks, and shaving bores him anyhow. He wept several times as he thought how sad war was and how his [story] of a little boy not knowing that his father was killed in the war and wondering what his mother was sick about, got under his skin and he could not go on at times. When he is full of beer he is so emotional that his work seems to him to be superlatively good. When he gets sober again, he usually says it is not as good as he thought.

"I feel that Scott is about the loneliest person in the world that I know," she continued. "His mother is old and doesn't understand him at all and he does not care to see her. His wife is crazy and the last time he went to see her [in Baltimore] he had an awful experience of having to tackle her like in football as she ran for a little railway. He is completely alone because no persons are near to him, and he has no religion to comfort him. He makes me think of a lost soul, wandering in purgatory -- sometimes hell. He tries so hard to drown it out with drinking and sex. Sometimes in the heights of those moments he forgets for a brief time -- then it all comes back in."

His drinking intensified that fall, prompting him to check himself into an Asheville hospital on September 13, 1935, for a week of drying out. There he did his final editing of a short story "The Finishing School" before sending it off. As he did he commented, "Drink heightens feeling. I wrote the fortune telling story sober and it was stupid -- all reasoned out. But when I drink, it heightens emotion and I put it in a story. But it is hard to keep reason and emotion balanced."

Fitzgerald then retreated back to Baltimore for the winter in order to be closer to both Zelda and their daughter Scottie, who was enrolled in a private boarding school in Connecticut. "It has been a wasted summer," he bemoaned to Laura Guthrie shortly before he left Asheville. "I never remember such a wasted summer."

Rendezvousing with 14-year-old Scottie that fall at their Baltimore apartment proved invigorating for Fitzgerald, and seemed to have a similar effect on Zelda, whom they visited at her nearby sanatorium. But, just as quickly, the glow faded. Fitzgerald began drinking again, which proved embarrassing to Scottie, prompting her rapid return to boarding school.

That winter, in a misguided attempt to break away from his familiar characters, plots and themes, Fitzgerald wrote "The Crack-Up." This lengthy, openly autobiographical essay detailing his own disintegration appeared in three monthly installments in *Esquire* in the spring of 1936. In it he confessed, "Suffice to say that after about an hour of solitary pillow-hugging, I began to realize that for two years my life had been drawing on resources that I did not possess, that I had been mortgaging myself physically and spiritually up to the hilt."

His self-absorbed confession caught the literary world off-guard, prompting his friend Ernest Hemingway to dismiss it as public whining. Biographers have since labeled it "a post-mortem on his nervous and psychological breakdown" of the previous year. Fitzgerald, in his own unique and naïve way, was pleased that he was being read again, and seemed to believe his harsh self-evaluation would signal the resurrection of his writing career.

At that time, however, Zelda's condition had worsened to the point where on April 8, 1936, Fitzgerald transferred her to Highland Hospital in Asheville, placing her under the care of Dr. Robert S. Carroll, whom he had met the previous summer. As his friend and author Tony Buttitta recalled, "He was impressed by the doctor and thought Zelda would be happier in the Carolina mountains, in a hotel-like atmosphere, than she would be in a clinic in the heart of Baltimore. She would be treated more like a guest in a supervised retreat than a patient in a mental institution."

Soon thereafter Fitzgerald returned to the familiar Grove Park Inn, located just two miles away from the lush, rolling grounds of Highland Hospital, where he again settled into rooms 441 and 443, one of which had been transformed into a sitting room for him.

His return, however, was greeted by yet another setback. As he explained in a letter to Scottie, "I thought I would be very smart and do some diving, and after a year and a half of inactivity I stretched my muscles too much in the air and broke my shoulder. It has all been very troublesome and expensive, but I have tried to be as cheerful as possible about it and everyone has been very kind; the people here [at the Grove Park Inn] have rigged up a curious writing board for me so that I work with my hand over my head. If I had not had this operation on my shoulder, the doctor tells me I would never have been able to raise my arm above my shoulder again."

His editor received a letter with a few additional details:

*I broke the clavicle of my shoulder, diving -- nothing heroic, but a little too high for the muscles to tie up the efforts of a simple swan dive. At first the doctors thought that I must have tuberculosis of the bone, but X-rays showed nothing of the sort, so it was left to dangle for twenty-four hours with a bad diagnosis by a young intern; then an X-ray, and found broken and set in an elaborate plaster cast. I had almost adapted myself to the thing when I fell in the bathroom [at the Grove Park Inn] reaching for the light, and lay on the floor until I caught a mild form of arthritis, which popped me in the bed for five weeks more. I have been within a mile and a half of my wife all summer and have seen her about half dozen times. Total accomplished for one summer has been one story, not very good, two articles, neither of them very good.*

The resulting pain and depression pushed Fitzgerald back over the edge, increasing his drinking even beyond what the staff at the hotel had witnessed in 1935. Albert Barnett, the hotel manager, had forbid his staff from serving Fitzgerald anything stronger than beer, which, according to one bellman who made regular deliveries to rooms 441 and 443, amounted to as many as 32 bottles a day. A few additional bottles of his favorites, namely whiskey and gin, may also have made their way to the fourth floor, as Fitzgerald had gained a reputation as a huge tipper. "When I bring the beer in," one bellman explained, "he never looks up, he just says, 'Set it over there and open me a bottle,' and he hands me a dollar without ever taking his eyes off the paper."

The secretary who worked for Fitzgerald after his diving board accident recalled that "his usual pattern was to start out having pots of black coffee served to us at intervals, but as the morning progressed into afternoon and the pain and the stress increased, he would advance to stronger stuff. At the end of the session he would slump over, overcome by exhaustion and drink."

After a 1967 interview with former employee Julia Lytle, who knew Fitzgerald, a Grove Park Inn historian recorded this recollection of the author's time at the Grove Park Inn:

*Every few hours Fitzgerald would order six bottles of beer sent up to his room. Mrs. Lytle arranged the orders and kept track of the number of beers sent up. When the count reached 32 bottles of beer, Mrs. Lytle asked the bellboy who had carried up the beer if Fitzgerald were throwing a party.*

*"No, he's by himself, and he's just sitting at a table writing."*

*Fitzgerald gave Mrs. Lytle an autographed copy of his novel,* Tender Is the Night. *"A day or two later," Mrs. Lytle said, "he asked me how I liked it. I said I hadn't finished the book yet. Actually I was just trying to beat around the bush. He knew I didn't like it.*

*"He was a very nice man. He wrote so many articles here. He'd type all night and then all the next day, and never come out for food. Ulysses Johnson, the bell captain, took care of him. He took food to his room, and I don't know whether he ever saw Fitzgerald or not, but he kept him well fed.*

*"Fitzgerald would stay in that room for days and just write, write, write. If those maids had been smart, they would have kept everything they emptied from his wastebaskets. Wouldn't those scraps of paper be worth something today?*

*"Fitzgerald's wife, Zelda, who was a patient at Highland Hospital, spent the weekends here. She stayed in an adjoining room, and if she was sick, she didn't look it."*

After an incident in his room in which Fitzgerald was believed to have fired a revolver into the ceiling, the manager Albert Barnett insisted that Fitzgerald would either agree to have a nurse in his room at all times or he would have to vacate the hotel. That summer Asheville resident Dorothy Richardson assumed the role of Fitzgerald's nurse mate, hotel companion and guardian against his excessive drinking.

The three installments of "The Crack-Up" that had appeared in *Esquire* that spring prompted an editor at the *New York Post* to send a reporter by the name of Michel Mok to the Grove Park Inn to interview F. Scott Fitzgerald for his fortieth birthday. Fitzgerald, however, was in no condition to grant an interview and initially declined. Mok persevered, playing upon the author's fragile ego and expressing a false admiration for his work. Finally, Fitzgerald relented and, according to one of his biographers, "received him wearing a tan suit and a soft green tie. He was boyish, keen, polite, but pale and unwell, and the nurse was giving him injections [morphine for the pain]. Mok stayed for several hours, and Fitzgerald thought the occasion had gone pleasantly enough until he read the story in the *New York Post*. The September 25 article opened:

*The poet-prophet of the post-war neurotics observed his 40th birthday yesterday in his bedroom of the Grove Park Inn here. He spent the day as he spends all his days -- trying to come back from the other side of paradise, the hell of despondency in which he has writhed for the last couple of years.*

*He had no company except his soft-spoken, Southern, maternal and indulgent nurse and this reporter. With the girl he bantered in conventional nurse-and-patient fashion. With his visitor he chatted bravely, as an actor, consumed with fear that his name will never be in lights again, discusses his next starring role. He kidded no one. There obviously was as little hope in his heart as there was sunshine in the dripping skies, covered with clouds that veiled the view of Sunset Mountain.*

*Physically he was suffering the aftermath of an accident eight weeks ago, when he broke his right shoulder in a dive from a 15-foot springboard. But whatever pain the fracture might still cause him, it did not account for his jittery jumping off and onto his bed, his restless pacing, his trembling hands, his twitching face with its pitiful expression of a cruelly beaten child.*

*Nor could it be held responsible for his frequent trips to a highboy, in a drawer of which lay a bottle. Each time he poured a drink into the measuring glass on his bedside table, he would look appealingly at the nurse and ask, "Just one ounce?"*

The article seemed to have all but sealed Fitzgerald's career and his literary reputation as a washed-up writer. Mired in despondency, Fitzgerald attempted suicide that night in room 441 by swallowing one of his bottles of morphine. Fortunately, his nurse Dorothy Richardson came back to his room just in time to find him lying on the floor in a pool of vomit.

As the shame and anger wore away, Fitzgerald recognized that unless he changed his life, he would become the writer Mok had portrayed. That same month a modest inheritance from his mother's estate eased some of the burden of his enormous debt, enabling him to move out of the Grove Park Inn and into the top floor of the Oak Hall Hotel in Tryon, 45 miles south of Asheville. He remained there, drying out, from January until July of 1937, when he moved to Hollywood to work for M-G-M studios on several movie scripts. Unable to control his drinking or to produce the scripts the studio executives expected, he was fired in 1938. Unemployed and living with Hollywood columnist Sheila Graham, he began work on a new novel, *The Last Tycoon.*

A few years earlier, on September 10, 1935, Fitzgerald had prophesied to his secretary, "You know that people aren't going to let F. Scott Fitzgerald act as he chooses now. Four years ago the publisher would have said, 'Oh, that's just Fitzgerald's way, and as long as he produced good stuff, it doesn't matter.' Today they wouldn't be so lenient if I told them the real story of this wasted summer."

"And four years from now?" she asked.

"I won't be here then."

In truth, it was just five years later, on December 21, 1940, that F. Scott Fitzgerald died at his home in Hollywood of a massive heart attack.

He was only 44 years old.

Like so many other famous writers, F. Scott Fitzgerald's life and his talents had been diluted by his dependency on alcohol. Just before his death, his friend and rival Ernest Hemingway's latest novel, *For Whom The Bell Tolls*, had been released to great fanfare, while Fitzgerald and his four out-dated novels languished in obscurity. It has been estimated, however, that since Fitzgerald's death more than twenty million copies of his books have been sold.

In 1999, the editors at Modern American Library surveyed literary critics, scholars, professors and authors across the country as they compiled a list of the Greatest Novels of the 20th Century.

James Joyce's *Ulysses* was voted #1.

Hemingway's *A Farewell to Arms* was ranked 74th and his *The Sun Also Rises* finished 45th.

F. Scott Fitzgerald's *Tender Is the Night* fared much better, coming in at number 28.

*The Great Gatsby* was voted the second greatest novel of the 20th century, making F. Scott Fitzgerald the highest-ranking American author on the list.

And Zelda?

From the time she was thirty, Zelda Fitzgerald spent the rest of her life in or associated with various mental institutions. After the crushing failure of her only novel, *Save Me The Waltz*, she turned to painting, with an equally disappointing reception. She then went through a period of reclusive and sometimes violent behavior. As previously noted, Scott had placed her under the care of Dr. Robert S. Carroll, a nationally-respected psychiatrist, whose original Dr. Carroll's Sanatorium had become Highland Hospital in Asheville. Dr. Carroll's preferred methods of treatment included occupational therapy, outdoor exercise and a carefully regulated diet.

After Scott relocated to Hollywood in July of 1937 in his failed attempt to become a screenwriter, Zelda remained behind at Highland Hospital. He returned the following year, signed her out and together they embarked on a disastrous trip to Cuba, the low point coming when she and Scott stumbled into a cockfight where he got beaten up trying to stop it. She returned to Asheville, he to Hollywood. It was the last time they ever saw each other.

Despite his ever-dwindling resources and declining health, Fitzgerald took on whatever writing projects he could manage in order to pay for Scottie's education and Zelda's medical expenses. Zelda continued to make progress at Highland Hospital, where in 1940, just months before Scott's heart attack, she was released and returned to her mother's home in Montgomery, Alabama. That year she and Scott wrote to each other weekly, sharing news of their daughter, their former friends and of his writing. No mention seems to have been made of his living with Sheila Graham or of Zelda ever coming to California. She was unable to attend either his funeral or their daughter Scottie's wedding a few years later.

Over the course of the next few years, Zelda returned to Highland Hospital whenever she felt in need of additional treatment from Dr. Carroll and his staff. She made one such trip in March of 1948, staying in her familiar fourth floor room with its sweeping views of the panoramic Blue Ridge Mountains in the distance. After a week the doctors announced that she was ready to return to Montgomery, but Zelda asked to remain an additional few days, just to be sure.

Late on the night of March 10, a fire started in the basement kitchen of Highland Hospital. The flames were soon sucked up an open dumbwaiter shaft, quickly shooting down each hallway of the aging wood structure. The small overnight staff struggled to get the

29 female patients out of the building and onto the lawn, but many resisted, unable to comprehend what was happening around them. Some were hampered by restraints, locked doors and windows covered by iron bars, placed there, ironically, for their own protection. Twenty of the women, nearly all in rooms on the lower floors, were quickly led to safety.

Miss Betty Uboenga, a staff assistant, described how she and supervisor Frances Render first went after the helpless patients. "We felt that the others were awake and would help themselves," she said. "As soon as we got the helpless ones out and safely put away elsewhere, we rushed back to help others. By then we knew some had been trapped. Some of them were awake, we know, and were rousing the others. It seemed no time at all until the entire building was like a furnace."

By the time the firemen arrived, the four-story wooden structure was a raging inferno, visible for miles, leaving them little to do but to stand and watch. Two additional women were carried out of the building, but each died shortly thereafter from their burns. Seven other women, all in rooms on the upper floors, were unable to flee, as the wooden fire escape below them was also engulfed in flames.

One of the nine victims that horrific night was the 48-year-old Zelda Fitzgerald, trapped by the bars over her fourth-floor windows. The following day the hospital staff was able to identify her body by one of her charred, red ballerina slippers.

*President Franklin Delano Roosevelt, with his trademark cigarette holder and friendly smile, was often photographed seated in his open touring car as he campaigned for re-election to the White House in North Carolina in 1936.*

# Chapter 16

# "A Presidential Secret"

*For thirty years I have been wanting to get to the Great
Smoky Mountains. I have planned at least a half dozen
trips to this section, but each time something happened
to prevent my coming. Today I finally made it. I am not
disappointed. I am delighted and thrilled. It was a grand trip.*

President Franklin Roosevelt
September 10, 1936

On August 11, 1921, a 39-year-old father vacationing in Canada with three of his children awoke to find that he could not move his left leg. By that evening the numbness had traveled to his right leg. The following morning his children discovered him paralyzed from the waist down and with a temperature of 102 degrees. Within days a team of physicians who examined him had come to a conclusion.

Franklin Delano Roosevelt had polio.

A rising star in the national Democratic party, young Franklin Roosevelt had served in the New York senate, had been assistant secretary of the navy under President Woodrow Wilson, and had been nominated the previous year as the vice-presidential candidate alongside James N. Cox. Though defeated, Democrats viewed Roosevelt, fifth cousin of former President Teddy Roosevelt, as their standard bearer of the future.

Now, however, his future seemed dim.

Determined to regain his ability to walk, Roosevelt vigorously attacked his disease, seeking out various cures, including the therapeutic waters of Warm Springs, Georgia, all the while remaining active in both state and national politics. In 1928 he was elected governor of the state of New York and was reelected in 1930, placing him at the forefront of candidates ready to take on both the embattled President Herbert Hoover and the challenge of pulling the country out of the Great Depression. Franklin Roosevelt defeated the incumbent president in 1932 and rallied hope in the American people, proclaiming, "The only thing we have to fear is fear itself."

Roosevelt's lifelong battle with polio was fought both privately and publicly. When first diagnosed, the announcement of his condition was carried on the front page of newspapers across the country. Although no cure for polio existed, Roosevelt was determined to rid himself of the wheelchair and crutches he had been forced to rely on. Fortunately for his political career, photographers of that era observed an unwritten code that they would not publish pictures of the president either in his wheelchair or on crutches. Prior to his election to the White House in 1932, Roosevelt spoke bluntly about his own condition, all the while urging Americans to support programs to assist those with severe handicaps, "because, as some of you know, I walk around with a cane and with the aid of someone's arm myself. People who are crippled take a long time to be put back on their feet -- sometimes years, as we all know."

"A Presidential Secret"

Seeing their president undeterred from his goals by his steel braces or a wheelchair gave the American people the impression that he was winning his battle against polio, providing hope for tens of thousands of victims and their families. A 12-year-old boy who had contracted polio several months earlier wrote, "I don't know when I shall be able to walk again, but I am not giving up hope. You had paralysis, but that didn't stop you from progressing." As one historian noted, "Roosevelt's own buoyant spirit and sustained support for a vaccine helped many Americans believe that polio could ultimately be vanquished."

And if so, they must have thought, surely he can also defeat the economic paralysis of the Great Depression. As one of his biographers explained,

*Roosevelt was able to convince many people that he was in fact getting better, which he believed was essential if he was to run for public office again. In private he used a wheelchair. But he was careful never to be seen in it in public, although he sometimes appeared on crutches. He usually appeared in public standing upright, while being supported on one side by an aide or one of his sons. For major speaking occasions an especially solid lectern was placed on the stage so that he could support himself from it; as a result, in films of his speeches Roosevelt can be observed using his head to make gestures, because his hands were usually gripping the lectern. He would occasionally raise one hand to gesture, but his other hand held the lectern.*

*Roosevelt was very rarely photographed while sitting in his wheelchair, and his public appearances were choreographed in such a way as to avoid having the press cover his arrival and departure at public events which would have involved his having to get in or out of a car. When possible, his limousine was driven into a building's parking garage for his arrivals and departures. On other occasions, his limo would be driven onto a ramp to avoid steps, which Roosevelt was unable to ascend. When that was not practical, the steps would be covered with a ramp with railings, with Roosevelt using his arms to pull himself upward. Likewise, when traveling by train, as he often did, Roosevelt often appeared on the rear platform of the presidential railroad car. When he boarded or disembarked, the private car was sometimes shunted to an area of the railroad yard away from the public for reasons of security and privacy.*

*In keeping with social customs of the time, the media generally treated Roosevelt's disability as taboo. News stories did not mention it, and editorial cartoonists often showed the president with normal mobility. The Secret Service interfered with any photographers who tried to take pictures of Roosevelt in a wheelchair or being moved by others.*

Like Teddy Roosevelt, his equally as famous cousin, President Franklin Roosevelt was unafraid to confront industry leaders on environmental issues, including the preservation of the dwindling stands of old growth timber in the Smoky Mountains. Civic leaders on both the Tennessee and North Carolina sides of the mountains had for years been urging their congressmen to push for the formation of a national park to preserve the rugged terrain, create desperately needed jobs and promote tourism in the region.

As early as 1924, an exploratory committee discovered that "timber companies controlled 85% of the land that would be proposed for a national park in the Smoky Mountains region. There were also smaller tracts of property owned by 1,200 farmers as well as 5,000 small individually owned lots. As many as 6,000 claims stood in the way of the Great Smoky Mountains becoming a new national park, and few were looking to sell their lands."

"A Presidential Secret"

The announcement of the discovery of more than 100,000 acres of virgin timber within the Smoky Mountains, however, inspired local civic leaders and Washington politicians to demand that the federal government protect the area. As support grew, the politicians in Washington finally took note, symbolized in 1926 by the signing by President Calvin Coolidge of a bill creating the Great Smoky Mountains National Park. The ensuing campaign to raise the necessary money to purchase thousands of tracts of lands from timber companies and private owners caught the imagination of the American people, prompting schoolchildren to send in their nickels and dimes -- and for the John D. Rockefeller family to donate an initial matching grant of $5 million.

Even so, President Roosevelt and supporters of the park faced stiff resistance from the timber companies, many of which hired teams of attorneys to fight the condemnation proceedings in court. Most, however, received ample compensation for the lands they were required to relinquish, including 92,000 acres of forests purchased by taxpayers from the Champion Fiber Company, at the time the country's largest manufacturer of paper goods. Despite the problems every family in America faced during the depths of the Great Depression, more than $12 million dollars was raised privately to buy the land necessary to create the Great Smoky Mountains National Park. President Roosevelt furthered the cause by earmarking nearly $2 million dollars in Civilian Conservation Corp money for the park.

All of their efforts were rewarded in 1934 when the Great Smoky Mountains National Park officially opened, just five tumultuous years after its creation. Considered a diamond in the rough, it encompassed more than 520,000 acres straddling the border of North Carolina and Tennessee. It remained for President Roosevelt to demonstrate his support for the park by making a highly publicized journey to the area in September of 1936.

The president's private train left Washington, D.C., on the evening of Tuesday, September 8, arriving in Knoxville the following morning. Local leaders were pleased with the president's decision to begin his combination tour and re-election campaign in their city, hoping it would send a message to future visitors that Knoxville would be the western gateway to the Great Smoky Mountains National Park.

Accompanied by the governors of both Tennessee and North Carolina, plus a pair of United States senators, the presidential motorcade traveled the Old Sevierville Pike to Gatlinburg, where they stopped so the president, while remaining seated in the back seat of his open car, could shake hands with local officials and admirers. Upon their departure from Gatlinburg and the drive toward the North Carolina border, a reporter noted that "the valley grew darker and the chimney tops were barely visible through the clouds. As the ascent quickened, the mist became rain that poured in torrents. After covering the president's car, the motorcade traveled up the steep incline, stopping near the third tunnel because one of the buses filled with out-of-town newspapermen overheated. Cooling water from a nearby creek was added to the radiator and the ascent continued."

The entire group ate lunch atop Clingman's Dome, where the manager of the Andrew Johnson Hotel in Knoxville had sent a truck full of "fried chicken, caviar and cheese sandwiches, crab salad, fruit, crackers, sardines and soft drinks, laid out on tables and served by waiters in white coats. Although the rain came again, Roosevelt studied the view and smoked a cigarette in a short holder after lunch. Governor McAlister asked Roosevelt what he thought about the park. The president told him he was 'very impressed by it,' but he was concerned that 'too many tourists will come to the park before we are ready for them.' "

At a brief stop at the Cherokee Reservation just inside the North Carolina border, the president was given an elaborate feathered headdress and conferred with the title of Chief White Feather. The president declined an offer to attempt a shot using a 10-foot blow-gun, as it would have necessitated him getting out of the car, something he was reluctant to do in public.

Although the Secret Service agents dressed in their white suits, dark ties and straw hats had problems getting all of the Cherokee children off the car's running boards, the motorcade finally headed down the eastern slope of the mountain range, passing through the towns of Sylva, Dillsboro and Waynesville on its way into the valley of the French Broad River and Asheville.

After a night spent sleeping on the train and a long day traversing from Knoxville through the Great Smoky Mountain National Park, the president was beginning to show his weariness. Ahead of him, though, lay Asheville, with more than 30,000 people expected to line the route leading through downtown, along Charlotte Street and up Macon Avenue, where a welcoming committee of 100 local notables awaited inside the Grove Park Inn. As one reporter observed, "The entire distance of the route the presidential party traveled was lined with men, women and children, white and colored."

Standing at the forefront of the welcoming committee was Colonel Edward Starling, head of the Secret Service, who had arrived the previous day to confer with the Grove Park Inn staff and to make arrangements for the president's comfort and security that evening. The entire south wing of the second floor had been emptied of all guests in anticipation of the president's arrival, and the corner suite, consisting of two rooms at the end of the corridor connected to each other by means of a private vestibule, prepared for him. One room remained set up as the president's bedroom, while the other had been transformed into a sitting and dining room.

As Julia Lytle, a former employee recalled, "He and his party occupied the entire second floor. He had the whole wing to himself. Dr. Bell [a guest] was there before President Roosevelt came and had to be moved to another wing. The Secret Service stayed on the fifth floor, and there were sixteen of them. I suppose they stayed up there and worked shifts guarding the President.

"While the president was here, there were so many flowers the halls were covered with them. Mr. Roosevelt was so pleasant. I shook hands with him. He would come out waving to everyone. It was nice having him here. He walked about on crutches while two men held him by the arms."

Colonel Starling had asked the reporters, photographers and welcoming committee, including Fred Seely, to wait for the president inside the Great Hall, thus enabling Starling and his staff to assist Roosevelt in getting out of the touring car beyond everyone's sight. The presidential motorcade, lead by six state police cars, two Asheville policemen on motorcycles, two Asheville police cars and two cars carrying officers of the Buncombe County Sheriff's Department, roared into the Grove Park Inn's parking area at 5:20 p.m., thirty minutes ahead of schedule.

Once alighted, the president's son John, a sophomore at Harvard, walked alongside his father, providing a firm arm on which the president leaned as he shuffled his stricken legs across the terrace and into the hotel. As one of the reporters noted, "To each member of the committee, the president expressed a few words of thanks for the welcome. Immediately upon shaking the hand of the last of the welcomers, Mr. Roosevelt continued on to the elevator, which took him to his suite of rooms on the second floor of the hotel. After washing up, he lay down for a short rest, while his son John returned to the lobby to greet friends and other notables."

Of the thousands of people on hand to greet the president in Asheville, only two were selected to have dinner with Roosevelt and his son that evening in the privacy of Roosevelt's corner suite: North Carolina Governor J. C. B. Ehringhaus and Fred L. Seely.

One can only wonder what discussions had taken place earlier in the day, as Fred Seely, in addition to no longer having any official connection to the Grove Park Inn, was neither an elected public official nor a ranking member of the Democratic party. Among those who were passed over for the coveted spot at the president's table were the mayor of Asheville, the head of the chamber of commerce, publishers of both of Asheville's newspapers, White House secretary Marvin McIntyre, Colonial Starling and members of Roosevelt's personal staff, as well as United States Senator Robert Reynolds, Senator Josiah Bailey, Congressman Zebulon Weaver and Tennessee Governor Bill McAlister.

All were present that evening and all ate together downstairs in the hotel dining room, while Fred Seely dined with the president of the United States.

Fred Seely still had clout -- and he still had connections.

According to a newspaper reporter who interviewed members of the staff the following day, President Roosevelt, his son, the governor of North Carolina and Fred Seely were treated to "assorted hors de oeuvres, consisting of foie gras, Beluga caviar, sardines and lobster Bellevue. He next had tomato juice frappe and then cream of chicken soup. His sirloin steak was garnished with tomatoes, mushrooms, sweet peas, carrots and potatoes. The president's vegetables requested by him from the regular menu were stewed corn, garden broccoli with Hollandaise sauce and whipped white potatoes. The corn was stewed in pure cream and the potatoes were whipped in cream and butter. The president also requested for his dessert fresh strawberry parfait Chantilly. A demitasse concluded the meal."

The reporter went on to note that "A. C. Dryer, chief steward of the Grove Park Inn, proved himself an ardent admirer of the president and the New Deal when he provided a clever ornament, modeled of mutton fat in the shape of a "horn of plenty" for Mr. Roosevelt's tray. Beautiful white, yellow and pink roses extended from the mouth of the horn. The chef said he meant the "horn of plenty" to show the state of the nation under Mr. Roosevelt. Mr. Dryer said the president expressed himself as greatly pleased with the meal and showed it by eating heartily."

The presidential suite, it was also noted, had been "decorated with a large assortment of flowers, including dahlias, asters and gladiolas," many of which were delivered the following day to a hospital in Gastonia en route to Charlotte.

At the conclusion of dinner, President Roosevelt excused himself, calling in his secretary with whom he worked the remainder of the evening in his room on the speeches he was scheduled to give the following day both in Asheville and Charlotte. As a reporter also observed, in addition to four United States marshals who, along with Colonel Starling, met the president upon his arrival at the Grove Park Inn, "the Chief Executive was well-guarded at the hotel last night. A Secret Service man maintained an all-night vigil in front of the presidential suite. Other presidential guards strolled about the lobby and grounds of the hotel. The city police department had nine plainclothes officers and eight or nine motorcycle policemen in the vicinity of the Grove Park Inn last night."

A sidebar article appearing the following afternoon in the *Asheville Citizen* revealed that the president's son John chose not to remain in his father's room after dinner:

*A score or more of Asheville girls received a genuine thrill last night at the Grove Park Inn, when they danced with John Roosevelt, the youngest son of President Roosevelt. The Harvard sophomore, who accompanied the president here yesterday, appeared to greatly enjoy the impromptu social function,*

*The dance was arranged early last evening at the request of some of the newspaper correspondents in the presidential party. The president's son was invited to attend and he readily agreed. Young Roosevelt, a tall, handsome boy, proved to have a pleasing personality and was very democratic. The Buccaneers orchestra played.*

The following morning the president had breakfast in his room as he put the finishing touches on his two speeches, the first to be delivered at eleven o'clock at nearby McCormick Field. After reading and signing papers a courier had driven overnight from Washington, Roosevelt's secretary announced that there were a few special visitors who wished to meet him, namely family members of local and state politicians, as well as "a group of small girls [who had been] permitted to go up to the presidential suite and shake hands with him. One returned to the lobby of the hotel carefully guarding her right hand, declaring she would be very careful not to wash off the chief executive's 'touch.' "

As another reporter noted, "More than a hundred guests and visitors assembled in the lobby and in front of the Grove Park Inn long before President Roosevelt made his appearance, anxiously inquiring if there was any possibility of shaking hands with him. Outside of the hostelry, uniformed policemen of the state highway department were busily engaged arranging automobiles in the motorcade that would escort the president to Charlotte. Both inside and out, Secret Service men hustled about, completing final arrangements for his departure. Newspaper photographers paced the driveway impatiently, waiting for a chance to photograph the chief executive as he left. One reporter noted:

"Before the president stepped from the elevator, Secret Service men cleared the spectators to one side of the lane, then quickly and methodically the men who form the president's bodyguards stepped closely around him, as he walked slowly to his car which had been pulled into the porte cochere."

Of the hundreds of photographs that were taken that morning, none were published showing the president struggling with his crutches, clutching the arm of his son or being lifted by Secret Service agents into his open Packard. Once the president had settled into the rear seat, he was joined by his son John and Governor Ehringhaus. As the Secret Service agents and the president's staff scrambled to get into their cars, a reporter noted that "an old lady who had been standing close by calmly stepped to the side of the automobile and shook hands with the chief executive."

By the time the presidential motorcade left the Grove Park Inn, it included the governors of North Carolina and Tennessee, six senators, congressmen and state representatives, a United States marshal and postmaster, and the mayor of Asheville. "Several more cars were added to the motorcade," it was noted in the Asheville newspaper, "which on Tuesday was limited to ten automobiles. Behind the president's machine were cars carrying Secret Service men, reporters and photographers, and in the rear of the procession was a service car driven by a mechanic."

The motorcade, by now more than thirty minutes behind schedule, slowly made its way down Macon Avenue and Charlotte Street, where "virtually every bit of standing room on the sidewalks leading to the entrance of McCormick Field was packed with people. The unbroken line extended across every intersection along the route." The same reporter described the president as "sunburned, and seemingly in the 'pink of condition' for the fall election campaign; [he was] in a genial mood and wearing a broad smile, and acknowledged the applause by waiving gaily. He responded with a wave of his hat and with a cheery 'hello' to children along the route."

Hours earlier, the first of more than 20,000 people began streaming into McCormick Field, quickly filling every available seat. A reporter estimated that "another 5,000 persons stood or sat in automobiles outside the municipal baseball park, unable to gain admittance when the gates were closed twenty minutes before the presidential party arrived at 11:40 o'clock."

The Secret Service, however, had no intention of letting anyone in attendance that day notice that the polio-stricken president relied on either crutches or a wheelchair. Members of the presidential advance team had arrived in Asheville ahead of Roosevelt, conferring not only with the Grove Park Inn's staff and local law enforcement officials, but with the groundskeeping crew at McCormick Field as well. By the time the president's Packard reached the stadium, a section of the outfield wall just wide enough for a car to pass through had been removed, and a lane cordoned off. When the president's car approached, the sea of people parted, allowing the president's driver to slowly guide the Packard through the opening, across the field to home plate, positioning the car to give Roosevelt a clear view of the crowd seated in the grandstand. Without even needing to stand, the president turned in his seat and spoke:

*Yesterday and today I am carrying out a promise to myself made nearly thirty years ago, because it was nearly thirty years ago that I was last in Asheville. In those days I said to myself that I wanted to come back. I wanted to see all this marvelous country and go up into these Great Smoky Mountains. I suppose in those days I could not have gotten there in an automobile or even in a horse and buggy.*

*So, I came on this pleasure trip, and it has been a pleasure every single minute. I have been tremendously impressed with what we are doing in opening up the Smoky Mountains through this great national park. I am not the only one impressed, because the number of visitors up there in the park has so far outstripped road building and facilities that it is a problem as to how to handle the people.*

*As some of you perhaps know, there is nothing in Nature I am as fond of as a tree. Here in North Carolina and across the line in Tennessee we have without question the most wonderful tree growth in all the United States -- trees that perhaps are not quite so big as some of the trees of the Pacific Coast, but I am told by all the experts and scientists -- you might call them 'brain trusters' -- that there are more varieties of trees and shrubbery and flowers down here than anywhere else.*

*I hope to come back in the years to come, either as a government servant or as a private citizen -- it makes very little difference which. I want to come back and spend some time seeing the new roads that are going to be opened, seeing more of this wonderful part of the United States. And I am quite sure that millions of other Americans are going to come down here, as I want to come, and spend more time. So, you might just as well get ready now to receive them.*

"A Presidential Secret"

At the close of his speech, which was interrupted several times by applause and laughter, the president thanked his supporters and, on cue, the driver started the car and slowly made his way in a large circle around the ball field and out through the opening in the outfield wall. After leaving McCormick Field, the presidential motorcade wound its way down the Charlotte Highway toward Lake Lure, crossing over the Eastern Continental Divide at the top of Hickory Hut Gorge, and passing through the villages of Bat Cave and Chimney Rock on its way to the Lake Lure Inn.

After a brief lunch under an umbrella on the inn's lawn, from which President Roosevelt could view the placid waters of the man-made lake, the group continued on its way. As one reporter observed, "Thousands of people lined the sidewalks of Rutherford County towns and villages to catch a glimpse of the president. A sudden, heavy downpour of rain failed to dampen their ardor. Those fortunate enough to possess a good vantage point along the road or street held their places, despite the soaking rain. Between ten and twelve thousand gathered in Forest City alone to greet the chief magistrate."

Anxious to see as many people as possible, the president declined the offer by his Secret Service agents to pull the top up on his open touring car. As a 13-year-old girl from nearby Hollis School recalled, "I was standing on the side of the road and was waving and calling to him. I felt that his eyes made contact with mine and that he waved directly at me. I was happy to see the President of the United States. I felt his greeting was personal."

In downtown Shelby, thousands of residents and school children had also lined the presidential route, "where banners of welcome had been displayed and thousands lined the street for miles, filling the windows of store buildings and perched in trees. For hours they waited in the boiling sun."

Just as the motorcade approached Shelby, however, the president's car suddenly veered off course, making an unscheduled detour down an empty side street. Unaware of what was happening, those in the crowd continued straining their necks waiting for the president's car to appear at the far end of Marion Street. By the time they realized the driver had taken an unexpected detour, the motorcade had reappeared behind them, headed on toward Charlotte.

It remained for the colorful former Governor Max Gardner to later reveal to a reporter exactly what had prompted the sudden change in the president's route. As the president's lunch began to settle, Gardner explained, Roosevelt "notified the pace-setting patrolmen that he needed to void his kidneys in a bottle that he always carried in the car. Seeing a patch of woods on West Warren Street as they approached the city from the west, the patrolmen routed the official car over a street one block from where the people had gathered and the banners of welcome had been displayed."

Once the president had finished relieving himself, the North Carolina highway patrolmen, anxious to stay on schedule, continued up Warren Street for several blocks before turning back onto Marion Street. They re-entered the main thoroughfare beyond the central business district, where the mayor, the town councilmen and several hundred disappointed citizens and schoolchildren stood stunned, still waiting beneath the red, white and blue bunting hanging from their porches and storefronts.

Despite possibly losing a few votes that day in Shelby, President Roosevelt rode his New Deal programs to re-election four months later, carrying North Carolina and 98% of the country's electoral votes on his way to the most lopsided victory in the history of presidential politics.

One sidebar:

In 1937, President Roosevelt established the National Foundation for Infantile Paralysis. His friend, the songwriter and actor Eddie Cantor, suggested a plan to help raise money for the foundation, whose goal was to provide care to polio victims and to support polio research. Cantor suggested that the president call the foundation "The March of Dimes," urging everyone send a dime for polio research to the president.

Tens of thousands of dimes soon began pouring into the White House, and in 1938 the March of Dimes made its first research grant to Yale University. By 1955, the year when the long-awaited Salk vaccine was declared safe and effective, the March of Dimes had raised more than $25 million dollars for research. Although Roosevelt did not live to see the vaccine, he was so closely associated with the March of Dimes that Congress honored his contribution by putting his image on the dime.

The first Roosevelt dimes were released on January 30, 1946, commemorating both the president's birthday and the start of the annual March of Dimes campaign.

*Harvey Firestone, Thomas Edison, and Harvey Firestone Junior pose for the photographers gathered outside the Grove Park Inn in August of 1918.*

# Chapter 17

# "Famous Early Guests"

*We feel that a glance at the list of our regular patrons*
*is sufficient proof of our claim that Grove Park Inn is the*
*Finest Resort Hotel in the World.*

Frederick L. Seely, President

When the Grove Park Inn opened on July 12, 1913, newspapers proclaimed it "the finest resort hotel in the world." Just an overnight train ride from New York, Washington, Pittsburgh and Chicago, the new hotel soon began attracting politicians, industrialists, entertainers and businessmen. Fred Seely, who served as president from 1913 through 1927, and as an unofficial advisor to the hotel's staff until his death in 1942, recognized the importance of such guests to his advertising and public relations plan, even going so far as to publish a list of notable guests on the back of the hotel's stationary and brochures. While many of these names have since faded from history, they serve to underscore the level of service the Grove Park Inn maintained during its early years of operation.

An entire book could be written just about the famous people who have stayed at the Grove Park Inn during its illustrious 100
years atop Sunset Mountain. Instead, included here is a sampling of
some of the guests who stayed at the hotel during its early years. Additional information, especially on some of the more recent guests,
can be gleaned from the photographs displayed in the hallways of
the Vanderbilt and Sammons Wings.

**Bela Bartok** (1881-1945) - Plagued by poor health, this great Hungarian composer left his homeland in 1940 rather than live under
Nazi rule. He came to America seeking solace in which he could
work. After a short stay in New York City, which proved too noisy
for the shy and quiet composer, he came to Asheville on the advice of
his physicians and friends, who hoped the surrounding mountains
would remind him of his homeland. He arrived in December of 1943
and is believed to have first stayed at the Grove Park Inn before set-
tling in the nearby Albemarle Inn, then a quiet boarding house just
a few blocks from the hotel. While in Asheville, Bartok completed
his famous "Concerto for Orchestra," as well as his "Solo Sonata for
Violin" and "Piano Concerto No. 3," also known as the "Asheville
Concerto." He returned to New York in April of 1944, dying the following year of leukemia at age 64.

**Gutzon Borglum** (1867-1941) - The famed sculptor of Mount Rush-
more was born in Idaho, trained at the Academie Julian in Paris
(where he met Auguste Rodin), then settled in New York City where
his reputation as a talented, but temperamental artist who preferred
to demonstrate his themes of nationalism on gigantic scales, was
soon established. In 1915 he began designing a memorial to the leaders of the Confederacy on Stone Mountain, Georgia. The first cut was

made in 1923, but Borglum soon began quarreling with the sponsors, the United Daughters of the Confederacy. Enraged with their suggestions, in 1925 he destroyed all of his drawings and models, fled the site and retreated to North Carolina, safely out of reach of the Georgia warrants being sworn out for his arrest. Borglum stayed at the Grove Park Inn that July, and reportedly traveled to Chimney Rock on July 20, where he deemed the exposed rock outcroppings unsuitable for a potential sculpture.

**William Jennings Bryan** (1860-1925) - A close friend of Fred Seely, Bryan delivered the keynote address at the opening on July 12, 1913, then returned that fall with Mrs. Bryan. They enjoyed Asheville so much that they eventually built a home at the foot of Sunset Mountain on one of E. W. Grove's lots. Bryan reportedly enjoyed eating 'possum stew' while staying at the Grove Park Inn.

**Asa Candler** (1851-1929) - While John Pemberton was the true inventor of Coca-Cola, it was Asa Candler who made the Atlanta-based soft drink famous through his astute marketing and advertising campaigns. Candler and Fred Seely are believed to have met while Seely was publisher of the *Atlanta Georgian* (1906-1912), and Candler subsequently made several trips to the Grove Park Inn.

**Enrico Caruso** (1873-1921) - After Fred Seely had his famed Skinner organ installed in the Great Hall of the Grove Park Inn, the Italian tenor was engaged to entertain guests gathered there. According to hotel lore, "Caruso was said to be quite demanding, requiring sixteen pure goose down pillows on his bed to comfortably support his large frame."

**Irvin Cobb** (1876-1944) - A popular American humorist often compared to Mark Twain, Irvin Cobb was at one time the highest paid reporter in the entire country (for the *New York World*). Cobb lived in New York, writing more than sixty books and 300 short stories, several of which were adapted into both silent and sound movies. He was once described as having "a round shape, bushy eyebrows, full lips, a triple chin and always a cigar in his mouth." In addition to appearing in at least ten films, Cobb also hosted the 1935 Academy Awards. Cobb often traveled on the vaudeville circuit, which may be what brought him to Asheville and the Grove Park Inn, although one reference has him coming there to recuperate from exhaustion. Given his prolific and varied career, that would not seem far from the truth.

Cobb is best known in the folklore of the Grove Park Inn for an incident that reportedly took place in the Great Hall. While entertaining a group of friends, Cobb is believed to have violated Fred Seely's rule for only speaking in low, subdued tones while in the hotel's lobby. A bellman, undoubtedly acting on orders either from Seely or the general manager, approached the comedian and handed him a small card. While none of the cards have survived, it apparently asked the recipient to speak more quietly so as not to disturb the other guests.

According to legend, Cobb read the card, then, in an exaggerated manner, proceeded to untie and remove his shoes, held them up for all to see before he tiptoed dramatically over to the front desk, where he asked for his bill so that he might leave.

**Ty Cobb** (1886-1961) - Like other players of his era, the famous third baseman for the Detroit Tigers traveled south for spring training and exhibition games in minor league stadiums. While in Asheville he stayed at the Grove Park Inn and took time to autograph baseballs for guests in the Great Hall. Ty Cobb set more than ninety records during his illustrious career, and still holds the record for the highest lifetime batting average (.367) and stealing home the most times (54). Ironically, he also still holds the record for most errors by an outfielder. When the very first balloting was conducted for the inaugural Hall of Fame, Ty Cobb received more votes than any other player in baseball history.

**Calvin Coolidge** (1872-1933) - Vice-President Coolidge and his wife chose the Grove Park Inn for two weeks of relaxation in February of 1921, shortly after Coolidge and President Warren Harding had been elected. When President Harding died in August of 1923, Coolidge became the 30th President of the United States. Fred Seely named a special red homespun cloth produced at Biltmore Industries "Coolidge Red," in honor of Mrs. Coolidge. The small token netted the company more national publicity than any amount of advertising could have generated.

**Thomas Edison** (1847-1931) - The famed inventor accompanied Henry Ford and Harvey Firestone on their widely publicized camping trip, which ended at the Grove Park Inn in August of 1918. Edison had actually opposed Ford's suggestion that they forego their cots and tents for a night of luxury of the Grove Park Inn, but had been convinced by Ford (who was bringing the group and several reporters as a favor to Fred Seely) to come to the Grove Park Inn for the benefit of 81-year-old John Burroughs (see Chapter 12).

**Harvey Firestone** (1868-1938) - The founder of the Firestone Tire and Rubber Company made his first trip to Asheville and the Grove

Park Inn along with Henry Ford and Thomas Edison in August of 1918 (see Chapter 12). He returned in June of 1931 when attending his son's graduation ceremony at Asheville School.

**Henry Ford** (1863-1947) - The world famous automobile manufacturer and his wife first visited the Grove Park Inn in 1916, but it was his return trip with his camping buddies Thomas Edison and Harvey Firestone in August of 1918 that was featured in newspapers across the country (see Chapter 12).

**Herbert Hoover** (1874-1964) - In 1900 Fred and Evelyn Seely reportedly met Herbert and Lou Hoover in China, and remained lifelong friends afterwards. When Hoover's son was diagnosed with tuberculosis and subsequently came to Asheville to recuperate, President Hoover and the First Lady visited him in November of 1930 and in April of 1931; they stayed both at the Grove Park Inn and in Seely's home.

**Harry Houdini** (1874-1926) - Born in Hungary as Erik Weisz, Harry Houdini gained fame for his amazing ability to perform death-defying escapes from chains, straightjackets and handcuffs while hung from skyscrapers, held under water, buried alive or locked in trunks. Critics remain divided on which of his feats were fabricated solely to keep his audience in suspense, but no one doubts his ability to twist, contort and disjoint his body as he made his escapes. Even his death remains shrouded in mystery. According to reports, while being interviewed by a student, the 52-year-old Houdini stated that his stomach was hard enough to absorb any blow, at which point the student slammed his fist into the magician's stomach. Unprepared, Harry Houdini doubled over in pain, and a few days later died of a ruptured appendix. Whether or not the blow led to his death remains a topic of speculation.

The "Handcuff King" toured Europe and the United States, performing his feats of escape on vaudeville tours to packed opera houses in major cities and small towns. For years he was the highest paid member of the troupe and became quite wealthy. In 1912 Houdini introduced his most famous act, the Chinese Water Torture Cell, in which he was suspended upside down in a water-filled case while he escaped his chains and padlocks. Doing so required that he be able to hold his breath for three minutes.

When in Asheville, Harry Houdini performed at the former Opera House, as well as at the Kenilworth Inn and in Montford's Homewood Castle, generally staying at the Grove Park Inn.

**Al Jolson** (1886-1950) - According to former employee Julia Lytle, the famous actor and singer "had a throat condition and stayed in the inn for several months. He always wore a black scarf around his neck and talked real low because of his throat. He liked to tease one of the bellhops -- asking him when he was coming up to his room to fit him for a casket."

**Bobby Jones** (1902-1971) - Known for his prowess on the golf course, Bobby Jones was also a Harvard graduate and respected attorney. In 1930 the "Grand Slam Kid" astonished the golfing world by winning the American Open, the American Amateur Open, the British Amateur Open and the British Open. He loved playing the Donald Ross courses in Asheville and often stayed at the Grove Park Inn.

**Margaret Mitchell** (1900-1949) - The famous author of the 1936 best seller *Gone With the Wind* (her only novel) honeymooned at the

Grove Park Inn after her first marriage on September 2, 1922. Unfortunately, her first husband was an abusive alcoholic, and the marriage ended after just four months. She later married John Marsh, her lifelong friend and the best man at her first wedding. Tragically, she was struck and killed by a speeding taxi as she and Marsh were on their way to see a play in Atlanta when she was just 49 years old.

**Dr. B. J. Palmer** (1881-1961) - The "Father of Chiropractic Medicine" was a close friend of both Elbert Hubbard and Fred Seely, and furnished his home and office with Roycroft furniture, including a grandfather clock similar to one in the Grove Park Inn. Palmer visited the inn frequently, where he reportedly worked on his famous book *The Bigness of the Fellow Within.*

**General John J. Pershing** (1860-1948) - Nearing the end of a national tour in 1920, General John J. Pershing, commander of the U.S. Army during World War I, arrived in Asheville in February. Despite an influenza quarantine, hundreds were on hand to see Pershing's private rail car, attached to the Carolina Special, pull into Biltmore Station. During his stay General Pershing was led on a tour by Fred Seely, including a stop at the Oteen Veterans Hospital. Among those who greeted the general at the Grove Park Inn was Margaret Wilson, daughter of President Woodrow Wilson. Seely hosted a luncheon for General Pershing and Margaret Wilson on February 20, 1920.

**Wiley Post** (1899-1935) - The famed American aviator who held the world record in 1931 for flying around the northern part of the earth, Wiley Post worked for Lockheed Aviation, often flying groups to Asheville to visit the Grove Park Inn. He and his good friend Will Rogers died in a plane crash in Alaska in 1935.

**Will Rogers** (1879-1935) - An Oklahoma cowboy turned humorist and vaudeville entertainer, Will Rogers traveled with the Ziegfeld Follies beginning in 1915 and became one of the highest paid performers of his era. When booked to appear in the Asheville Opera House, he stayed at the Grove Park Inn. He may have first met Fred Seely when Seely published the *Atlanta Georgian* (1906-1912). Rogers made a successful transition from the vaudeville stage to Hollywood, appearing in more than seventy films between 1918 and his death in 1935. In 1934, he was voted the most popular male actor in America.

Will Rogers also reigned as one of the most popular newspaper columnists and reporters of his day, penning more than 6,000 columns and six books, while also becoming a radio personality noted for his folksy humor and gentle criticism of politicians. He developed into a nationally respected political pundit, and became a regular guest of Presidents Calvin Coolidge and Franklin Roosevelt at the White House.

Tragically, the private plane carrying Will Rogers and Wiley Post to an Alaskan fishing trip crashed on August 15, 1935, killing both men. Will Rogers was 55. President Roosevelt dedicated his memorial a few years later. Among Will Rogers' most famous lines are the following:

*Everything is changing. People are taking the comedians seriously and the politicians as a joke.*
*A fool and his money are soon elected.*
*Americans will feed anyone that's not close to them.*
*Our foreign policy is an open book -- a checkbook.*
*I belong to no organized party -- I'm a Democrat.*
*People who fly into a rage always make a bad landing.*

*If there are no dogs in Heaven, then when I die I want to go where they went.*

*The income tax has made more liars out of Americans than golf.*

*If stupidity got us in this mess, why can't it get us out?*

*When I die, my epitaph, or whatever you call those signs on gravestones, is going to read: "I joked about every prominent man of my time, but I never met a man I didn't like." I am so proud of that, I can hardly wait to die so it can be carved.*

**John D. Rockefeller Jr.** (1874-1960) - In a newspaper interview published in 1967, former employee Julia F. Lytle told the story of how John D. Rockefeller Jr., head of the Standard Oil Company and U.S. Steel, and his wife stopped at the inn. The couple, which she described as "devout churchgoers," attended Sunday services at First Baptist Church, where Rockefeller left what must have been a sizable check in the collection plate. An account of what happened afterwards appears in the Grove Park Inn archives:

*The Rockefellers returned to the Grove Park Inn and left word at the desk with Mrs. Lytle that they didn't want to be disturbed for a while.*

*"Once the pastor of the church got a look at the check," said Mrs. Lytle, "he just dropped everything and came to the Grove Park Inn to thank Rockefeller. I told the minister I couldn't disturb Rockefeller -- and that he and his wife were resting."*

*"Wealthy visitors at the inn," she went on, "usually tipped the bellhops and other service personnel well before they left -- in the range of $10 to $20 a person."*

*However, Rockefeller proved to be different, according to Mrs.*

Lytle, "He tipped me $2 when he finished his stay at the hotel, and I had gone to bat for him, keeping the people off his back."

"In contrast," she added, "novelist Zane Grey tipped everybody $10 when he left the Grove Park Inn."

According to hotel reports, John Rockefeller Jr. returned to the Grove Park Inn several times to rest and play golf. Despite his reputation at the Grove Park Inn as a poor tipper, Roosevelt was a major contributor to the development of the Great Smoky Mountain National Park project.

**Eleanor Roosevelt** (1884-1962) - The wife of President Franklin D. Roosevelt often traveled on her own, generally accompanied on her journeys by her own personal staff. On July 4, 1934, she stayed at the Grove Park Inn for the first time as part of her trip through the South in search of information on handcrafts, especially weaving. She met Fred Seely at Biltmore Industries, who also took her to Tryon to tour Tryon Toymakers. The First Lady returned to Asheville and the Grove Park Inn in April of 1937. Her April 15 newspaper column included the following: "I had very pleasant memories of Grove Park Inn, so we went there for the night, arriving about 5:00 o'clock. The view from our windows out over the golf course is very pleasing and the hotel itself is a most restful spot."

**Charles Schwab** (1862-1939) - The American steel magnate and first president of U.S. Steel had accumulated an enormous fortune by the turn of the century. As a wedding gift, he gave his wife a 60-carat diamond ring and a $4 million dollar (in 1905 dollars) mansion in Palm Beach. After a vacation in Asheville, he wrote back to his host Fred Seely, "I have always the most delightful recollections of your splendid establishment, and be sure that when we do have time to spend away from our own home, we will come to visit you."

**William Howard Taft** (1857-1930) - After serving as the 27th President (1909-1913), Taft was appointed Chief Justice of the Supreme Court, serving in that capacity from 1921 until his death in 1930. While Chief Justice, Taft contracted bladder cancer and stayed at the Grove Park Inn from January 16 until February 3, 1930. When his condition worsened, he returned to Washington, where he died on March 8. According to the *Citizen-Times*, his favorite pastime at the Grove Park Inn was to "pace back and forth on the terrace, where he could look out across the French Broad Valley in the direction of the Blue Ridge Mountains."

**Bill Tilden** (1893-1953) - "Big Bill" Tilden was the most popular tennis player of his era, winning seven U.S. singles championships and the British singles crown three times. His tours often included Asheville, where he played at the Grove Park Inn and the Biltmore Forest Country Club, and stayed at the Grove Park Inn.

**Edith Vanderbilt** (1873-1958) - While the mistress of the 250-room Biltmore Estate may never have found it necessary to actually sleep at the Grove Park Inn, she did visit it and the adjacent Biltmore Industries on several occasions. What remains unclear is whether or not her husband, George Vanderbilt, ever toured the hotel in the brief time between it's opening on July 12, 1913, and his sudden death eight months later on March 6, 1914, in Washington, D.C.

## Other Notable Guests

Between 1921 and his departure in 1928, Fred Seely published on the back of the official Grove Park Inn stationary a list of prominent individuals who had stayed at the hotel. Among more than 200 other notables, including company presidents and founders, who stayed at the Grove Park Inn during those early years were:

| | |
|---|---|
| H. J. Heinz (Heinz Foods) | E. M. Statler (Statler Hotels) |
| Sir John and Lady Eaton | Sir Edward and Lady Murray |
| Charles Mayo (Mayo Clinic) | William Mayo (Mayo Clinic) |
| George F. Baker (industrialist) | Louis Swift (industrialist) |
| Dr. John Harvey Kellogg | Horatio Seymour (reporter) |
| John Burroughs (author) | Helen Keller (author) |
| H. J. Funk (Funk & Wagnalls) | Josephus Daniels (Sec. of the Navy) |
| Jane Addams (author) | Tracy Drake (Blackstone Hotels) |
| Margaret Woodrow Wilson | John Morron (Portland Cement) |
| H. S. Scott (Detroit News) | W. T. Noonan (B.R. & P. Railway) |
| Pleasant Stovall (ambassador) | William Proctor (Proctor & Gamble) |
| Henry May (Pierce-Arrow Co.) | W. H. Danforth (Ralston Purina) |
| Mitchell Palmer (Attorn. Gen.) | W. C. Greer (Goodrich Company) |
| Arthur Hunger (Atlas Steel) | Ernest Skinner (Skinner Organ Co.) |
| H. G. Chilton (British Embassy) | F. R. Scoffield (Lake Eric Iron Co.) |
| Senator Clarence Case | W. E. Moss (American State Bank) |
| John Carstensen (N.Y. Railroad) | Senator Harry Reynolds |
| Gov. Jason Higgins | F. L. Klingensmith (Ford Motor Co.) |
| A. Houghton (Corning Glass) | George Jay Gould (Financier) |
| Judge W. L. Carpenter | George Crosby (Rock Island Lines) |
| Amy E. Du Pont | Gov. Edwin Warfield |
| Cornelius Vanderbilt | Duchess de Chaulnes |
| Senator George Oliver | Arthur Davis (president, Alcoa) |

*More than a few brides and servicemen, who married just before they enlisted, later celebrated their honeymoons during a two-week furlough at the Grove Park Inn.*

# Chapter 18

# "World War II:
# The Grove Park Inn Enlists"

*The selection of Asheville for these purposes is, of course,*
*a great compliment to the community. By this token it*
*is recognized as one of the most desirable places for leisure*
*and recreation in the country. For those soldiers who may*
*come here, this community will show the utmost courtesy*
*and hospitality. They deserve from us the best that we*
*have, and the best they will receive.*

*Asheville Citizen-Times*
*July 23, 1944*

As America struggled to emerge from the deadly grip of the
Great Depression, news began filtering into Asheville of the tension
steadily building in Europe. The rise of the Nazi Party in Germany
under the leadership of Adolph Hitler may initially have seemed like
distant political drama to many, but when the German army invaded Poland, prompting France and then Great Britain to declare war

on Germany, history seemed ready to repeat itself. Just as President Woodrow Wilson had struggled to maintain the country's neutrality from 1914 through 1917, President Franklin D. Roosevelt, while sympathetic to the plight of the French and British people, continued to resist Winston Churchill's entreaties to join the Allies in their fight to curtail Nazi domination of Europe.

The quiet uneasiness which had settled over the United States was shattered on the morning of December 7, 1941, when the Japanese air force launched an unprovoked attack on the United States' military base in Hawaii. Within days the battle lines were drawn, as the United States officially joined the war against Japan, Italy and Germany.

Like other cities across the country, Asheville immediately began contributing to the war effort. As young men lined up at the local recruiting stations, families began gathering scrap metal, planting victory gardens, buying war bonds and curtailing their consumption of gasoline and other precious commodities diverted to the soldiers and sailors making their way across the Atlantic and Pacific Oceans. Even the Biltmore House played a role, as hundreds of priceless works of art from the National Gallery of Art were secretly crated, shipped and stored inside the 250-room limestone mansion until the end of the war.

Ownership of the 141-room Grove Park Inn had recently fallen back into the hands of the St. Louis Union Trust Company, albeit reluctantly, which had held the mortgage on the property. The trust company then formed the Grove Park Inn, Inc., with John L. Nordman serving as president. Struggling just to keep the inn open, the staff and general manager Lawrence I. Hollandsworth soon discovered the Grove Park Inn was about to play a unique and unusual role in the war effort.

Once congress had declared war, the United States government moved quickly to arrest hundreds of German, Japanese, Hungarian, Bulgarian and Italian diplomats, along with their families and household staff, then living in Washington. The government wanted the diplomats removed from Washington, yet confined in safe living quarters until they could be exchanged for American diplomats being held in foreign countries. In addition to seizing their offices and papers, the United States government also froze their personal bank accounts. They presented the owners of the Grove Park Inn with a simple plan: in lieu of their regular guests, the Grove Park Inn's staff would provide accommodations for a minimum of 225 diplomats and family members. Money was not an issue, as the government would pay the hotel with funds withdrawn from the diplomats' bank accounts.

As the March 30, 1942, edition of the *Asheville Citizen* reported, "Members of the diplomatic and consular corps of three countries, Italy, Bulgaria and Rumania, and possibly Hungary, will be the guests of the United States government at the inn until an exchange of diplomatic internees can be arranged, or for the duration. More than 200 persons, including the members of the families and servants of the diplomats, are expected to be brought here. It was explained by the state department that the best of treatment, by old custom, was always accorded to interned diplomats, in order that the persons representing this or other nations in enemy countries might receive the same treatment."

On April 3, 1942, without any public announcement, two trains arrived in Asheville carrying 242 of the diplomats and their families from Washington. They were quickly loaded onto busses and driven directly to the Grove Park Inn, where they were met by representatives from the state department and the hotel staff. Though treated by the staff as guests, the diplomats and their families were completely cut off from the outside world. They were not allowed to send or receive telegrams, to make telephone calls or to meet friends or outside family members.

The grounds of the hotel remained unfenced, but armed guards patrolled the perimeter, preventing any of the new guests from leaving. Anxious to secure the return of American officials being held abroad, the government quickly arranged for an exchange of diplomats. Just as quietly as they arrived, one month later the diplomats and their families were bussed back to the railway station and returned to Washington and, eventually, to their homelands.

Life at the Grove Park Inn, however, was not about to return to normal. The owners were again approached, this time by the Special War Problems Division of the U.S. State Department, which ran a small group of their own internment facilities during World War II. "Special war problems," the staff learned, "included diplomats and consular corps staff, as well as executives from Axis-owned businesses, from both the United States and Latin American countries. These prisoners were housed in hotels and elegant resorts, pending repatriation." In addition to the Grove Park Inn, foreign nationals were also confined within the Greenbrier Hotel in West Virginia, as well as the Homestead Hotel, the Cascade Inn, the Ingleside Hotel and the Shenvalee Hotel, all in Virginia.

A State Department memorandum in 1942 reported that 785 people were interned in these hotels, including "363 Japanese, 212 Germans, 113 Italians, 71 Hungarians, 16 Bulgarians and 10 Romanians. Of this number, 655 diplomats, officials and dependents actually resided at internment hotels from December 1941 to early September 1942." A group of 63 Japanese and 155 German officials and their families arrived in Asheville in late May. They remained at the Grove Park Inn throughout the summer under terms and conditions similar to that enforced upon the diplomatic corps from Italy, Bulgaria and Rumania.

On October 17, 1942, however, the Asheville newspapers announced that the Navy Department had signed a lease with the Grove Park Inn to utilize it "as a rest and recreation center for naval officers who have returned from the war zones. At present," the article went on to state, "the Grove Park Inn is being used for interned enemy nationals, and about 260 Japanese and Germans are now at the hotel. The internees will be moved in the next two or three weeks." The first naval officers were expected to arrive in mid-November, greeted by new general manager Burton S. Frei, a long time employee at the Grove Park Inn.

"Studying the experience of Great Britain," the newspaper explained, "the Navy has learned that men working under strain must be watched. There is a point at which their nerves near the breaking point. Before that point is reached, the plan is to send the officer to the Grove Park Inn for whatever period is necessary to put him back in perfect nerves and physical condition. Periodic rest and recreation have been found necessary, especially in the case of fliers, and most of the guests are expected to be naval aviation officers."

The writer also observed, "since the departure of the last [Japanese and German] aliens, Mr. Frei and his staff have been doing a thorough job of housecleaning in preparation for the new guests. Each of the 141 rooms has been gone over, every piece of furniture cleaned and redecorated where necessary, and a lot of painting has been done. Under the new set-up, the 38-acre grounds will be under guard. The naval officers will be here for rest, and every precaution will be taken to prevent them from being disturbed. No sightseeing will be permitted at the inn or in the grounds."

The Navy's lease expired in June of 1943, at which time the St. Louis Union Trust Company began negotiations to sell the Grove Park Inn to Ike Hall (1896-1986), a well-known Oklahoma real estate developer. On October 27 of that year, Hall reportedly paid between $230,000 - $252,000 for the 30-year-old inn. With no prior hotel experience and a country still locked in a world war, Ike Hall struggled from the very beginning of his tenure. He did, however, acknowledge the need to adopt a new policy in regards to the relations of the hotel to the people of Asheville.

"It will be the policy of the new owners," Ike Hall's statement to the press read, "to promote a better friendship between the inn and the people of this city, and to give it a more important and active place in the life of the community." He went on to say, "Burton S. Frei will continue as manager and the inn will remain open during the winter. The special privileges that have always been accorded guests at the Grove Park Inn by the Asheville Country Club will continue under the new ownership."

On July 23, 1944, Ike Hall and the people of Asheville awoke to discover that the United States government was again coming to Asheville. The front page of the *Citizen-Times* announced that the government was taking over four Asheville hotels and the basement of the city auditorium "as a redistribution center for soldiers who have returned from combat duty." Among the hotels named in the story was the Grove Park Inn. The terms of the lease, which were never officially disclosed, reportedly paid Ike Hall $100,000 per year, plus refurbishments upon the termination.

Officially named the Asheville Redistribution Center, operation of the four hotels and the city auditorium, plus some adjacent vacant retail stores, would require approximately 400 officers, enlisted men and civilians. As the government sources explained, "The returnees sent to this center will be physically and mentally well. All returnees will have had 45 or more days of front line combat duty. They need -- and the army feels they are entitled to -- rest and relaxation and recreation, and under the best and most pleasant conditions possible."

The release went on to explain, "Upon arrival in the United States, the returnees -- officers and enlisted men -- will be given 21-day furloughs to visit their homes. Upon expiration of the 21-day furlough periods, they will be under orders to report to the Asheville Redistribution Center, with permission, if they wish, to bring their wives here to be with them during their stay. The wives will be here at their own expense, but at special government rates. No other members of the returnees families will be permitted to stay with them in the hotels. They will be guests at the hotel, at government expense, just as though they were civilians -- free to rest and play. At some of the other redistribution centers in other parts of the country, Negro soldiers will be cared for."

At the close of their stay in Asheville, estimated to be two weeks long, the soldiers were to receive their next set of orders. Based on the amount of time they had spent in a combat zone, they were either assigned to serve as instructors at one of the military bases or shipped back overseas.

Of the four hotels, the Grove Park Inn was the first designated for those soldiers who were bringing their wives with them. Starting August 20, 1944, the couples were to have use of the inn's recreation facilities, including the riding stables, skeet range and miniature golf, as well as the Asheville Country Club golf course, the club's swimming pool and the two tennis courts.

The first returning soldier to bring his wife with him to Asheville was Corporal Harry Paczynski of Erie, Penn. Assigned to a room at the Grove Park Inn, the couple was able to enjoy their honeymoon courtesy of the United States army. Harry and Mary Paczynski had been married in January of 1942, just days before he was shipped overseas. "We didn't get to have a honeymoon then, so this is our first honeymoon," she explained. As an article in the *Asheville Citizen-Times* reported:

*Both of them were pretty well sold on the inn and the whole setup of the distribution station. "This is certainly a great advantage to fellows coming back. They're 'beat up' and if married have been away from their wives so long that this is a great help," the corporal said.*

*"Yes," added pretty brunette Mary Paczynski, "it helps their morale."*

*"That's it," he emphasized, "it builds up their morale. This place is so nice and quiet. Most fellows who've been in combat will enjoy a nice quiet place to sleep and rest."*

*What was Mrs. Paczynski doing while her husband was overseas? She was working on an assembly line at a plant making bombers for two years. Now she will have about two weeks with him.*

*"They'll have a hard time getting rid of me in two weeks," she said. "I really like it up here. The room, the meals, the scenery -- they're all really nice. All the conveniences you need are right here," Mrs. Paczynski continued.*

*"Yes, sir," the corporal emphatically agreed. "This rest will do a lot of boys a lot of good."*

News of the leasing of Asheville's four major hotels by the government, while viewed as a compliment to the scenic beauty and surroundings of the city, was not welcomed by all concerned. An editorial in the *Citizen-Times*, after describing Asheville as "being a patriotic community," declared that "the War Department has acted unwisely in appropriating for such use so large a portion of the city's hotel facilities. This action will, of course, impose very severe hardships on this community and will result in grave derangements of our civilian life and economy. It will strain to the breaking point our already overtaxed housing, eating and transportation facilities. It will mean that for the duration of the occupancy, Asheville must in effect close its doors to visitors."

In closing the writer was careful to note, however, "that Asheville will do its best to live up to this honor. To the fighting man who has risked the supreme sacrifice in defense of this country and, indeed, in defense of this community, and who may go forth with that high mission again, we will extend the warm, patriotic welcome which is his just due. Nothing less could be expected of us."

The war in Europe ended on May 8, 1945, followed on September 1 with the signing of the terms of surrender with the Japanese government. By 1946, the last of the military personal had left Asheville, and Ike Hall was again in charge of the Grove Park Inn. The lucrative lease with the Department of the Navy had helped offset the cost of the hotel, but now he had to deal with a return to civilian life and a new generation of vacationers.

From nearly all accounts, it would seem that Ike Hall was rarely happy at the Grove Park Inn. According to Asheville businessman Harry Blomberg, who had purchased Biltmore Industries from Fred Seely's heirs, Ike Hall was known to be a heavy drinker, and his drinking increased after his wife and daughter moved back to Oklahoma City. Blomberg was in the Grove Park Inn one evening when Ike Hall got into a heated argument with one of his managers over where a small orchestra should be seated in the Great Hall. When the manager refused to move the musicians, Ike Hall reportedly went back to his office, pulled a gun out of his desk and threatened to shoot him.

While some cosmetic changes had been made to the hotel in the years since the departure of Fred Seely in 1927, what had once been hailed as "the finest resort hotel in the world" was now approaching forty years of age, and was beginning to show it. Ike Hall had neither the resources nor the interest to resurrect the hotel, which also faced the reality of a new style of vacations for the American public. In place of plush railcars and stately hotels, a new, postwar generation of married couples and their families were opting for sleek automobiles and roadside motels.

No one said it any better than television star Diana Shore, who in the early 1950s was urging families watching their new Zenith black-and-white television sets to "See the U.S.A. -- In your Chevrolet."

Tucked away near the top of Sunset Mountain, miles from the nearest major highway, the Grove Park Inn soon began to slip into obscurity, her future becoming as hazy as the clouds which hung over the Blue Ridge Mountains in the distance.

*Returning servicemen and their wives are seen here in 1944 enjoying the view over downtown Asheville from the Arts and Crafts rocking chairs on the Sunset Terrace.*

*Of the five quaint cottages that once stood on the grounds, only the Anne Hathaway Cottage, since renamed the Presidential Cottage, still remains intact and in use.*

# Chapter 19

# "A President in Exile"

*I would rather have a country run like hell by Filipinos*
*than a country run like heaven by the Americans,*
*because however bad a Filipino government might be,*
*we can always change it.*

Manuel L. Quezon, President
Philippine Commonwealth

Soon after the Grove Park Inn opened in 1913, Fred Seely was faced with a problem. While himself a father of four, Fred Seely did not want his guests, those "tired businessmen" he courted with promises of peace and quiet, rest and relaxation, to be bothered by loud and boisterous children running among the plush wicker chairs and rockers in the Great Hall.

But many of his best clients also wanted to bring their entire families with them to the Grove Park Inn.

Fred Seely solved the problem of noisy children in the hotel's restaurant by also including a children's dining room in the lower level, adjacent to the recreation room and the indoor swimming pool. In 1914 he also started construction on a series of cottages snuggled into the hillsides to the east of the hotel. Records indicate that they were named the Van Dyke Cottage, the Sunset Cottage and the Anne Hathaway Cottage. Two other structures, simply called the Engineer's Cottage and the Night Clerk's Cottage, were also erected.

Over the years, as the Grove Park Inn has expanded its parking lots, built the Sammons and Vanderbilt Wings and constructed the Sports Center, all but one of the original cottages has been demolished. The remaining cottage was originally called the Anne Hathaway Cottage, having been inspired by the original cottage where Anne Hathaway, future bride of William Shakespeare, grew up in Stratford-on-Avon. After visits by two notable presidents during the 1940s, however, the cottage was renamed the Presidential Cottage.

At the outset of World War II, only weeks after the Japanese attack on Pearl Harbor in December of 1941, the Japanese army and navy invaded the Philippine Islands. Despite reinforcements provided by the American military under the command of General Douglas MacArthur (1880-1964), the weak and inexperienced Philippine army was soon defeated. In April of 1942, General MacArthur was forced to retreat to Australia, prompting his famous line, "I shall return." He took with him the president of the Philippine Commonwealth, Manuel L. Quezon (1878-1944), who escaped with his family on an American submarine.

Quezon had risen from a modest upbringing to become a respected attorney, military leader and politician, serving in the Philippine congress for three decades. His efforts to obtain Philippine independence were rewarded by his election as the country's first president in 1935. Quezon was so popular that at the close of his second term the country's constitution was amended to allow him to serve as president for a third term.

"A President in Exile"

Quezon, his wife and three children remained in Australia only briefly before being invited by President Franklin D. Roosevelt to establish a government in exile in Washington, D.C. By this time, however, Quezon was suffering from an advanced stage of tuberculosis. He spent the winters of 1942 and 1943 in Miami, where his physicians hoped his health would improve. In April of 1944, rather than returning to Washington, President Quezon and his wife announced they would be traveling to Asheville, where arrangements had been made for him to establish a government in exile in the Anne Hathaway Cottage on the grounds of the Grove Park Inn.

"Asheville will become the temporary capital of the Philippine government while President Quezon is here," the *Asheville Citizen* reported. "Other officials of the Philippine government are functioning in Washington, but during Quezon's stay here the Anne Hathaway Cottage will be the executive headquarters of the government. Direction of official business from here will be by telephone and correspondence."

On April 19, 1944, the 65-year-old president arrived in Asheville from Miami on a private railcar, "The Pioneer," attached to the rear of the Southern Railway train. The chief of staff of the Philippine army, the president's military aide and his secretary, two physicians and their nurses, his chaplain, three servants, a housekeeper and a chauffeur accompanied him and his wife. Their three grown children remained in Washington, D.C.

Quezon had suffered a setback in his recovery shortly before leaving Miami, prompting the decision to travel to Asheville. Word of his pending arrival was kept out of the press until the last possible moment, in part because Quezon was so ill that he had to be transported from his private railcar to the Grove Park Inn in an ambulance. Reporters and photographers were asked not to attempt to interview or photograph the exiled president during his transition.

"The president," his aide was quoted as saying upon their arrival, "has been working incessantly throughout his illness, preparing for the day when his land would be rid of the invading Japanese, and the work of rebuilding his country could begin." With his staff occupying rooms within the Grove Park Inn, Quezon and his wife settled into the Anne Hathaway Cottage, described by a newspaper reporter as being "tastefully furnished, containing a living room with open fire, dining room, kitchen and three bedrooms. Everything was in readiness. In addition to the flowers inside the cottage, jars of white dogwoods adorned the porch of the white-painted stone cottage." As the reporter continued:

*Colonel Nieto, military aide to the president, explained that Asheville's comparative nearness to Washington will make it possible for President Quezon to summon cabinet members and other officials who are there to Asheville for conferences when necessary. The cabinet in Washington carries on the routine governmental affairs, he added, but President Quezon acts upon all matters of major importance, and the staff here will be in daily communication by long distance telephone with the cabinet in Washington.*

*The length of the party's stay in Asheville, he said, will be a minimum of several weeks, and possibly they may remain here for months. It depends chiefly, he added, upon how rapidly President Quezon recovers here. He went from Washington to Miami last December, the military aide said, and some progress was noted there, but Miami is now becoming warm.*

*He emphasized that President Quezon is happy to be here, and expressed the belief that his mental state will greatly aid in his recovery.*

Unfortunately, President Quezon's health continued to decline during his sojourn in Asheville, as his tuberculosis-ravaged lungs weakened daily. In June it was decided to move him once again, this time to a health sanitarium near Saranac Lake, New York. He died there on August 1, 1944, just weeks prior to General MacArthur's successful attack on the Japanese forces occupying the Philippines, prompting his memorable line, "People of the Philippines: I have returned."

--------

Three years later, at dusk on Sunday, April 13, 1947, the chief of staff of the United States Army, General Dwight D. Eisenhower and his wife Mamie, secretly arrived at the Grove Park Inn, where they were greeted by general manager H. L. Thomas and shown to the Anne Hathaway Cottage.

News of the arrival of the Eisenhowers on Sunday evening had been one of the best-kept secrets in Asheville. The general and members of his staff had just finished a grueling fourteen-day inspection of major military bases in the South, traveling by car nearly all of the way. On their way back to Washington, it was decided that the group would rest for two days at the Grove Park Inn, with no public appearances planned for the general.

Accompanying General Eisenhower were his aide Colonel James Stack, War Department officer Major Robert Schulz, his driver Master Sergeant Leonard Dry and Sergeant William Murray.

On Monday, Colonel Stack met with reporters from the *Asheville Citizen-Times* with a proposition: in exchange for providing them with the basic information regarding General Eisenhower's visit, the reporters would need to promise not to reveal where the Eisenhowers were staying in Asheville.

As Colonel Stack explained, "The past two weeks have been strenuous days for General Eisenhower, and they purposely came here unannounced to avoid public appearance and to give the general an opportunity to get a much needed rest before returning to his duties in the nation's capital." Stack also remarked that the stop in Asheville was planned "to give the general an opportunity to view the scenic beauty of Western North Carolina."

*General Dwight Eisenhower and wife Mamie.*

"A President in Exile"

Guests at the Grove Park Inn that weekend may well have never known that the mastermind behind D-Day, the June 6, 1944, invasion of Europe that brought the German army to its knees, was also staying at the hotel. Since the Anne Hathaway Cottage featured its own living room and kitchen, the future president and his wife were able to enjoy their meals in private. Colonel Stack did hint that the couple would be dining at the Grove Park Inn on Monday before their departure Tuesday morning.

The press remained true to their word, reporting in the next day's edition that General and Mrs. Eisenhower were in Asheville, but without any mention of the Grove Park Inn. By the time news of their stay had swept through Asheville, the couple had concluded their visit and were on their way back to Washington.

*Elaine and Charles Sammons, accompanied by general manager Herman von Tres-*
*kow and Ed Leach (right), president of Jack Tar Hotels, pause to admire the historic*
*photographs on display in the Sammons Wing, which opened in 1984.*

# Chapter 20

# "Bought in a Bathroom"

*If the right kind of people got a hold of that old hotel,*
*it could make money.*

Harry Blomberg
Asheville businessman

The year was 1955 and the Grove Park Inn was in trouble.

Once the pride of Asheville, the grand hotel on Sunset Mountain was now 42 years old, and beginning to show her age. Edwin Wiley Grove and Fred L. Seely were but memories of days gone by. Nearly five years of occupation by the United States government, with rooms filled with German diplomats, Japanese prisoners of war and families of returning American servicemen, plus another ten years of neglect, had turned the once-stately queen of Sunset Mountain into an aging spinster dressed in tattered gowns.

Plumbing pipes had begun to leak, the oak Arts and Crafts furniture was out of style, window drapes were unraveling and Fred Seely's famed French rugs were threadbare and faded. Many of the staff had fled, including the wife of owner Ike Hall, taking with her back to Oklahoma their two young daughters. Ike had moved into the Ann Hathaway cottage, located on the hillside just below the sagging gates at the main entrance to the hotel grounds, where he nursed his sorrows with a bottle of Jack Daniels.

War-weary Americans, released from the shackles of government restrictions on everything from sugar and meat to gasoline and tires, enjoyed a newfound prosperity under President Dwight Eisenhower. Returning servicemen and their young families found banks anxious to loan them money to buy homes in the suburbs, where they could escape industrialized downtowns, growing racial friction, failing infrastructures and over-crowded school systems. In their place they could buy a patch of green grass, a modest one-story home, a paved driveway and an attached garage for their new automobile -- and began using their two-week vacations to explore America on an ever-expanding highway system and gasoline that cost only 25 cents a gallon.

While Interstate Highway 40 brought many of them to Asheville, it did not lead them up Sunset Mountain to the Grove Park Inn. Too young to be considered historic and too old to be trendy, the famed hotel that once had served United States presidents, New York socialites and millionaire industrialists sat nearly empty, as shiny new Fords and Buicks filed into the 'motor hotel,' now better known as the motel.

Unable to compete with flashing neon signs, sun-drenched swimming pools and convenient drive-in restaurants, the Grove Park Inn soon teetered on bankruptcy. Ike Hall had neither the money nor the experience to resurrect the spirit of the once-grand hotel. He appeared unable to appeal to young families drawn to Western North Carolina and its growing number of theme parks and attractions, from the Biltmore Estate and the Blue Ridge Highway to the nearby Grandfather Mountain and the Great Smoky Mountain National Park.

Not since July 9, 1912, when Gertrude Grove turned over the first ceremonial shovelful of dirt, had the Grove Park Inn been in such desperate need of a strong leader with a plan for the future and the means to accomplish it.

A man such as Charles A. Sammons.

Born in Ardmore, Oklahoma, on June 5, 1898, Charles Sammons and his two sisters found their world turned upside down when in the span of two years both of their parents died. Separated from his sisters and sent to live with relatives, 13-year-old Charlie went to work picking cotton, a job he immediately found distasteful. Instead, he began devising a plan, and within a few years he had bought a horse and wagon, and started a delivery service in Ardmore.

At the tender age of nineteen, Sammons decided to expand his business. He began buying and selling cotton, and soon had his own small commodities business. While he never went to college, he used the money he earned to pay for both his sisters' education while he remained in Ardmore, betting on the futures market. "The hay and grain business was feast or famine," he later recalled, "and for me it ended in famine." The stock market crash of 1929 wiped out his entire savings and left the 31-year-old entrepreneur penniless.

Never one to remain discouraged for long, Charles Sammons moved to Waco, Texas, where he partnered with a wealthy farmer to again begin buying and selling cotton. Two friends, however, persuaded Sammons to join them in a new venture -- an insurance company called the Postal Indemnity Company. Each contributed a few hundred dollars in savings for an office and typewriters, then began selling $1,000 life insurance policies for $3.65 a year -- "a penny a day" was their slogan.

But before they had hardly gotten settled, one of their first policy holders died, forcing the three young businessmen to make a hard decision: borrow the $1,000 payout or go bankrupt. For Charles Sammons, who sixty years later could state with pride that he never once failed to pay a legitimate claim or let a company he owned go bankrupt, there was no decision to be made. He found a bank willing to lend them the money and wrote out a check for $1,000 to the family. Looking back, he later chided loan officers for "lending me money with which to go into businesses in which I had no experience whatever."

At the time, however, Sammons and his partners were relieved to find the means to stay in business, and Sammons found a way to turn near-disaster into a successful marketing plan. "We made thousands of pictures of that check," he explained, "and mailed them to doctors all over the United States to show them how important such small policies could be."

By 1938, at the age of forty, Charles Sammons had bought out his partners, paving the way for a new and even larger company, the Reserve Life Insurance Company. Throughout the 1940s and 1950s, Charles Sammons aggressively expanded Reserve Life, buying up smaller mutual insurance companies whenever possible until he had established a national network of firms and offices. Throughout it all he relied on tight cost controls to help build his company, often casting himself as a 'penny-pincher' who insisted that paper clips be re-used and that pencils not be thrown away as long as they could still function. One of his secretaries recalled that more than once, when approached by a staff member requesting a salary adjustment, Sammons would pause for a moment, then ask, "I see. Up or down?"

No one at the Reserve Life Insurance Company could complain that Charles Sammons did not work as hard as they did, as he set the bar by which others were judged -- and expected the same from each of them. Doris Hartman, his secretary of 47 years, explained, "After hours, he'd often go around and check people's desks to make sure they did their work for the day. He wouldn't necessarily say anything, but he was definitely aware." Though demanding, Sammons' personal work ethic inspired those who worked for him. "We never minded the hard work or long hours," she explained. "It was fascinating, because there was always something new happening."

A heart attack at age 50, however, caused Charles Sammons to reassess his life and his business. He began to travel more with his wife Rosine and their children, including stays at the Jack Tar Hotel in Galveston. "My family and I enjoyed stopping there," he later recounted, " so when it was for sale, I thought it would be nice to own it."

The purchase gave Charles Sammons a new focus and fresh energy, as he began buying hotels and resorts to place under his Jack Tar brand. Numbering thirteen at one time, Jack Tar hotels could be found from California to South Carolina, including the Grand Bahamas Hotel and Country Club, into which he poured more than $70 million for improvements. Vacations for the Sammons family became inspections of the various properties he owned. As his friends and associates joked, like the Queen of England, Charles Sammons didn't like to step on land he didn't own.

And not that much different than another real estate investor -- Edwin Wiley Grove.

And in what could only be described as an irony of fate, it was Edwin Wiley Grove who brought Charles A. Sammons to Asheville.

By 1955, after the deaths of Fred Seely in 1942 and Evelyn Grove Seely in 1953, the Seely children had decided to sell the brick downtown Battery Park Hotel. The fourteen-story hotel had been built by their grandfather, Edwin Wiley Grove, in 1924, in a move which sparked a bitter lawsuit filed in 1925 by Fred Seely against Grove (see Chapter 13). The towering Battery Park Hotel, which still stands, was designed to cater to traveling businessmen and tourists who, according to Grove, might be seeking less expensive accommodations than the prestigious Grove Park Inn. An enraged Fred Seely declared that the new hotel would compete against the Grove Park Inn, thus violating the terms of his lease for the inn with E. W. Grove. The lawsuit took several years to resolve, in part because of Grove's death on January 27, 1927, in his suite atop the Battery Park Hotel.

And although Fred Seely eventually lost both the lawsuit and the Grove Park Inn, years later he and Evelyn, in a yet another twist of fate, were handed the deed to the Battery Park Hotel as part of the settlement of E. W. Grove's estate.

With no interest in owning the hotel -- and anxious, perhaps, to be rid of the symbol of the public fight which split their family -- the Seely children put the Battery Park Hotel up for sale. Word of its availability filtered down to Dallas, where Charles Sammons decided to send Ed Leach, the president of Jack Tar Hotels, up to Asheville to inspect it.

Leach arrived on August 10, 1955, and was given a tour of Asheville and the Battery Park Hotel by Fred Seely Jr. Leach didn't feel that the downtown hotel was something he and Sammons would want to add to the Jack Tar brand, but was curious to see what was happening at the famed Grove Park Inn. As he recalled years later, he could not help but notice a rather bedraggled man sitting on the steps of one of the outlying cottages, "dressed in an old pair of dungarees and an undershirt, sitting with a bottle of bourbon in his hand."

"Bought in a Bathroom"

Leach walked beneath the portico, through the double oak doors and into the cavernous Great Hall, nearly deserted except for an aging bellman. "The place was gloomy," he recollected. "The drapes were dusty, the furniture old. It didn't look like a thing had been done to it since 1913. I walked around, had a meager lunch in the dining room and, like any good hotel man, started asking questions. When the old bellman let it be known the place was for sale, I asked 'Where's the owner?' "

"Up there," came the reply, as he gestured out the door, "sittin' out front of his cottage."

Ike Hall had been trying unsuccessfully to find a buyer for the Grove Park Inn for nearly five years, but he was not about to simply give it away. He took Ed Leach on a tour of the hotel and grounds, stopping by the Biltmore Industries workshops located on the north side of the property. There they ran into Harry Blomberg, a savvy Asheville businessman who in 1953 had purchased from the Seely family the five Biltmore Industries buildings and the homespun weaving operation Fred Seely had built in 1917. As the story was often told, Harry Blomberg had driven out to Biltmore Industries in 1953 hoping to buy an antique copper moonshine still someone had left in one of the buildings. When he asked the price of the still, he reportedly was told that the only way he could get it was to buy the entire Biltmore Industries. So he did.

As the two men talked about the condition of the hotel and its prospects for the future, Blomberg remarked, "If the right kind of people got a hold of that old hotel, it could make money."

That evening Ed Leach called his boss. "Mr. Sammons," he said, "you got to come up here."

Never one to make a rash decision, instead Charles Sammons summoned Ed Leach back to Dallas, where they discussed the hotel at great length, all the while letting Ike Hall wonder if he had let his last legitimate buyer slip away. A few weeks later, Ed Leach called Hall and arranged a meeting in Sammons' office in Dallas.

From the beginning it was clear that Ike Hall and Charles Sammons had differing opinions as to the value of the Grove Park Inn. Hall opened by stating that his price was $600,000. Sammons, after pointing out that the hotel had only 142 guest rooms, hardly enough to generate a positive cash flow, and was in need of a complete refurbishing, offered the oilman $400,000. A long and frustrating debate ensued, but when Sammons rejected Hall's reduced price of $500,000, Hall announced he was leaving. Still determined to pursue the hotel that he had yet to see in person, Sammons rode to the airport with Leach and Hall. The discussion continued even as the three men walked toward the gate and the waiting plane, but they remained $100,000 apart. When Ike Hall suddenly turned and ducked into the men's bathroom, Charles Sammons and Ed Leach followed.

As Leach later recalled, as Ike Hall and Charles Sammons stood there, facing the bathroom wall and taking care of business, Sammons made one final offer.

"Ike," he said, "how about $450,000 -- in cash?"

Ike Hall thought for a moment, then sighed, zipped up his pants and said, "I'll take it."

An editorial that appeared a short while later in the *Asheville Citizen-Times* stated what everyone in Asheville already knew. "It is no secret that this world famous hotel has been on the decline for some years because many of its facilities had become inadequate and outdated." Sammons' plans for the hotel, it continued, include "a new 600-seat meeting hall, a new swimming pool, a new 100-car parking lot, expanded recreation facilities, redecorated lobbies, dining and guest facilities, along with other improvements."

## "Bought in a Bathroom"

What may have proved equally as shocking was the announcement that the Grove Park Inn would also undergo a change of names. "It will have a new name," the newspaper announced. "It will reopen next year [1956] as 'The Grove Park.' We salute The Grove Park that is soon to be, and the imaginative and progressive spirit that it signifies. It will be an inspiration for the community -- and an example well worth our attention."

Just as not all ideas work, the attempt to rename the hotel 'The Grove Park' soon fizzled and the original name was quietly reinstated.

That fall of 1955, after the last guest of the season had packed their bags and checked out of the hotel, a team of interior designers and workmen descended on the Grove Park Inn. They worked under the direction of the new general manager George J. Stobie, an experienced hotel man Ed Leach had hired away from the Stanley Hotel in Estes Park, Colorado. Their initial budget was $100,000, but it eventually swelled to $250,000 before they were finished. While the *Citizen-Times* may have thought the Sammons-Leach plan was "progressive," general manager Stobie had his doubts. Lead by interior decorator Thomas M. Price of Galveston, Stobie recalled that "the designers who were redecorating the inn wanted to plaster over the fireplaces, but I wouldn't let them do it." He claimed they covered the columns while he was on vacation or else he would have stopped them from doing that, too. Fearful he might lose his job before the hotel even re-opened, Stobie fought what battles he felt he could win, then left the rest alone.

It remained for another *Citizen-Times* reporter to later describe what the team of decorators had done to the six original pillars in the Great Hall. "Stone facing has been removed from the central pillars and walls flanking the great fireplaces in the main lobby.

Pillars are now oval with aqua and citron as the prevailing color scheme." Another added, "This huge room has been livened up with a color scheme of aqua and citron, and all the furniture has been reupholstered in gay new fabrics." And as chief engineer Bill Nielson explained, "they removed the rocks from the Great Hall columns to place around the outdoor swimming pool." Some also made their way into a new exterior wall enclosing one of the outdoor terraces.

The original dining room was also targeted by the decorators, the newspaper reported. "The Plantation Room has been decorated in olive and turquoise with new furniture throughout. The redecorated cocktail lounge has been named 'The Jug.' "

Among the casualties of the refurbishing of the Grove Park Inn were the original 1913 Roycroft chairs in the dining room and the White Furniture Company rockers in the guest rooms. According to Asheville residents, the chairs, rockers and other unwanted furniture were lined up on the front porch of the hotel and sold for five dollars each. For decades afterwards, the famed Roycroft chairs still bearing the "GPI" initials could be spotted in a local nursing home, a bar on Eagle Street and on porches around Asheville -- until Arts and Crafts collectors began gathering them up.

The message Charles Sammons and Ed Leach had sent to George Scobie and the interior decorators was simple and direct: transform this old hotel into a family-oriented resort. Go after the convention business, but make them want to bring their families with them. Indicative of the means by which staffs of all of the Jack Tar Hotels sought to attract families was their trademark "Operation Kidnap, that assures youngsters of a separate vacation from their parents (and vice-versa) and at no extra charge. Trained counselors lead the kiddies on a round of activities, such as swimming, hiking, exploring, field trips, games, picnics and arts and crafts."

"Bought in a Bathroom"

Upper most on everyone's mind was the immediate need for an outdoor heated swimming pool. The logical location seemed to be on the open terrace just below and to the left of the original west veranda off the Great Hall. In June of 1956, a modern cloverleaf swimming pool made its debut at the Grove Park Inn, along with resurfaced tennis courts, a large indoor play area and a game room. A new brochure described the hotel as "completely redecorated, [and offering] mountain climate, new heated swimming pool, sports, dancing and scenic trips."

"Prepare To Be Pampered" was their new motto.

And the marketing department back in Dallas was not about to let young newlyweds slip out of their grasp. While describing all that the Grove Park Inn had to offer, one copywriter declared, "in the unspoiled wilderness around it, you may spend the ideal honeymoon." And as if what the hotel had to offer was not quite romantic enough, he invented a few natural features of his own, including "an unadvertised waterfall [and] the calmness of a mountain-rimmed lake."

"Unadvertised" only because neither the waterfall nor the lake existed at the Grove Park Inn.

Not even Fred Seely had dare assume those creative powers of invention....

In what was touted as the hotel's second grand opening, on Friday, May 4, 1956, more than 150 select guests, including members of the press, radio and television, were greeted by none other than Charles Sammons and his wife Rosine as they walked through the oak doors of a remodeled Grove Park Inn. The theme of the evening was "New Year's Day in May" and all were handed noisemakers and paper hats.

"Coming from all parts of the country by train, plane and automobiles, guest cars wound down the steep incline to the main entrance of the massive structure literally carved out of Sunset Mountain," one reporter wrote. And those historians who wonder where such myths get started need only read the press release handed out that night, boldly, but inaccurately, proclaiming "Fred Seely designed it without an architect and built it in less than a year without a contractor."

No apologies were made to architect and engineer William McKibbin or to general contractor and foreman Oscar Mills. Or to the fact that the Grove Park Inn was still not complete when it opened one year and three days after groundbreaking. But as Mark Twain once said, "Never let the facts get in the way of a good story."

The Saturday night party the favored guests enjoyed the next night also deserves mention. "Dressed in denim skirts and sunbonnets with the men in blue jeans and 'farmers' hats of straw with bandanas at their necks, the guests forgot their big city backgrounds and joined in the hillbilly atmosphere as they danced to mountain music by Panogen Pete, whose tall sparse frame held a collection of homemade instruments, as well as a drum, a harmonica and a mandolin. These he manipulated at all times with amazing dexterity as he sang and played folk songs of the mountains. Another highlight of the evening was the perfection clog dances done by children nine to eleven who brought the guests to their feet in tribute...."

A truly hillbilly night in Asheville.

And just as work had continued after the opening banquet on July 12, 1913, the workmen returned to the Grove Park Inn the following Monday to resume work on the cloverleaf swimming pool, a new parking lot and the beginning of the second phase: the Fairway Motor Lodge. But even before groundbreaking could take place, the hotel was honored with visits in 1956 from Vice-President Richard Nixon and evangelist Billy Graham.

Opening in 1958 where the Sammons Wing currently stands, the Fairway Motor Lodge resembled a modern roadside motel. More important, it added fifty more rooms to the hotel and served to offer a modern flair alongside an aging hotel. Two years later a covered walkway connecting the original south terrace and outdoor fireplace to the Fairway Lodge was completed.

The efforts of George Scobie, Ed Leach and Charles Sammons to bring the famed Grove Park Inn back to life did not go unnoticed in Washington, D.C. At a time when the Cold War with the Soviet Union was escalating and the real possibility of a nuclear war was looming, the United States government reached a secret agreement with the new owners. A document dated April 3, 1956, that has only recently been discovered, stated: "This agreement provides that the Supreme Court will take possession of the Grove Park Inn in the event of an enemy attack or the imminence thereof. As soon as possible thereafter, the Government will enter into negotiations with you for the execution of a formal lease...." Additional correspondence indicates that the agreement to house the members of the Supreme Court at the Grove Park Inn in the event of a war was continued into the administration of President John F. Kennedy.

In addition to providing an interesting footnote to history, the agreement between the Grove Park Inn and the United States government contained an accurate inventory of what Charles Sammons had purchased in 1955 from Ike Hall: 141 guest rooms, four cottages, a forty-person staff dormitory, a 23-car garage and a 140-car open parking lot.

In 1965, Charles Sammons provided an additional wing, simply called the North Wing, on the site presently occupied by the

Vanderbilt Wing. While adding another 46 guest rooms, the North Wing was primarily designed to provide the hotel with a spacious ballroom and the meeting rooms needed to attract the latest rage: business conventions.

Despite the accolades heaped upon Charles Sammons and his designers by the local newspaper, not everyone in Asheville was as enamored with the wealthy Texans from Dallas. In particular, the staid members of the Asheville Country Club, who had since 1913 only reluctantly shared their fairways and putting greens with guests from the Grove Park Inn, bristled at the growing influx of fresh tourists and their noisy families.

In 1969, after their traditional winter season when the hotel was closed from November through April, the Grove Park Inn's staff assembled for their first meeting with general manager Rush Hays. His remarks were recorded by the secretary, as he announced, "The president of the Asheville Country Club came to the hotel to inform me that no guests will be allowed to play golf at the Country Club. In the past we have had privileges at the Country Club; however, due to a recent ruling by their Board of Directors, they no longer take guests unless accompanied by a member."

The announcement was heard all the way to Dallas. Two months later, in a move that caught nearly everyone off guard, the Sammons Corporation announced that it was selling the Grove Park Inn. Frustrated, perhaps, by years of butting heads with the Asheville Country Club and adjusting to the retirement of Ed Leach, his close friend, advisor and president, Charles Sammons may well have decided to begin divesting himself of some of his responsibilities.

The buyer of the hotel, a group of Florida developers named the Osias Organization, Inc., simultaneously announced their plans to build a clubhouse for Grove Park Inn guests adjacent to a different golf course located three miles away. In addition, believing perhaps that Asheville was located further north than it actually was, the new owners also announced that they were going to construct an ice skating rink and ski slope next to it, and afterwards would then be open year round. The Osias Organization, however, proved to have more dreams than money. Two years later they defaulted on their payments, and Charles Sammons quickly took the steps necessary to reclaim his favorite hotel.

The return of Charles Sammons to the helm of the Grove Park Inn in 1972 prompted two moves that forever altered the course of the famous hotel. First, Sammons let it be known that he was prepared to do whatever was necessary to gain control of the golf course belonging to the Country Club of Asheville. Prompted by Sammons' statement, a Miami millionaire with close ties to Asheville developed an unusual proposal for a three-way deal dubbed "The Big Swap." As a result, in 1978 Charles Sammons was finally able to purchase the course, renaming it the Grove Park Country Club. The story of the Big Swap and the history behind it are detailed in the next chapter.

The second move was actually made by a woman few in Asheville had ever heard of, yet few would ever forget.

Her story is just three chapters ahead of you.

But first a round of golf, and then a long-awaited ghost story.

*The golf course at the Grove Park Inn pre-dates the hotel by several years. Members of the Asheville Country Club had laid out the first course at the base of Sunset Mountain on land E. W. Grove was never able to buy. Note how few trees were on the course in the 1920s compared to today.*

# Chapter 21

# "Fore!"

*He wanted to test every facet of a golfer's game; he wanted
the well-rounded player to play his courses.*

Kris Spence,
Restoration Architect

On July 12, 1913, as he stood in front of the 400 gentlemen
assembled to celebrate the opening of his magnificent hotel, Edwin
Wiley Grove recalled, "After a long mountain walk one evening, at
the sunset hour, I sat down here to rest, and while almost entranced
by the panoramic view of these encircling mountains and a restful
outlook upon green fields, the dream of an old-time inn came to me."

A portion of those green fields, he failed to mention, was the
golf course belonging to the Asheville Country Club.

And when in 1912 Grove and Fred Seely carefully selected
the building site for the hotel, not only was it high enough on Sunset
Mountain to provide guests with that same panoramic view Grove
had enjoyed, it also had as its front lawn the rolling slopes of a lush
eighteen-hole golf course.

But there was one small problem: it was not for sale.

Although E. W. Grove had amassed more than 800 acres of land around the Grove Park Inn and would eventually buy nearly 300 more, there in the midst of it all stood a veritable island, a small oasis that Grove's fortune could not buy.

The Asheville Country Club.

Established in 1894, it proudly bore the banner of the oldest country club in continuous operation in North Carolina, and the second oldest in the entire South.

Not long after the much-heralded opening in 1886 of the sprawling Battery Park Hotel on the highest knoll in downtown Asheville, a group of prominent citizens gathered to form what was first called the Swannanoa Country Club. The name was inspired by the nearby Swannanoa River, which flowed into the French Broad River south of the city. Around Asheville it was simply known as The Hunt Club, for its early members would gather at the Battery Park Hotel before crossing the bridge over to West Asheville. There they would mount their horses at the club's stables and release their prized dogs, trained to pick up the scent of one of the many fox who lived in the area, or, when in season, pheasant and quail.

Their original letters of incorporation clearly stated their intention "of fostering and encouraging the engaging and taking part in hunting, the preservation of game, the breeding of blooded stock and of blooded dogs, and for the purpose of encouraging and taking part in athletic sports of every kind and nature." Afterward, the hunters would return to their clubhouse, provided by Colonel Frank Coxe adjacent to his towering Battery Park Hotel, where they would play cards or a game of billiards, listen to someone play the piano, and socialize.

"Fore!"

As the number of fox declined and the number of members increased, however, talk turned to building both a golf course and tennis courts for their pleasure. As one historian enjoyed noting, "Neighboring farmers were beginning to complain about the fox hunts causing damage to their farms and fences, not to mention a severe decline in the local fox population. It was an easy decision to drop fox hunting in favor of golf ball hunting. Golf balls were easier to find and did not require a horse."

A slight name change in 1896 to the Swannanoa Golf and Country Club reflected the addition of a five-hole golf course to their facility. The first greens were simply mowed more closely to the ground than the fairways, but later were replaced with a packed and rolled clay surface that the members covered with a thin layer of fine river sand.

Their first course, however, was soon abandoned, not for lack of interest, but for a more convenient location closer to their downtown social clubhouse. A five-hole course laid out in north Asheville also proved temporary, as members had to share it with a herd of hogs and cattle owned by a consortium of local butchers. An Asheville newspaper observed, "it was a strange sight to see the game played amidst the ranging of cattle and accompanying disagreeable features of a slaughter house. The swellness, elegance, verse and spirits comprising the cream of Asheville society was mixing with -- shall we dare say it? -- swine."

One of Asheville's most famous benefactors, George Willis Pack, came to the club's rescue. Pack reportedly did not golf, but Mrs. Pack did, so in 1898 Pack presented the Swannanoa Golf and Country Club with a five-year lease on nearly 130 acres of land he owned at the north end of Charlotte Street, adjacent to Macon Avenue. The lease included a clubhouse Pack had built for the members at his own expense, and called for the sum of one dollar per year, stipulating that the land was "to be used for the games of golf, cricket, tennis and other athletic sports."

When George Pack died in 1906, however, his heirs did not feel quite so generous. They reportedly sold the land and clubhouse to five Asheville citizens for the price of $26,000. The five then offered to resell the property to the Swannanoa Golf and Country Club. Unwilling to assume such a large debt, the members declined to act on their offer, and the land became the neighborhood around Edgemont and Woodlink Roads, which today includes the stately Albemarle Inn.

Having seen their most recent facility slip from their fingers, the members renewed their attempts to secure a permanent home and to form an organization that would be a legal entity in its own right. In 1907 the newly incorporated Asheville Country Club took the first steps by purchasing nearly 100 acres of land and constructing a clubhouse. J. J. McCloskey, one of their most active members, laid out a new nine-hole course on land that remains to this day a part of the Grove Park Inn links.

All those costs, however, prevented the membership from quickly being able to enlarge the golf course from its original nine-hole configuration. At some point in the discussions, one of the members must have suggested hiring noted golf course designer Donald Ross, for included in their minutes for one of their meetings in 1909 was the notation, "It was decided that the club would not for the present invite Donald Ross of Pinehurst to offer suggestions for the improvement of the course. Still involved with finishing the new clubhouse."

The year 1909, however, brought with it a new era in the history of the Asheville Country Club. That was the year Edwin Wiley

Grove first publicly acknowledged that he was seriously entertaining the idea of building a resort hotel on land adjacent to the Asheville Country Club's golf course.

When word reached the influential Coxe family, owners of the Battery Park Hotel, that E. W. Grove was planning to open a competing hotel adjacent to the Asheville Country Club, Tench Coxe set in motion a plan to build a new golf course several miles away. Under his plan, he would then sell his new eighteen-hole course to the Asheville Country Club in exchange for shares of stock -- plus their current golf course, which in all likelihood he was prepared to plow up in order to derail Grove's hotel project.

As Grove noted in a letter to his property manager, "It seems to me that the citizens of Asheville should be deeply interested in securing these grounds at the best possible location, and that they should subscribe liberally to keep them where they are now located. It is very evident that Mr. Coxe's motive is a selfish one in fighting over the location of these grounds."

Coxe, regardless of his money and his influence, may have underestimated his adversary. Grove, though he lived in St. Louis, had two younger and aggressive men on his side in the battle to keep the golf course in its present location: Fred L. Seely and Thomas Dudley Raoul.

Thomas Raoul's father, railroad magnate William Greene Raoul, had begun construction in 1898 on the Manor Inn and a series of rental cottages located on 32 acres of land in north Asheville. In contrast to most tourist hotels, William Raoul envisioned a residential park complete with summer cottages, a central inn where meals would be served, walking and riding paths winding through the property, a stable, a small park with a natural amphitheater for outdoor performances, and the preservation of native trees and shrubbery. Raoul called upon architect Bradford Gilbert and land-scape designer Samuel Parsons to help create Albemarle Park, as it is still called, which was to be managed by his son Thomas Dudley Raoul.

The Raouls were early supporters of the Asheville Country Club and its attempt to establish a permanent golf course and club-house within walking distance of the Manor Inn. Thomas Dudley Raoul and Fred Seely joined forces in their attempt to thwart the Coxe family's plan to move the Asheville Country Club's golf course two miles further north. In 1909 they approached the club's members with a proposition which included a pledge of $15,000 from E. W. Grove and one of $10,000 from the Raoul family, plus their assistance in generating an additional $25,000 through a city-wide subscription drive. In return, the Asheville Country Club agreed in November "to maintain the golf links at the present location for five years from this date." With their support and an influx of funds, the Asheville Country Club was able to purchase the additional land nec-essary to both enlarge and improve the course. The move effectively killed Coxe's plan for a new golf course that would have crippled the ability of the Manor Inn and the Grove Park Inn to draw golfers to their hotels.

Shortly thereafter, the Asheville Country Club appears to have contacted not Donald Ross, but one of his fellow Scotsmen and a two-time victor at the British Open -- William "Willie" Park (1864-1925). While not as well known as Donald Ross, Willie Park paved the way for an entire generation of golf course designers. In addi-tion to being an accomplished golfer, Willie Park is credited with improving the design of the golf ball and several golf clubs, for which he received numerous patents. In 1896, he was the first professional to write a book on the subject entitled *The Game of Golf*, which he then followed in 1920 with *The Art of Putting*. Later in his career he turned to golf course design and has been credited with the design of 170 courses in Great Britain, Canada and the United States.

Park, however, was not given free rein at the Asheville Country Club, but was only requested to add nine more holes to the existing course. A few years later the members must have reconsidered their decision. In 1913, the same year that the Grove Park Inn opened, the members voted to have Donald Ross redesign the entire eighteen-hole course.

Born in Scotland, Donald James Ross (1872-1948) spent most of his life in the United States, where he played on the professional circuit for several years, finishing fifth in the U.S. Open in 1903. By that time, however, he had become the golfing instructor for the Pinehurst (N.C.) Country Club and began devoting the majority of his time to teaching and golf course design, eventually forming Donald J. Ross and Associates with offices in North Carolina and Rhode Island. He is credited with more than 400 golf courses, including four at Pinehurst and another four in Asheville.

Donald Ross was noted for creating courses that disturbed the natural terrain as little as possible. As Jack Nicklaus observed, "His stamp as an architect was naturalness." As another author noted, "Ross often created holes which invited run-up shots, but had severe trouble at the back of the green, typically in the form of fall-away slopes. In the 1930s he revolutionized greens-keeping practices in the Southern United States, when he oversaw the transition of the putting surfaces at Pinehurst No. 2 from oiled sand to Bermuda grass."

An early description of the eighteen-hole course at the foot of Sunset Mountain, to which Donald Ross reportedly returned in 1924 to make additional improvements, noted, "the lands of the Country

Club are admirably adapted to its purposes. The acreage of the entire tract is gently undulating, affording the natural hazards desired -- just such territory as the golfer delights in traversing. The broad reaches slope away from the eastern foot of Sunset Mountain in the city's northern suburb.... [and] will doubtless maintain the natural attractions that now form such considerable portion of their extensive expanse. Painstaking efforts will build the greens for permanent grass covers."

The opening of the Grove Park Inn in 1913 prompted E. W. Grove and Fred Seely to take steps to ensure that hotel guests would have playing privileges on the course. First, they continued their practice of buying whatever shares of stock in the Asheville Country Club became available, just to prevent any adversary from owning a majority stake in the corporation. In addition, Grove offered to pay, as did the Raoul family, an annual assessment to the Asheville Country Club for that right. In return, their guests would be allowed, for a fee each guest would pay, to play alongside the club members.

In 1917, however, when Fred Seely was leasing the hotel from E. W. Grove, the subject of the assessment became contentious. Thomas Raoul and Fred Seely, despite being perceived as hotel competitors, had actually become close friends in their earlier struggle to expand and keep the golf course located between their two hostelries. They did take differing approaches to their "hotel tax" paid to the Asheville Country Club, which was based on the number of hotel guests who elected to play the course each year.

Raoul felt strongly that the Manor Inn and the Grove Park Inn should continue to pay the additional assessment to the country club, fearing "it would have no money left for making improvements. Personally, I believe that if we let this Club go backwards instead of forward, it will be a very serious blow to the hotels of Asheville."

Seely had taken the stand that their two hotels are "bringing the people here and producing the players on the links, rendering the biggest service and yielding the largest amount of money; and that reducing, or even eliminating, the tax they are charging us would not rob the Club of the many thousand of dollars of new revenue they are now receiving from your and my activities in the hotel line."

Sensing, however, that Raoul's concern was legitimate and that the course might deteriorate without the additional funds the two hotels contributed, Seely concluded, "Rest assured, also, that I am willing to stick with you for whatever you think is right, for you could not have been any more unselfish in what you have done." Later, when Thomas Raoul asked for Seely's advice in an unrelated matter, Fred replied, "I want to assure you that it will give me pleasure to assist you, for I have often said you are about the most decent competitor I have ever had, and I really don't feel that you are a competitor. I think we are going to have good business this summer, and I sincerely hope you will get yours."

Women were always welcome to play either golf or tennis at the Asheville Country Club. The club proudly pointed to two of their most illustrious members, George and Edith Vanderbilt. Despite George Vanderbilt's untimely death in 1914 due to complications after an appendectomy, Edith Vanderbilt remained a member and was considered a respectable golfer. According to Asheville lore, however, on one of her outings to the clubhouse on the grounds of the golf course, Edith Vanderbilt reportedly began smoking a cigarette in a public area. The manager is believed to have approached her, requesting that she either extinguish her cigarette or move to one of the private rooms, as women were not allowed to smoke in public at the clubhouse.

While Edith Vanderbilt's actual response did not survive, her reaction has: she revoked her membership, built the competing Biltmore Forest Country Club and hired none other than Donald Ross to design a new and larger golf course.

The fate of the hapless manager is unknown.

The Roaring Twenties came roaring into Asheville with an economic boom that sent real estate values soaring to unsustainable levels. In their wake the city experienced a frenzy of construction projects, from the mansions lining the fairways of the Biltmore Forest Country Club to Douglas Ellington's Art Deco designs along downtown streets to an eclectic mixture of expensive houses in E. W. Grove's recent Kimberly Avenue and Griffin Boulevard subdivisions.

Members of the Asheville Country Club were swept up in the fervor, building a new clubhouse designed by English architect H. T. Linderberg in 1925. Described as a "rambling stucco-on-masonry structure designed in a vaguely Franco-English manorial style," the three-story clubhouse featured no fewer than seven different interior levels, a massive exterior chimney laid in a Flemish bond pattern, an archway drive and a circular tower with a conical roof.

Like Asheville and the adjacent Grove Park Inn, the Asheville Country Club struggled to survive during the Great Depression, as many of its members found themselves unable to pay their annual dues and greens fees. In response to the challenging times, the Country Club formed a partnership with another golf course near Beaver Lake, a few miles north of the Grove Park Inn. Owned by Lakeview Properties, which had in 1925 retained Donald Ross to design the course, the Beaver Lake links had once been called "longest and hardest in the country."

Despite a series of absentee owners in the 1930s, the Grove Park Inn continued to make an annual payment of $2,000 to the

Asheville Country Club, motivated by its desire to have the course maintained at a level of excellence that would continue to attract guests to the hotel.

In 1944, as part of yet another reorganization plan that would reduce the club's debt and solidify its financial footing, the name was legally changed to the Country Club of Asheville. As part of the plan, guests at the Grove Park Inn, which then included hundreds of returning servicemen enjoying reunions with their families, were still permitted to use the country club's swimming pool, tennis courts and golf course. Over-crowding was overlooked in the name of patriotism during the war years, but once tourists began replacing soldiers, members began to complain about the number of Grove Park Inn guests using their facilities.

The relative stability of the Eisenhower era and an increase in the popularity of golf brought members back into their fold, further heightening the friction between club members and guests from the Grove Park Inn. In addition to the never-ending maintenance required by eighteen fairways and putting greens, the thirty-year-old clubhouse was now in need of updated plumbing, wiring and structural repairs. Despite -- or because of -- increased members and guests, the Country Club of Asheville again found itself in a dangerous financial situation.

The arrival of Charles Sammons as the inn's new owner in 1955 had also signaled a new era in hotel management and services. Crucial to the success of the "new" Grove Park Inn was a first class golf course catering to their guests rather than to a country club rules committee. But like E. W. Grove, Charles Sammons was unable to find a way to buy the golf course in his front yard. Friction grew into hard feelings between club membership and inn management, until negotiations reached an impasse and ground to a halt.

Then came the "Big Swap."

Mitchell Wolfson (1900-1983) was a Miami-based business-man who turned a single movie theatre bought in 1926 into a media empire that at the time of his death was worth more than $1 billion dollars. Like many Florida millionaires, Wolfson often vacationed in Asheville where, like E. W. Grove fifty years earlier, he began invest-ing in property on the north side of the city. Among his extensive holdings was the Beaver Lake Golf Course he had purchased from the failed Lakeview Properties.

Laid out by Donald Ross in 1925 along the Beaverdam Creek as it flowed toward Beaverdam Lake, the eighteen-hole course had been described as being in a "placid Blue Ridge glen three miles long and one mile wide, with towering mountain ramparts to the north, east and west, pointing toward the dawn at its head and open the other way to sweeping sunsets." The planned development sur-rounding the golf course, however, had become mired in the Great Depression. Threatened with unwanted commercial encroachment as Asheville developed north along the Route 25 corridor, the prop-erty remained a fragile ecosystem until purchased by Mitchell Wolf-son, who had no other agenda than to save it from untrustworthy developers.

In 1976, Wolfson orchestrated a real estate transaction that few could have envisioned, let alone have pulled off. The key to the success of the transaction, as everyone involved soon realized, was Wolfson's willingness to forego the profits he could have made had he divided and developed his north Asheville property along Bea-verdam Creek.

On November 18, 1976, after weeks of negotiating with both sides, Mitchell Wolfson brought all of the affected parties together for the formal signing of the papers. In the first step of the swap, the

Country Club of Asheville sold its entire 100-acre golf course and clubhouse to the Grove Park Inn for $2,900,000. Next, the Country Club of Asheville purchased from Mitchell Wolfson the former Beaver Lake Golf Course and property for the below-market price of $1,675,000. The Country Club of Asheville then invested the balance of its profit in a new clubhouse, tennis courts, swimming pool and improvements to the golf course.

Much was written at the time in the local papers about the Big Swap, but one historian placed it in perspective when he wrote, "The role of Mitchell Wolfson in these transactions, so important to the Club's future at that time, deserves more credit than one could gather from the days' newspaper accounts. He was a man of wealth, true, and could spend it where and when he chose. But he also had a deep commitment to the preservation of the environmental beauty of Asheville, his adopted summer home. What Mitchell Wolfson recognized was a fantastic opportunity to preserve and protect forever the natural beauty of an area he loved."

Back inside the offices at the Grove Park Inn, Charles Sammons and his staff finally had the freedom to manage and develop the golf course that, more than sixty years earlier, had inspired Edwin Wiley Grove to build the Grove Park Inn on the spot where it stands today.

By that time, however, the design which Donald Ross had envisioned for the golf course below the Grove Park Inn had long since been altered by subsequent changes. The largest reconfiguration prior to the inn's purchase occurred in 1969, when the board spent $20,000 "to make maintenance easier, lengthen and toughen up the course, afford bigger tees and greens, and give some holes a complete new prospect. We're going to make it more appealing." Charles Sammons followed after the Big Swap with another major facelift for the golf course, further reducing the dwindling evidence of the original design as conceived by Donald Ross.

It remained for Elaine Sammons, widow of Charles Sammons, who died in 1988, to make a commitment to restoring the Grove Park Inn's golf course back to the design, which Donald Ross had intended in the 1920s. On June 1, 2001, the golf course was closed and the bulldozers rumbled in to begin an eighteen-month, $2 million dollar renovation headed by noted golf course architect Kris Spence. His firm, Spence Golf, Inc., specializes in new golf course design and the renovation of classic Donald Ross designed courses.

"Our over-riding goal at the Grove Park Inn," Kris Spence explained, "was to bring back the character of the course as Donald Ross had intended it. The popularity of golf on television and the courses designed by modern architects had influenced many changes that erased the signs of a Donald Ross course. They lost sight of the heritage of Donald Ross and his designs. Bunkers had been removed, others added; greens had been reinvented and fairways rerouted, and hundreds of trees and shrubs had been planted that obscured the original layout."

Making Kris Spence's task even more challenging was the fact that he was never able to locate Donald Ross's original plans for the Grove Park Inn course.

"We first had to create a master plan, but without the original plans we had to resort to other means. We studied historic photographs in the inn's archives, but what we really needed was an aerial photograph. As it turned out, the father of one of the groundskeepers had been a surveyor, and he actually found in his files a 1938 aerial photograph of the course."

Kris Spence's research also took him on several journeys, tracking down and examining documented Donald Ross golf cours-es. There he learned first hand the unique features characteristic of the famed designer's layout: the shape and contour of the greens, and the dark, distinctive, deep bunkers -- similar to those of Ross's native Scotland -- left like clues by Ross to help guide the golfer to what he felt was the best approach to the hole.

"I walked as many of his courses I could," Spence recalled, "and each time I tried to put myself in Donald Ross's shoes."

Long before the first backhoe arrived, Spence returned many times to the Grove Park Inn's course, walking in search of remnants of former bunkers and buried greens. To his amazement and delight, he discovered -- tucked between two modern fairways -- the original seventh hole, neglected and overgrown, but still intact and retaining the Donald Ross characteristics Kris had learned to recognize from those other courses.

Before the completion of his research for the master plan, Kris had determined that four of the modern day holes -- the 4th, the 6th, the 11th and the 18th -- were original to the course as Ross had intended it to be played in the 1920s. "I consider the 18th hole," he added, "to be a classic example of his work."

One of the greatest challenges Kris Spence faced was what to do with hundreds of non-original pine trees now growing on the course. Early photographs reveal Ross's preference for an open, wind-swept course with very few trees. "Ross often did leave native trees on his courses," Spence explained, "but he knew not to design a hole around a tree, for trees eventually die. Plus, he wanted golfers to be able to access the greens from several different approaches." Dur-ing the 1980s, however, a movement toward golf courses with a more park-like appearance led to long rows of fast-growing pine trees being planted along the fairways.

By the time Kris Spence arrived in 2001, those mature trees had become a familiar part of the character of the Grove Park Inn's course. But turning a golf course renovation into a major logging operation would have raised protests from both guests and neighbors. As a compromise, Spence's crew thinned out secondary shrubs and smaller trees, then removed lower limbs on the larger trees to recapture as closely as possible Donald Ross's original, open layout.

Those rows of towering pine trees lining the fairways, Spence also pointed out, had grown into an important safety feature, as they prevent many an errant drive off the tee from careening into an adjacent group of golfers. With far more golfers on today's courses than Donald Ross had to contend with in the 1920s, architects like Kris Spence cannot neglect the safety of their golfers when attempting to retrieve an older course design. When it reopened in September of 2002, the restored and renovated Grove Park Inn course measured 6,720 yards and plays as a par-70.

And when asked about how he feels when he plays the course today, Kris Spence replied, "In truth, I don't play it that well. I always seem to get distracted -- by Donald Ross."

"Fore!"

*Pictured here soon after the Sammons Wing opened in 1984, the golf course officially became a part of the Grove Park Inn in 1976. A subsequent remodeling of the course further eroded the original design of Donald Ross, which was largely restored in 2002.*

*The Grove Park Inn's resident ghost, the Pink Lady, has appeared most frequently in the Palm Court, prompting many to speculate that a beautiful young woman in a flowing pink gown may have fallen to her death here.*

334

# Chapter 22

# "A Beautiful Ghost"

*"I was never afraid of her -- ever."*

Sharon Ponder
Former Employee

Is the Grove Park Inn haunted?

Long before it became popular for historic sites to each have their own resident ghost -- from author Nathaniel Hawthorne roaming about the House of Seven Gables to Presidents Abraham Lincoln and Andrew Jackson, plus First Lady Dolly Madison, all refusing to leave the White House -- Grove Park Inn employees have for decades quietly shared with each other the unusual encounters they experienced while working in the historic hotel.

While each encounter might vary somewhat, a common thread links many of them together: a fleeting vision of a beautiful young woman in a flowing pink gown.

The Pink Lady.

A guest, perhaps, who met her untimely death inside the Grove Park Inn?

A guest no one missed?

A death that, just as mysteriously, seems to never have been reported in either of the two Asheville newspapers?

Could there be a ghost without a reported body, without a confirmed death?

Would it be possible for someone, possibly a young, beautiful woman, to have died inside the Grove Park Inn without the story being reported in the local newspapers?

Many questions waiting to be answered.

First, we cannot be sure that such a story did not appear in either of the Asheville newspapers. No one has yet taken the weeks, possibly months, required to search through the 14,600 editions of the two daily newspapers published just in the first twenty years after the inn had opened.

Second, such a story, especially if it did not involve a famous celebrity or a heinous crime, might not even appear in the newspaper. People do die in hotels while on vacation, and their deaths, especially if from natural causes, do not always warrant a front-page story, if any at all.

One story describing the tragic death of a beautiful young woman did appear in the local newspapers the day after the opening of the Grove Park Inn. Despite its lurid details, the small article was buried on an inside page. As reported, on July 12, 1913, a train carrying the hotel's guest of honor, Secretary of State William Jennings Bryan, was unable to stop in time to avoid striking and killing a young tourist, as she walked along the railroad tracks a few miles outside Asheville.

"A Beautiful Ghost"

As the reporter assigned to write the story of the death of Miss Annie E. Williams noted:

*It is said that her head was almost decapitated by the train, Southern No. 15, a few miles out, on a trestle. She had no time to jump before the engine struck her. The young woman was picked up by the train crew under the trestle 20 feet below. The body was carried to a house nearby and will be conveyed to her Florida home, probably today, for interment.*

A century later, how much imagination would it take for a ghost hunter to envision the ghostly spirit of Miss Annie Williams, her dress turned pink from her faded blood, following the train carrying William Jennings Bryan all the way to the Grove Park Inn?

How many other Annie Williams might have died, even inside the Grove Park Inn, with their newspaper stories forgotten, now relegated to a single frame on a strip of microfilm locked in the basement of the city library?

In addition, small town newspaper publishers of that era had a far cozier relationship with their major advertisers than they do today. Had there been a mysterious or even a totally plausible death that might have reflected poorly on the Grove Park Inn, a publisher might well have elected not to delve into it, for fear of losing a major source of revenue for years to come.

But, even without a newspaper article or an obituary, the questions still persist:

Is the Grove Park Inn haunted?

Does the Pink Lady exist?

And, if so, where might she be seen?

The stories swirling around the hotel prompted Joshua Warren, author and noted authority on paranormal activity, to launch an extensive investigation in 1995 seeking an answer to the question: Is the Grove Park Inn haunted? His research resulted in the opening chapter to his popular book *Haunted Asheville*.

Joshua Warren began his investigation by interviewing current and former employees, as well as guests who had seemingly unexplainable experiences inside the Grove Park Inn. Many of these stories have since become familiar, as they have been read, shared and re-told, with perhaps an occasional personal embellishment, by everyone from tour guides and bellmen to elevator operators and local residents.

Among the stories Joshua Warren recites in great detail in his book are the following:

- a night watchman, some seventy years ago, who feels someone grab his arm, but turns to find no one beside him;

- the buzzing of the elevator call button on the fifth floor, at a time when the hotel was closed for the winter and void of any guests;

- every room in the entire sixth floor lighting up at midnight, again at a time when the inn was closed for the winter, then going dark, only to light up again a few minutes later; a feat, according to hotel staff, which would be impossible for one person to accomplish with the throwing of a single switch;

- a fleeting glimpse of a pink blur, late at night, in the old portion of the basement or along the hallways in the Palm Court;

- a similar apparition in the former kitchen, now occupied by storage rooms and a few offices;

- a child, alone in a secured, fourth-floor room taking a nap, awakes to ask his parents who had remained in the adjoining room, "Where did the nice lady go?"

- Main Inn bathroom doors -- equipped with a sliding bolt lock that only operates manually from the inside -- found locked with no one inside the bathroom;

- the country club elevator traveling up and down in the middle of the night with no one in it;

- a guest reporting that he could feel someone sit down next to him on his bed in a fourth-floor room;

- another guest who purposely left the closet door open while she slept in her fourth-floor room, only to find it closed and latched when she awoke;

- electric typewriters that, even after being inspected, continue to randomly start typing;

- a plumber who refused to go back into the tunnels under the Great Hall after having the Pink Lady hover around him;

- employees, especially nighttime security officers, who after an unexplainable incident, suddenly quit their job, refusing to come back to the Grove Park Inn.

In yet another story reported by the Grove Park Inn, "a housekeeper once reported seeing a 'lady dressed in pink' walk into a lavatory. After waiting an appropriate amount of time for the woman to come out, the housekeeper decided to investigate, and discovered no one was there. More than a little distraught, the housekeeper reported the whole event to her manager, who calmly replied, 'That's just the Pink Lady.' "

It remained for Joshua Warren and his two associates to get permission from the Grove Park Inn's staff to bring an assortment of photographic and recording equipment to the Palm Court for a total of ten nights between December of 1995 and May of 1996. Again, his study was carefully documented in *Haunted Asheville*, with the following summary of his findings:

- "unexplainable fields of electromagnetic energy fluctuating throughout the hotel;"

- a photograph taken in the Palm Court with "an uncanny grey mist shown hovering over a chair;"

- another photograph in the Palm Court with "a strange orange light glowing outside of room 545;"

- persistent problems operating the electronic locking mechanism in the door to room 545. "Once we were inside the room, we detected huge masses of fluctuating electromagnetic energy;"

- also in room 545, his two associates and Warren each "felt a strange sensation on the surface of his skin... an unexplainable feeling of weight pressed down on top of my hand, and the hair on my knuckles stood up... as though some strange field had passed each of us on its way through the room;"

- an associate who later described "seemingly coming out of nowhere, a white streak of illumination [that] passed across his range of vision and disappeared." A portion of the white streak was captured by Joshua Warren in a subsequent photograph.

For those believers anxious to catch a glimpse of the Pink Lady, Joshua Warren found the greatest amount of paranormal activity, based both on his observations and the stories he gathered from guests and employees, to be around room 545 in the Palm Court and, surprisingly, in the nightclub Elaine's built in the lower level of the 1988 Vanderbilt Wing.

Why in a modern nightclub?

For years, Elaine's was largely forgotten by the staff and overlooked by guests. More often than not it was closed, providing anyone -- or anything -- looking for a dark, locked corner of the hotel with their own quiet, peaceful retreat.

In addition, while difficult to imagine amid the labyrinth of hallways throughout the hotel, the site of the lower level Elaine's is actually very close to the original lawn outside and just beneath the original rooms in the north wing of the hotel. It is also adjacent to the 1913 Main Inn basement, where many reports of sightings have also taken place.

And what obstacles could a few modern walls present to a vaporous spirit?

In *Haunted Asheville*, Joshua Warren also proposed a possible link between sightings in the Grove Park Inn and those he also documented immediately next door in the former Battle House, a sprawling 1928 mansion. The Battle House, it should be noted, was demolished in 2008 to make room for The Fitzgerald, a collection of 24 luxury condominiums overlooking the hotel and golf course. What effect that demolition might have had on any spirits in either the Battle House or the Grove Park Inn remains open to conjecture.

For whatever reason, reports of sightings of the Pink Lady had declined in recent years, but in the summer and fall of 2012 she appeared to have made her return -- and seems to have liked room 444. In one instance, a guest looked into the mirror in room 444 and could see a woman in a pink gown -- but only in the mirror. Her mother remained skeptical until she, too, saw the apparition. "About an hour later," according to a hotel report, "[the guest] felt something push down on her arm. At this point she began freaking out, and called down to the front desk and spoke with [a staff member] who informed her about the Pink Lady phenomenon." The guest must have felt some sense of relief, for she and her daughter declined the offer to move them to a different room -- but did sleep with the lights on that night.

That same month the Pink Lady may have made another appearance, this one near the original 1913 storage room on the seventh floor of the Vanderbilt Wing. As a staff member recounted:

*I had arrived early to meet a group from the hotel, and so was standing in the area near the offices of Accents on Asheville. I turned around and saw the most beautiful young girl standing against the low wall near the glass elevator. She was dressed in a three-quarter length formal pink gown. It had pink tooling and silver sequins, nothing like what you would expect to see today -- very decadent looking!*

*She had one sandal off -- it was lying on its side on the floor -- and had long brown hair and peachy skin. She looked to be in her late twenties. I needed to walk past her and thought to myself, "Well, I'll say 'hello.' " When I did -- and I was just three feet away from her -- she opened her mouth to say "Hello" in return, but nothing came out.*

*She just mouthed the word. I walked on past her, then thought to myself, "How strange," and so I turned back around.*

*But she was gone.*

*And there was nowhere she could have gone without walking past me.*

When asked if what she saw looked like a ghost, the staffer replied, "Goodness, no. She was a beautiful young woman, playing with her long, brown hair. Until I turned around and she was gone, I thought she was a real person just standing there. But her dress was so formal, so unusual, and with the way she just disappeared, I said to myself, 'I just saw the Pink Lady.' "

Regardless of what conclusions anyone might draw from all of this, no one who has had any encounter with the Pink Lady, from the night watchmen and housekeeping staff to Joshua Warren and his investigators, ever felt threatened by what they saw.

As one former staff member who often worked late at night in her office in the original kitchen area recalled, "To me, she was more of a prankster. She liked to play tricks. She liked to have contact. She liked to let me know she was there. I was never afraid of her -- ever."

Note: Joshua P. Warren continues to track and document ghosts utilizing scientific methods and equipment, as well as appearing regularly on the *Discovery Channel*, the *Learning Channel*, the *Travel Channel*, and the *History Channel*. Additional information on his many exploits, publications and activities can be followed at www.JoshuaPWarren.com. Copies of his paperback books, including *How To Hunt Ghosts* and *Haunted Asheville*, called a "reading tour of Asheville," are readily available in bookstores around Asheville and online.

*Elaine Sammons cuts the ribbon officially opening the Vanderbilt Wing in 1988.*

# Chapter 23

# "Building for a Second Century"

*If Charles Sammons represented the second E. W. Grove,*
*then Elaine Sammons could have been the second*
*Frederick Loring Seely.*

Grove Park Inn historian

Growing up as an orphan in Oklahoma, Charles Sammons (1898-1988) had known adversity. He left school to work to send his two sisters to college, only to lose everything he had earned in the stock market crash of 1929. A few years later, with the added responsibilities of being a husband and a father, his first insurance business nearly went bankrupt. None of this, however, prepared him for the tragedy that struck just when it seemed like the 64-year-old millionaire had reached the pinnacle of his success.

On Sunday, August 26, 1962, Rosine, his wife of 34 years, had driven over to inspect the new house the couple was building in Dallas. While on an upper floor, she apparently stepped off a temporary wooden walkway onto a plasterboard ceiling that was unable to support her weight. Plunging through the plasterboard, she fell more than twenty feet to the marble floor below. Although rushed to Baylor Hospital, she was unable to survive her traumatic injuries.

In his characteristic fashion, Charles Sammons poured his grief into his work. While his management team operated Reserve Life Insurance Company, Sammons doubled his efforts to diversify his holdings. He formed or purchased companies in the telecommunications fields, cable television, bottled water, printing, importing of ceramics and gift items, nationwide distribution systems and financial services, as well as several travel agencies and hotels.

Under his aggressive direction, Sammons Enterprises eventually grew to include nearly 70 different companies. Sammons traveled extensively, continuing to inspect businesses he considered buying. He had purchased his first hotel ten years earlier, the modest Jack Tar Motor Court in Galveston, Texas. He and Rosine, he explained, "enjoyed stopping there, so when it was for sale, I thought it would be nice to own it."

Sammons soon formed the Jack Tar Hotels chain, elevating Ed Leach from manager of the original Jack Tar motel to president of Jack Tar Hotels. Leach's first job was to oversee the $1 million expansion of the Jack Tar Motor Court into a 225-room hotel that would serve as the jewel in the Jack Tar Hotels crown. Over the course of their sixteen-year career together, Sammons and Leach purchased a total of thirteen different properties stretching from San Francisco to the Bahamas, including the Grove Park Inn.

When in 1959 Sammons bought the Grand Bahamas Hotel and Country Club, it was in desperate need of a complete remodeling. Sammons and Leach, however, looked past the peeling paint to the potential offered by the lush 2,000-acre property located only fifty miles off the coast of Florida. By the time it was finished, Charles Sammons had invested more than $70 million dollars in the resort, building an airport runway to accommodate passenger jets, adding a second golf course and increasing the number of rooms to 575.

By far the most ambitious project he had ever undertaken, the Grand Bahamas Resort provided Sammons with a needed distraction after Rosine's death. On his way to the resort he often stopped by his travel agency in Miami, where he met 45-year-old Elaine Schloff Dewey, one of his employees. After a brief courtship, they were married in November of 1963.

Born in Pontiac, Michigan, Elaine Dewey had settled in Florida after the dissolution of her first marriage, eventually taking a job with a travel agency in Miami. Her chance meeting with Charles Sammons set her life on a different course, as she soon became his trusted advisor in the renovation of several of the Jack Tar Hotels properties. In addition to the Grand Bahamas Resort, Charles and Elaine Sammons also flew to Asheville, where she was able to view the progress his designers had made over the course of the past eight years.

It was not until after Charles Sammons had made one of the few hasty and regrettable decisions in his business career -- selling the Grove Park Inn to the Osais Organization in 1969 -- did Elaine Sammons begin to assert herself in the affairs of Sammons Enterprises. Two years later, she undoubtedly must have encouraged him to take back the Grove Park Inn when the new owners defaulted on their payments. Once the Grove Park Inn had been returned to Sammons Enterprises, it became her lifetime pet project.

Buoyed by the acquisition of the Country Club of Asheville's golf course and clubhouse in 1976, Elaine Sammons was determined to set the Grove Park Inn on a stable course destined for year-round occupancy. One of her first moves was to abandon the Jack Tar Hotels' practice of annually rotating general managers through their thirteen hotels. Instead, in 1978 she selected Herman von Treskow, a 34-year-old graduate of the famed Heidelberg School of hotel management in his home country of Germany, to serve as the inn's general manager.

Together the pair soon discovered that the Grove Park Inn was in need of much more than a fresh coat of paint and a new team of interior decorators. The closer they looked, the more trouble they found. While his intentions had been noble, much of the money Charles Sammons had first poured into the hotel had been hastily spent. The superficial facelift his interior decorators had given the hotel in 1955 looked outdated by 1978, especially as the country, fresh off a bicentennial celebration, had begun to embrace historic restoration over hysteric renovation.

The cloverleaf swimming pool, constructed on unstable fill dirt, had slowly begun to sink. Cracks appeared in the concrete liner and water from the pool steadily seeped down the mountainside. The 1958 Fairway Lodge had been designed only for summer occupancy and by 1978 looked as outdated as other roadside motels of that era. The 1965 North Wing tacked onto the end of the hotel looked as natural as a hastily arranged marriage, sharing nothing in common with the Arts and Crafts architecture and craftsmanship of the Main Inn. The canvas awning stretched over the Sunset Terrace conveniently served as an ashtray for guests leaning out the bedroom windows above it. Holes left by burning cigarettes provided little protection for anyone on the terrace during an afternoon rain shower.

What began as a series of small steps -- constructing a permanent roof over the Sunset Terrace in 1980, filling in the cloverleaf swimming pool, adding oak Arts and Crafts style woodwork and antiques to the Great Hall -- culminated in the 1984 completion of a ten-story, 202-room addition with an indoor swimming pool, a spacious ballroom, additional meeting space and a new restaurant.

In deference to the original hotel, it was deliberately designed with a roofline lower than that of the Main Inn.

In honor of the man who signed the $20 million check, it was called the Sammons Wing.

But Mrs. Sammons was just getting started.

With the 1984 transformation of the Grove Park Inn into a year-round resort, she and her husband invested another $1 million in renovating the Donald Ross golf course, the 1925 clubhouse and the outdoor swimming pool next to it. The following year saw the completion of a new 32,514-square-foot Sports Center, providing guests with indoor and outdoor tennis courts, a squash court, two racquetball courts, a weight training room, an aerobics rooms and an indoor swimming pool.

The only remaining eyesore, the drab and outdated North Wing, was reduced to rubble on December 15, 1986, with a series of carefully placed detonation charges. In its place rose the Vanderbilt Wing, adding 413,250 square feet and pushing the total number of guest rooms to 510. In addition, the new wing boasted additional meeting space, retail shops, a glass elevator, a second spacious ballroom and a new restaurant.

On November 12, 1988, three months after the dedication of the Vanderbilt Wing, the 90-year-old Charles Sammons quietly passed away in Dallas, knowing full well that the fate of the Grove Park Inn lie in the safe hands of his wife. Her management skills were not limited to just the restoration of the Grove Park Inn, however, as this spry and sometimes testy woman was soon elected as chairman of the board of Sammons Enterprises, Inc.

Her additional duties at Sammons Enterprises, with assets totaling an estimated $55 billion, did not distract Elaine Sammons from her goal of preparing the Grove Park Inn for its second century of excellence. Along with new general manager James France, in 1991 she turned her attention to restoring the Arts and Crafts heritage of the Grove Park Inn, starting with the historic Palm Court.

Many of the guests relaxing in the Great Hall have no idea that the Grove Park Inn actually has two lobbies: the famous Great Hall flanked by its two enormous fireplaces, and the more intimate Palm Court tucked away on the third floor, directly above the Great Hall. Little do they realize that the twelve-inch concrete ceiling above the Great Hall is the floor of the Palm Court. To get there, guests can either take one of the two original elevators hidden inside the fireplaces or can climb the stairs located next to each one *(see pg. 334)*.

When, in 1913, Fred Seely was building the 150-room hotel, he had many challenges to overcome, including the lack of air-conditioning and the need to provide every guest with a breathtaking view from the window in their room. The Palm Court provided a solution to both of these challenges.

By placing all of the sleeping rooms on the outside walls, Seely created a hollow core reaching from the third floor (the ceiling of the two-story Great Hall) up to the roof above the sixth floor. The doors of the third floor rooms in this atrium open onto what became known as the Palm Court, decorated with chairs, tables and four large oak planters sprouting leafy palm trees. The doors from the sleeping rooms on the fourth, fifth and sixth floors open onto a narrow walkway bordered by a low wall that enables them to safely peer down onto the third floor Palm Court.

The Palm Court and open atrium also solved Seely's air-conditioning problem. Above each door, in an area now filled with wood, had originally been a hinged transom window that each guest could open or close from inside their room. Far above the third floor Palm Court, Seely installed a skylight in the roof; glass panels in the skylight were also hinged and could be opened by means of a wheel mounted on the sixth floor wall.

In warm weather, guests could simply open the outside windows in their room to allow fresh air to enter. By also opening the transom window above their door, the fresh mountain air would be drawn through the room. To complete the transfusion, the warm air in the Palm Court atrium would naturally rise and exit through the open skylight. As the warm air exited the roof, additional fresh air would be pulled through the outside window, across the length of the guest room, out the transom window and into the Palm Court, where it would rise to the open skylight.

It was classic Fred Seely: observe the laws of Nature, then use them to your advantage.

Simple, yet efficient.

By the time Mrs. Sammons had turned her attention to the Arts and Crafts heritage of the Grove Park Inn, the Palm Court had largely been neglected by the staff and forgotten by the guests. Mismatched and sometimes broken chairs littered the Palm Court, whose walls had been painted countless times, each time with a color more bland than the previous one.

Fred Seely, however, once again provided the solution to the challenge.

At various times, both shortly after the completion of the Grove Park Inn in 1913 and later during his fourteen-year tenure as president and general manager, Fred Seely had hired professional photographers to document the design and furnishings of the hotel. Fred Seely utilized many of these photographs in advertising and promotional booklets; others simply were filed away. Fortunately, nearly all were saved and somehow survived the various purges that took place each time a new owner or team of interior decorators arrived on the scene.

A close examination of these photographs provided Elaine Sammons and her staff with a blueprint for restoring the Palm Court. In addition to revealing how the Palm Court had been furnished, the historic photographs also documented the stenciling that Fred Seely had selected for the parapet walls ringing the fourth, fifth and sixth floors. Layer upon layer of paint had long since obscured the original geometric Arts and Crafts design that had once enlivened the poured concrete walls. It fell to Asheville restoration expert Mark Ellis Bennett to uncover and duplicate the original stencils.

Working for an entire summer atop a tower of scaffolding, Bennett began by meticulously scraping away more than a dozen layers of paint on the north section of the fourth-floor wall. Layers of paint slowly fell away beneath Bennett's scrapers to reveal not one, but two stencils. On top of the original 1913 stencil, which was primarily a geometric design, Bennett also discovered that in the 1920s Fred Seely had the stencils altered, adding some greenery, but still keeping the Arts and Crafts flavor. His discovery was born out by comparing a 1913 photograph of the Palm Court to one taken nearly ten years later. In the end it was decided that Bennett would duplicate the later stencil. Over the course of the summer he slowly worked his way around the three parapet walls, using a series of templates to duplicate the design on the other sections.

The original section of wall that Mark Ellis Bennett had scraped was left in its original state, along with some careful touch-ups to restore the stencils to their 1920s appearance. Also on that same section of wall is a display of original room keys that Bennett discovered quite by accident at an Asheville flea market that same summer. Had he not recognized the room numbers stamped in the keys, which contained no G.P.I. initials or name, the keys would undoubtedly have languished unrecognized in their cardboard box, destined to someday be melted down for their scrap value rather than being displayed inside the Grove Park Inn.

Outside, work was also progressing on some badly needed improvements. The original tile roof and Palm Court skylight had performed admirably for more than 87 years, but by the turn of the century it was obvious that patching leaks was not going to suffice any longer. Rather than opting for less-expensive asphalt shingles, Elaine Sammons was determined to find a way to replace the existing roof without changing its appearance. The Ludowici Tile Company had provided roof tiles for the Biltmore House in 1895 and the Grove Park Inn in 1913, so they were again tapped to provide roof tiles for the Main Inn. Four different shades of red tiles were created by the craftsmen at Ludowici to duplicate the age and the mottled patina of the 87-year-old tiles, but they also had a special challenge: creating curved tiles to match the undulating roofline of the sixth-floor dormers.

After a great deal of research and experimentation, it was decided that the curved tiles over the dormers would be secured using modern adhesives rather than being nailed as they had been in 1913. The painstaking process required hundreds of sections of scaffolding erected on all sides of the hotel, scaffolding that had to be modeled and assembled so as not to block the view from any of the guest rooms. Workmen began removing and saving the original tiles in 1999, discovering and repairing sections of deteriorated concrete before they could begin installing the first of nearly a half million new tiles. Eighteen months and $3 million later, general manager Craig

Madison slipped the final ceremonial tile into place in the year 2000, expecting that the new roof would last as long as the original 1913 one had.

But such was not the case.

Before long guests and staff began noticing a white substance leaching out over the tops of the new clay tiles around the 'eyelid' dormers on each side of the sixth-floor roof. Some thought it was "salt spalling," a reaction caused by rainwater depositing dissolved salt on top of the tiles, leaving behind a white film once the water evaporates. Closer inspection, however, determined that the residue was, in fact, the adhesive leaching out from between the new tiles. Attempts to determine the precise cause led to numerous meetings and negotiations between the Grove Park Inn, the architects, the tile manufacturer and the contractor. Dissatisfied with the answers they were given, the Grove Park Inn presented their case against the contractor in a court of law and eventually prevailed.

In 2009, the scaffolding once again rose around the Grove Park Inn as the workmen returned, this time to remove the nine-year-old tiles from each of the dormers. The project required another eighteen months, but was completed in October of 2010.

By far a more ambitious and more costly project, the construction of a 40,000-square-foot spa remains the most impressive of all of the contributions that Elaine Sammons made to the Grove Park Inn's heritage. As she explained in an interview, "I had been traveling around and found that most of the finer resorts have spas. I thought that the Grove Park Inn needed a spa, for it is the trend of the future."

Most resort owners, however, do not have the dual responsibility of protecting the historical integrity of the building while providing guests with the modern conveniences they expect to find. It fell to noted architect Robert LeBlond to design a world-class spa that would reflect the Arts and Crafts heritage of the hotel while not detracting from it. His solution: put it underground.

Nestled between the two wings to which it is connected by underground tunnels, the only clue to the spa's existence are the peaked skylights surrounded by shrubbery, rocks and waterfalls. The three-story structure is nearly all built below ground, with a sun-drenched pool and patio spilling out beneath the lower end. As expected, construction both took longer and cost more than initially hoped, with the price tag rising from $12 million to more than $42 million. But when it opened on February 28, 2001, Mrs. Sammons never faltered in her endorsement of the project. Sounding every bit like a typical homeowner, she explained:

"Everything costs more than you expect it to."

Like Edwin Wiley Grove before her, as Elaine Sammons grew older she became even more attached to the Grove Park Inn. Her visits became more frequent, becoming less of the rigorous, white glove inspections of her earlier years and more of an opportunity to relax and take delight in the projects she had proposed and approved.

When Charles Sammons died in 1988, the Grove Park Inn was but one minor accomplishment in a life filled with achievements. But for Elaine Sammons, in addition to her philanthropy in Asheville and Dallas, the Grove Park Inn had been her palette of expression, her creative outlet, her opportunity to leave behind evidence of a life well lived, a life dedicated to preserving and protecting the heritage of this historic structure.

On January 14, 2009, at the age of 92, Elaine Sammons died peacefully in her sleep at her home in Dallas.

Her death marked the end of the most illustrious era in the history of the Grove Park Inn, paving the way for a second century of excellence.

*President Barack Obama met with Breanne Hall, club manager and head golf professional for the Grove Park Inn, soon after his arrival on April 10, 2010.*

# Chapter 24

# "A Presidential Weekend"

*For 72 hours, the Grove Park Inn <u>was</u> the White House.*

Ron Morin, Grove Park Inn
Vice President and General Manager

President Obama loves to golf.

And, as it turns out, he loves Asheville.

Not a bad combination.

As a presidential candidate, Barack Obama first came to Asheville on Saturday, October 4, 2008, just a few days before his nationally televised debate with Senator John McCain. Before his arrival, in what had to have been one of the best kept secrets in Asheville, the candidate's advance team and the Grove Park Inn's staff had quietly transformed one portion of the hotel's ballroom into a replica of the Tuesday night debate hall: stage, podium, audience, moderator, even mock television cameras.

Making their task even more difficult, the Grove Park Inn was also hosting the state Democratic party's annual Vance-Aycock dinner that night. The scheduling, as it turned out, was no coincidence. To the surprise of the Democrat attendees, Barack Obama crashed their Saturday night party, appearing unannounced to throw his support behind the slate of Democratic candidates vying for office that fall.

Afterwards, Obama and his campaign staff remained in Asheville and at the Grove Park Inn, where he rehearsed for the upcoming debate. That Sunday afternoon he took time off to address the crowd gathered at the historic 1929 Art Deco-designed Asheville High School, where he spoke before a crowd of an estimated 28,000 people, promising "affordable, accessible health care" to every American by the close of his first term. In the midst of "the worst economic crisis since the Great Depression," he said, "the question is not 'if' we can afford, but why we cannot afford health care."

On Monday, Barack Obama took a break from his debate preparations to grab lunch at a local eatery, 12 Bones Smokehouse, and to shake hands with many of the surprised diners. Before leaving the Grove Park Inn that afternoon, he took time for a photo shoot with local officials and hotel staff in the inn's parking garage. As he was getting into his car, Obama stopped, walked back to where the hotel staff still stood, and announced, "I really love this place. They wouldn't let me golf this time, but I'm going to bring my wife back here."

As the motorcade pulled away from the hotel, the staff began buzzing with anticipation of a return visit. Ron Morin, then vice president and general manager who helped coordinate the candidate's stay, warned the group not to get too excited. "He's a candidate," Morin pointed out. "He's being gracious; he's being a nice guy. I'm sure he tells everyone that."

## "A Presidential Weekend"

Seventeen months later, on a Saturday afternoon in April, Ron Morin received a phone call at home from his sales manager. The president was coming back.

"When?" Morin asked.

"In three weeks."

And three weeks later, on April 22, 2010, after countless gallons of paint and polish, Ron Morin and his staff were again standing in the hotel parking garage. "We arrived an hour early," he recalled, "and we waited, and we waited, and we waited. Then, the 'sweep' car, a police cruiser, rolled through the garage, checking everything. Next, we could hear the motorcycles coming, roaring into the parking garage, followed by a string of vans full of counter assault guys. It made the hair stand up on your neck. Here we were, just a hotel staff, waiting to greet the most protected man on the planet. Finally, the president's car pulls up, he hops out, helps the First Lady out of the car, then comes up to me and says, 'I told you I was going to bring my wife back.' "

The Secret Service team was anxious to get President Obama and the First Lady out of the parking garage and into their room, Morin explained, but the president suddenly stopped and remarked to the hotel staff, "Wait a minute. I bet you guys would like some pictures." He turned to the White House photographer. "Lets take a couple of pictures for these guys."

Billed from the beginning as a romantic weekend for the President and First Lady, Barack and Michelle Obama had arrived in Asheville without their two daughters. No speeches were planned or given. No public appearances were made, not even at 12 Bones Smokehouse, where a crowd had gathered in hopes of getting a second glimpse of the president.

This time he had one thing in mind: golf.

For Ron Morin and the Grove Park Inn staff, the president's visit presented a unique set of challenges. In addition to complying with special requests and considerations from the Secret Service and the presidential staff, they also had to continue to ensure that their regular guests were not inconvenienced, that their Grove Park Inn experience was not sacrificed for the benefit of the president. It was a delicate balance, and one that the Grove Park Inn's staff handled flawlessly.

The Obamas were looking forward to a weekend similar to what any guest at the Grove Park Inn might envision: some tennis, a round of golf, browsing the shops, taking time for a hike and enjoying some private, relaxing meals prepared by the staff. Their schedule, however, was neither haphazard nor spur of the moment. Twelve hours prior to arriving at any location in the hotel, whether it be at the Sports Center or in the retail shops, the Secret Service did a "lock down" of that area. They set up metal detectors and portable X-ray machines to scan both staff and guests in the area, but, as Ron Morin noted, "the president's staff was every bit as gracious as the President and First Lady, and did not want to disrupt any of the other guests."

Even though this had always been billed as a private weekend for the Obamas, the national press corps was still on hand. In addition to providing a well-stocked press room for approximately thirty reporters that weekend, the Grove Park Inn also had to allow the president's staff to set up a meeting room from which, in the case of a national emergency, he could immediately address the country. Complete with desk, podium and American flag, the room remained poised and ready during the president's entire three-day visit. In addition, the White House Communication Office and officers from the Pentagon had also requested meeting rooms for their staff and equipment.

## "A Presidential Weekend"

"For 72 hours," Morin explained, "the Grove Park Inn was the White House."

In a tradition dating back to President Franklin D. Roosevelt, the president of the United States is always accompanied on his travels by Navy corpsmen who serve as his personal assistants, handling or overseeing everything from the purchase of personal items and favored snacks to the preparation of his meals and the cleaning of his hotel room each morning. While the corpsmen do not necessarily prepare his meals, as Ron Morin explained, "they worked with our chef on each meal, overseeing our staff while the food was being prepared."

As much as the president enjoyed the food and the service at the Grove Park Inn, his focus that weekend remained on getting onto the famed Donald Ross golf course. As Breanne Hall, club manager and head golf professional for the Grove Park Inn, explained, "A couple of weeks before the president came we were told about it, but had to keep it all very hush-hush. At first we thought I would be giving his two daughters a lesson, but we later found out the president would be playing with some college buddies from Chicago. At first we worked with the Secret Service over the phone, then, as it grew closer to the time, it became one-on-one with them. They sent some staff down a week ahead and scanned every inch of the property, looking for hidden spots. They wore just regular clothes and were very low key; you wouldn't have known what they were doing. And I think they did background checks on everyone who might be in contact with the president."

As she went on to explain, "We were told the president wanted to take a lesson on Friday evening with a private instructor. The Secret Service brought the president down the back way from the hotel, by the spa, out onto the sixteenth hole. From about 6:00 p.m.

until 7:30 p.m. he worked on his swing on the sixteenth hole, while I worked with his friends on the green at number fifteen, working on their short game. The president played just two or three holes Friday evening."

On Saturday morning the Grove Park Inn's course was completely closed to guests and the general public as the president and his friends teed off at eight o'clock. "We didn't go around with him," she explained, "but he had about twenty golf carts of Secret Service agents and staff following him around. There must have been thirty to forty of them."

"Meeting the president," Breanne went on, "was one of the coolest things ever. Afterwards we really didn't think he would take the time to talk with us, but he wanted to meet our staff. And when he saw me Saturday morning, he remembered my name and said, "How are we doing today, Breanne?"

"At the end of his round," she recalled, "some staff had gathered at the club house just hoping to see the president as he left. We really didn't expect to talk to him, but he walked over and posed for some pictures with us, and laughed and really seemed to be enjoying himself.

"Then, his staff finally got him into his car and we thought they were pulling away, but then he got back out and came over to us. I could see he had something in his hand. "Here," he said, "I bet you won't find these anywhere." I looked and he was handing me three special golf balls that Titleist makes only for the president, each stamped with the number "44," since he is the 44th president.

"It was unbelievably awesome."

*After completing his round of golf on Saturday morning, President Obama took time to gather many of the country club staff for a photograph outside the clubhouse.*

*In the fall of 1913 Fred Seely took Secretary of State William Jennings Bryan, along with Mary Baird Bryan (back left), Evelyn Grove Seely (center) and an unidentified friend, for a ride along the roads traversing Sunset Mountain.*

# Chapter 25

# "A New Era Begins"

*The Grove Park Inn is a unique structure, built on an entirely different plan from the average resort hotel. The idea was to build a big home where every modern convenience could be had, but with all the old-fashioned qualities of genuineness with no sham. Things made by Nature, assisted by artists, carry sentiment.*

Frederick Loring Seely, 1918

The bigger the building, the bigger the rumors.

And for 100 years, the Grove Park Inn has been no exception.

When World War I erupted in Europe, it was rumored that Edwin Wiley Grove was going to close the hotel.

He didn't.

And when E. W. Grove died on January 27, 1927, it was rumored his son was going to sell the hotel.

He did.

When the Great Depression took a death grip on the country's economy, it was rumored the new owners of the Grove Park Inn were going to declare bankruptcy.

They did.

And when World War II started, it was rumored the United States government was going to turn the hotel into a prisoner of war camp.

It did.

Afterwards, when the Grove Park Inn sat nearly empty in the early 1950s, it was rumored it was going to be demolished.

It wasn't.

Then, when longtime owner Charles Sammons died in 1984, it was rumored the hotel would be sold.

It wasn't.

And when his wife Elaine Sammons died in 2009, it was again rumored the Grove Park Inn would be sold.

It was.

And so, for almost as long as the Grove Park Inn has stood on Sunset Mountain, people have enjoyed speculating on it's immediate and long term future.

Spreading rumors.

*Was it going to become part of a hotel chain?*
*Or were the employees going to own it?*
*Are the rocks going back onto the pillars -- or staying down?*
*Is the Great Hall bar moving -- or staying?*
*Will the north fireplace be working -- or remain cold?*
*Will the Arts and Crafts furniture stay -- or again be sold?*

"A New Era Begins"

After the passing of Elaine Sammons in 2009, there seemed to be a rumor for every rock lining the Great Hall. For nearly three years people wondered what was going to happen to the historic hotel. In the spring of 2012, however, the rumors were replaced with real news regarding the future of the Grove Park Inn. On May 1st it became official: KSL Resorts, a branch of the investment firm KSL Capital Partners, LLC, officially became the new owners of the historic Grove Park Inn, prompting the question: "What is KSL?"

The answer soon became clear: KSL Capital Partners, LLC, was a private equity firm specializing in buying under-performing resort properties, investing several millions of dollars in capital improvements, reorganizing departments under KSL employees transferred from other properties, and then making the resorts available for purchase.

The firm had been formed in 2005 by Michael S. Shannon and Eric C. Resnick, both of whom had worked as investment specialists at KSL Recreation from 1992 until that firm was sold in 2004. Shannon and Resnick then formed KSL Capital Partners, LLC, which continues to be funded by a combination of corporate and state pension funds, university endowments, financial institutions, and private individuals. They subsequently formed KSL Resorts, whose staff manages and operates the firm's resort properties.

With offices in both Denver and New York, KSL Capital Partners then had more than $3.5 billion in travel and leisure business assets spread across 26 states and four countries. According to their website, KSL Capital Partners focused "on acquisitions of complex, operationally intensive businesses, and strives to unlock 'hidden value' by re-envisioning and repositioning these enterprises through targeted capital expenditures, operational efficiencies and enhanced marketing strategies."

Internally, KSL Resorts began making major personnel and organizational changes immediately after taking over on May 1, 2012, prompting the departure of scores of employees who had worked under the Sammons family for several years. Many left feeling unhappy with both the transition process and the new management style. "It was all about improving the 'bottom line,'" one former employee stated. "Gone was the feeling of 'family.' We were told what to do and how to do it. And it was 'their way or the highway.'"

Behind the closed doors of the management offices it was well known that KSL Partners was planning to make a series of major improvements designed not only to make the hotel more attractive and to improve its profitability, but to prepare it to be sold in five to eight years.

In a matter of months the plans for improvements to the hotel became clear, starting with the new owners' intent to enhance the "sense of arrival" for guests by re-configuring the courtyard to reduce the number of cars and shuttle busses blocking the view of the front entrance. They next turned their attention to the Great Hall, reducing congestion by eliminating the bellstand, downsizing and moving the front desk and the concierge station, redesigning the wooden covers around the concrete pillars, downsizing the bar, and eliminating the stage for bands. They invested $250,000 in the north fireplace, which had not functioned properly for several decades.

KSL Resorts next embarked on a major remodeling and upgrading of all of the rooms in the 1988 Vanderbilt Wing, as well as the public hallways throughout the hotel. Their single largest project of the estimated $25 million invested may well have been the creation of the Edison, a combination indoor-outdoor sports bar between the original Main Inn and the Sammons Wing, intended to further reduce the congestion and noise in the Great Hall.

## "A New Era Begins"

In May and June of 2013, however, while many of these projects were still underway, the directors of KSL were approached by managers of the Omni Hotel & Resorts corporation interested in purchasing one of their Texas resorts. In just a matter of days, however, the deal mushroomed, eventually resulting in the purchase of five KSL properties for an estimated $900 million dollars. The headliner of the deal was none of the than the Grove Park Inn.

Thus, as plans were being finalized for an elaborate celebration commemorating the Grove Park Inn's 100th birthday on July 12, 2013, staff members at the hotel were being introduced to yet another new owner, new management team, new business philosophy, and a new name: the Omni Grove Park Inn.

How people will respond to all of the changes set in motion by KSL Partners during their brief tenure and the plans yet to be announced by Omni Hotels & Resorts for the immediate future of the historic hotel remain uncertain at this writing, but if the first hundred years has been any indication, each decision will be carefully watched by those who have grown attached to the history and the heritage of the stately queen of Sunset Mountain.

# A Timeline of Grove Park Inn History

## Edwin W. Grove Era: 1850 - 1912

1850    Edwin Wiley Grove is born in Bolivar, Tennessee.
1871    Fred Loring Seely is born in Monmouth, New Jersey.
1874    E. W. Grove becomes a pharmacist in Paris, Tennessee.
1877    Evelyn Grove (Seely) is born in Paris, Tennessee.
1878    E. W. Grove develops his first malaria preventive.
1887    Grove forms the Paris Medicine Company.
1891    Moves the Paris Medicine Company to St. Louis.
        Edwin W. Grove Junior is born in St. Louis.
1897    E. W. Grove establishes a second home in Asheville.
1898    Grove meets Fred Seely at Parke, Davis in May.
        Fred Seely marries Evelyn Grove in October.
1900    Fred and Evelyn Seely move to St. Louis.
1903    Seely leaves the Paris Medicine Co., moving to Atlanta.
1906    Seely and Grove establish the *Atlanta Georgian*.
1909    Grove starts planing a hotel on Sunset Mountain.
1912    Seely and Grove sell the *Georgian* to William R. Hearst.

## Fred L. Seely Era: 1912 - 1928

1912    Fred Seely becomes the contractor for the Grove Park Inn.
        Groundbreaking takes place on July 9.
1913    The Grove Park Inn opens on July 12.
1914    Fred Seely leases the hotel from Grove through 1927.
1917    Seely buys Biltmore Industries from Edith Vanderbilt;
        begins construction of five workshops next to the hotel.
1918    Ford, Edison and Firestone are guests in August.
1920    E. W. Grove buys the Manor Inn and cottages.
1922    Grove demolishes the original 1886 Battery Park Hotel.
1924    The new Battery Park Hotel opens in downtown Asheville.
1925    Fred Seely files a breach of contract lawsuit against E. W. Grove.
1927    Edwin Wiley Grove dies on January 27 at age 77.
        Fred Seely's lease on the hotel expires in December.
        Fred Seely loses his lawsuit against the E. W. Grove estate.
1928    Gertrude Grove dies at age 64, leaving entire estate to her son.
        A Baltimore investment group buys the Grove Park Inn.

# An Era of Turmoil: 1928 - 1955

1930    Presidents Hoover and Taft are guests at the hotel.
1932    The Grove Park Inn owners declare bankruptcy.
1935    F. Scott Fitzgerald stays for the summers of 1935 and 1936.
1936    President Roosevelt visits during his fall campaign tour.
1942    Axis diplomats and their families are interred at G.P.I.
        Fred Seely dies on March 14 at the age of 71.
1943    Oklahoma real estate developer Ike Hall buys the hotel.
1944    Hotel serves as redistribution center for returning military.
        The Philippine president in exile stays at Grove Park Inn.
1947    General Dwight Eisenhower stays in one of the cottages.

# Charles A. Sammons Era: 1955 - 1988

1955    Charles Sammons purchases the Grove Park Inn from Ike Hall.
1958    The Fairway Lodge is built to the south of the Main Inn.
1963    Charles Sammons marries Elaine Dewey.
1964    The North Wing addition is completed.
1973    Hotel named to the National Register of Historic Places.
1976    Sammons buys golf course from the Country Club of Asheville.
1982    The Fairway Lodge is demolished for the Sammons Wing.
1984    The Sammons Wing opens, increasing number of rooms to 410.
1985    The Sports Center is completed.
1986    The North Wing is demolished for the Vanderbilt Wing.
1988    The Vanderbilt Wing opens, increasing number of rooms to 510.
        Charles Sammons dies on November 12 at the age of 90.

# Elaine D. Sammons Era: 1988 - 2013

1999    The Sports Center receives a major overhaul.
        Battle House (1927) and Bynum House (1924) purchased.
2001    The spa opens at a cost of $42 million.
        The original tile roof on the Main Inn is replaced.
2002    The golf course is restored to the original Donald Ross layout.
2006    The Battle House razed for Fitzgerald condos, opening in 2008.
2009    Owner Elaine Sammons dies on January 14 at age 92.
2010    President and Mrs. Obama arrive for a private weekend.
2012    KSL Resorts takes ownership on May 1.
2013    Omni Hotels & Resorts purchases the Grove Park Inn in June.

# Want to learn more?

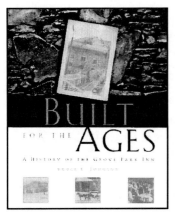

*Built For the Ages: A History of the Grove Park Inn* (hardback, 128 pgs., 2004) chronicles the design, construction and furnishing of the Grove Park Inn in 1913, then traces its history from its opening through the building of its award-winning spa in 2001. Author Bruce Johnson also provides insight into the relationship between owner Edwin W. Grove and his son-in-law and manager, Frederick L. Seely.

*The Grove Park Inn Arts & Crafts Furniture* (hardback, 175 pgs., 2009) provides an in-depth examination of the Arts & Crafts heritage manifested in one of the most important Arts & Crafts buildings in the country. Author Bruce Johnson explores the relationship between the historic hotel and the Roycrofters, who provided many of the original furnishings and lighting in 1913. Included in the book are detailed drawings for woodworkers interested in building their own Arts & Crafts furniture.

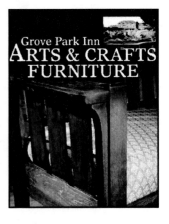

The novel *An Unexpected Guest* (softcover, 298 pgs., 2012) is set at the Grove Park Inn on the night of August 27, 1918, when Henry Ford, Harvey Firestone and Thomas Edison were guests at the hotel. That night, however, general manager Fred Seely discovers yet another guest, this one unexpected -- the body of a young woman dressed in a pink gown. First time novelist Bruce Johnson's blend of history and fiction has been called "an unexpected marvel" and is sure to surprise and delight every reader.

# Bruce E. Johnson

has been researching and writing about the Grove Park Inn since first coming to Asheville on assignment from *Country Living* magazine in 1986. In 1988 he founded the National Arts and Crafts Conference and Antiques Show, which he has directed each February since then at the Grove Park Inn. He has written several books on the American Arts and Crafts movement and on the history of the Grove Park Inn. Additionally, Johnson has been the corporate spokesperson for the Minwax Company since 1992, appearing on the *New Yankee Workshop*, the *Today Show*, the *Martha Stewart Show* and numerous other television shows, as well as hosting three television shows for the DIY Network and HGTV. He has two grown sons, Eric and Blake, and lives with his wife Leigh Ann on a small farm outside Asheville.

He is still hoping to someday meet the Pink Lady.

CPSIA information can be obtained
at www.ICGtesting.com
Printed in the USA
FFOW01n2334160718
47408974-50603FF